AF575471

WARHOL
THE TEXTILES

WARHOL
THE TEXTILES

Geoffrey Rayner
and Richard Chamberlain

Yale University Press, New Haven and London

In memory of Matt Wrbican, whose knowledge and enthusiasm steered us in the right direction with this book.

CONTENTS

FOREWORD

Zandra Rhodes

Andy Warhol entered my world right at the beginning of my career – when I was at the Royal College of Art in London in the early sixties – with his soup cans and images from popular culture. Before this time, these were just objects we had around us, ignored and definitely not considered as art.

Andy made me look at everything differently. I started to re-evaluate my surroundings and their place in my life. His Pop art imagery influenced my early textile designs of the 1960s, such as the prints 'Top Brass' and 'Mr Man'.

Warhol progressed from Pop artist to Pop icon, leading the way with his unique grasp of everyday imagery. His influence stretched worldwide and inspired all the realms of art. He was a child who never grew up; an observer, a voyeur and a creative sponge – capturing the world around him with a unique, new perspective. I met Andy several times when I visited the Factory in the sixties and seventies. My dresses were photographed on Paloma Picasso and other star models for his magazine *Interview*.

In my first grand London dress show at The Roundhouse some of the Warhol girls were modelling: Catherine Milinaire and Donna Jordan. Many years later, in 2011, I was in Pittsburgh where Bizet's opera *The Pearl Fishers* was being performed: I had designed sets and costumes for the production. While there, I was lucky enough to have some downtime and visited the Andy Warhol Museum. On the top floor were Andy's videos of my fashion show for the visionary New York charity Girls' Town of Italy. This show, which took place in September 1982 at the Pierre Hotel, I did for the chic Park Avenue shop Martha's. It brought back fabulous memories of my incredible fantasy shows, and there it was playing permanently in the Warhol Museum: what a tribute!

Before Warhol became this icon he worked as a freelance illustrator and graphic artist. He had his own studio in the fifties and sixties, and became extremely successful. Andy developed his own signature style of commercial illustration with hard, stark blotchy outlines, the shapes then filled in with bright colours. His drawings of fifties shoes were particularly notable; they were impossibly slim and chic.

His textile work reveals a joyful, free but exact penmanship. The designs were drawn in a specific way: abundant ink was then blotted when wet to produce the signature blotchy line. The result was lovely wearable prints. But at the time, because they were commercial and wearable textiles there was no name attached. Although the print 'makes' the garment, the print designer is the Cinderella of the industry – never mentioned.

Warhol's textiles are rare and hidden gems from this time, evocative of classic American fifties imagery from shops like Bonwit Teller and I. Miller Shoes to magazines such as *Vogue, Harper's Bazaar* and the *New Yorker*. Never mentioned and largely bypassed, they reveal what a great designer and multi-talented artist he was. These works are too good to be forgotten.

Geoffrey Rayner and Richard Chamberlain have had to search extensively to put this collection together. While the designs are clearly Warhol, the 1950s is now seventy years past and because of this the treasured fabrics were caught up in the mists of time and had drifted into obscurity. Thanks to Geoffrey and Richard's persistent endeavours, these works have now been found and can be properly memorialised.

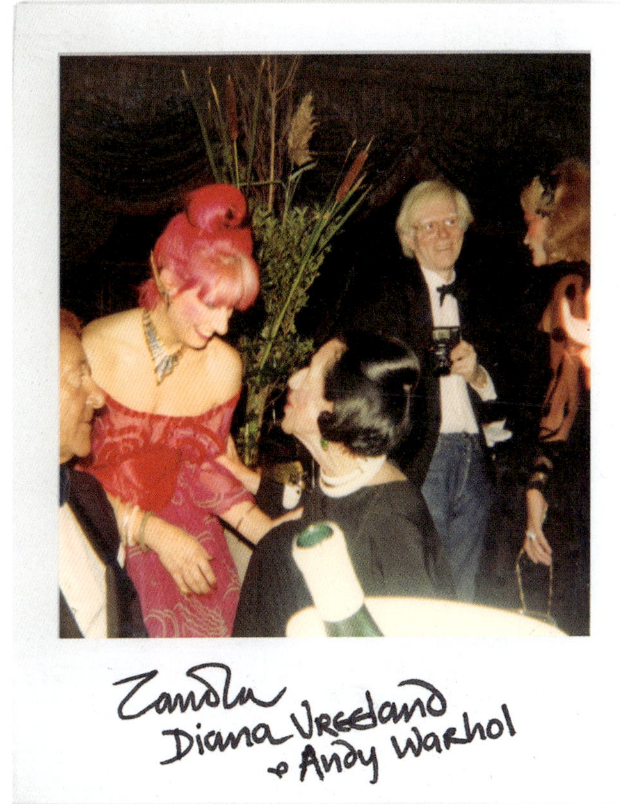

Zandra Rhodes show for Martha's, Park Avenue, filmed by Warhol Studio and choreographed by Ron Link. Attended by Diana Vreeland (in picture) with Zandra Rhodes and Andy Warhol, 1982. Photographer: Joan Agajanian Quinn.

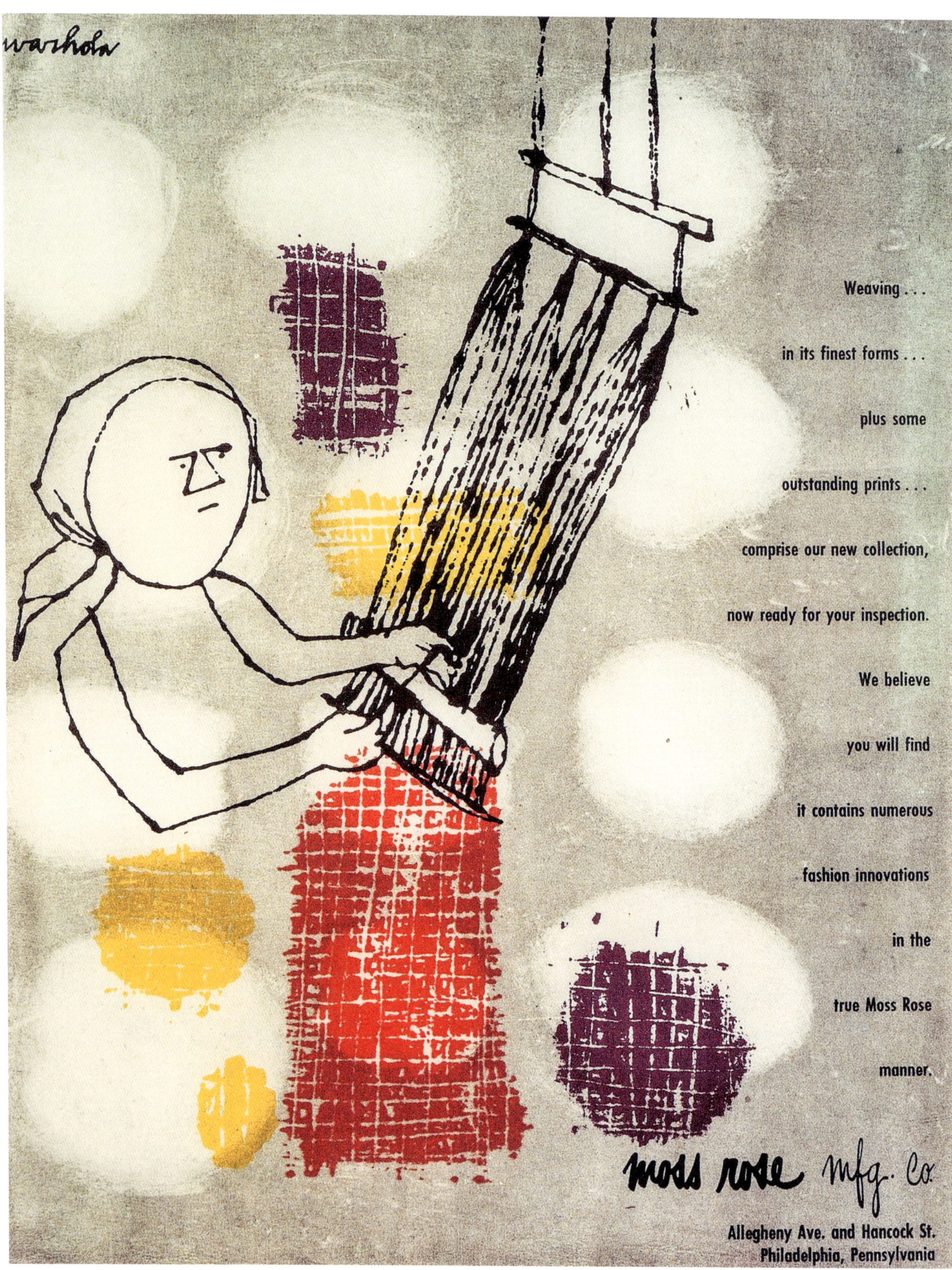

Printed advertising mailer by Warhol for the Moss Rose Manufacturing Co., *c.*1949. This is from the earliest period of his career when he was still using the name 'Warhola'.

INTRODUCTION

Geoffrey Rayner

Andy Warhol is now recognised internationally as probably the most influential and significant artist of the second half of the twentieth century. However, what is not so widely known is that his career in the fine arts was preceded by work in New York in the 1950s and the early 1960s as an extremely successful commercial illustrator and graphic designer. Although much of his pre-Pop commercial artwork, such as that for the New York-based company I. Miller Shoes, has become better known, awareness that he also designed commercial textiles is only now beginning to grow. Many of these textiles, a fascinating aspect of his work as a designer, are also closely allied to his early Pop art paintings and other works of art that date from about 1962 or a little later.

Warhol was born in 1928 as Andrew Warhola, to Slovakian emigrant parents living in Pittsburgh, Pennsylvania. He spent his formative years in the industrial city of Pittsburgh, graduating from the city's Carnegie Institute of Technology in 1949. Later that year, with a degree in his pocket as a Bachelor of Fine Arts in Pictorial Design, he arrived for the first time in New York, then the most glamorous and exciting city in the United States of America. The city's great sophistication and razzmatazz very much appealed to him, and from then onwards New York remained his place of both residence and work until his death in 1987.

Warhol's career in New York as a commercial designer also began in 1949, initially with an assignment for illustrations from the art editor of *Seventeen* magazine. However, of far greater significance for himself was a commission that came the same year from Tina Fredericks, then the art editor of *Glamour* magazine. It was due to the misspelt credit line in this assignment that his name first appeared in print as 'Warhol' instead of 'Warhola', something he very much liked, and from then on the name by which he was known. A little later, in 1951, he was joined in New York by his mother Júlia, who not only generally cared and cooked for him until shortly before her death in 1972, but also became his first 'commercial' assistant. She is credited with creating Warhol's 'trademark' lettering, which was, in fact, an elaboration of her own highly idiosyncratic handwriting, for which she eventually received two professional awards, in 1957 and 1959. The success of his 1950s pre-Pop art career made Warhol one of the most well-known illustrators and graphic designers in New York City. His design work covered the whole gamut of advertising, from campaigns for companies such as the luxury leather goods manufacturer Fleming-Joffe Ltd to promotional material and elaborate window displays for swanky New York stores such as Tiffany's and Bonwit Teller. Among the many other commercial items he designed were dust jackets for books and covers for long-playing records. For himself, he created privately printed cookery books such as *Wild Raspberries* (in collaboration with Suzie Frankfurt, 1959) and self-promotional books such as *Twenty-five Cats Named Sam and One Blue Pussy* (1954), which he chose to send to art directors and other designers as gifts to advertise his abilities and originality.

The wide breadth of the commercial work he undertook in the 1950s was, in part, accounted for by a constant need for money, not only to support himself, his mother and his general lifestyle but also to give some financial support to members of his family back in Pittsburgh. It was also necessary to cover the costs of studio assistants Vito Giallo and a little later Nathan Gluck, if Warhol was to accomplish the increasing demands of his ever-burgeoning workload.

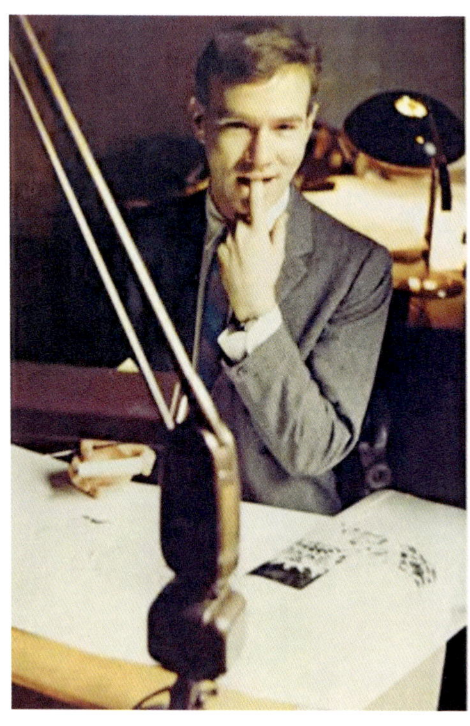

Photograph of Warhol at his desk, 1957. Photographer unknown.

The artist and illustrator John Rombola, who knew Warhol and his mother well in the 1950s, has said that, back then, 'Andy was completely commercial in outlook and considered doing any work as long as there was fifty dollars in it for him'.[1]

Warhol, who once called himself a 'business artist', said in 1975 in his book *The Philosophy of Andy Warhol: A to B and Back Again* that 'Being good in business is the most fascinating kind of art. Making money is art and working is art, and good business is the best art.' However, unlike most other aspects of his pre-Pop artwork, his textile designs were not intended to promote a company or institution, or to deliberately sell a product.

Instead, they were very much an art form; pure pattern with little agenda or brief attached. As the doyenne of American textile design, the artist Ruth Reeves, expressed it in 1946: 'it is my personal opinion that fabric design rightfully belongs in the category of the Fine Arts … as an art, it is just as important as good architecture, and certainly is more closely associated with our everyday living than are paintings'.[2]

Fine artists' involvement with textile design was an increasing phenomenon throughout much of the twentieth century. In the United States, this was particularly so. For instance, the American Modernist painter and illustrator Rockwell Kent designed a very striking series of furnishing textiles in 1949 for Bloomcraft, as part of the company's Happily Married collection, while, also in the 1940s, the New York textile converter Wesley Simpson, Inc. sold Surrealist-inspired textiles designed by Spanish and Hungarian émigré artists Salvador Dalí and Marcel Vertès, for which they received considerable positive publicity.

Warhol, an acutely sharp observer of New York City's creative and commercial scenes, would have been well aware of this artistic development in textile design in the 1950s. The city had a thriving garment manufacturing industry, and the island of Manhattan was then the centre of fashion for the whole of the United States, with most of the big names in fashion and high style concentrated there. The offices of many textile converters, both large and small, had by this time accumulated in an area known as the Garment District, which was considered to mainly lie between Fifth and Ninth Avenues, on the 34th to 42nd streets of Manhattan.

Probably the most prestigious collaboration in America between fine artists and the textile industry occurred in 1954, between the New York converter Dan Fuller of Fuller Fabrics, Inc. and some of the most internationally renowned artists of the twentieth century, among them Pablo Picasso and Joan Miró. Like many others involved in New York's advertising and marketing sector, Warhol would have been well aware of the large publicity campaign that accompanied

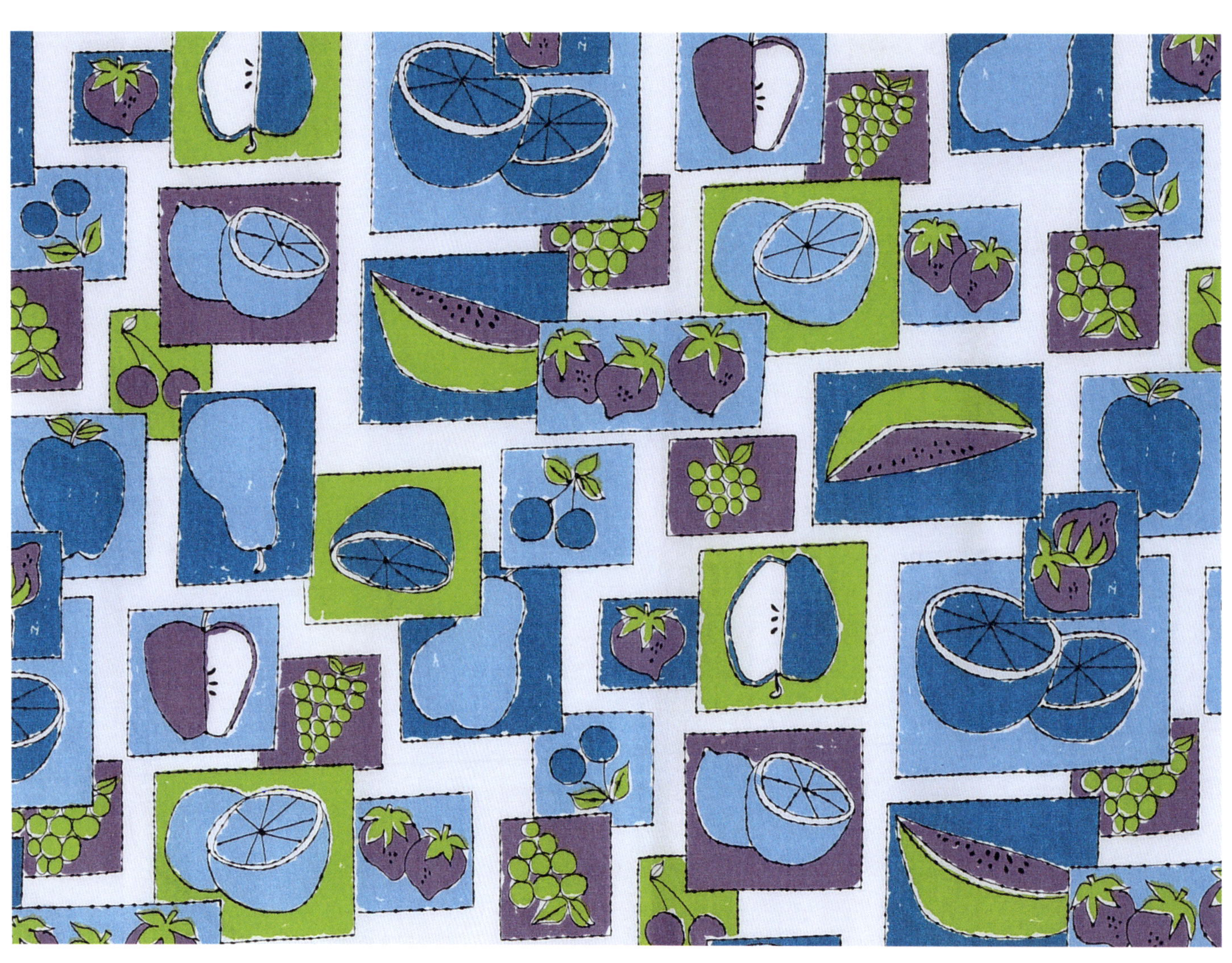

Fruit-themed textile by Warhol, manufactured by Crompton-Richmond, printed cotton, *c.*1957–8. Chosen by the manufacturer as suitable for use on summer frocks and skirts. Warhol's drawings for advertising and editorial projects often feature fruit cut to reveal their inner core of seeds and pips.

the launch of this event. As part of the promotions, a major travelling exhibition of work by the various artists involved in the project opened in October 1955 at the Brooklyn Museum in New York. This exhibition was held in tandem with a touring 'coloured film' documentary of the artists involved working on the textile designs in their studios.

A little later, as John Rombola clearly recalls, 'never one to miss an opportunity, Andy himself also did three or four textile designs for Dan Fuller, somewhere about 1956 or 1957'.[3] Although Rombola cannot now remember exactly what the subjects were, he recalls that they were 'florals'. At that time, Rombola himself was a leading designer for the upmarket textile converter Patterson Fabrics, Inc., and occasionally worked on a freelance basis for Fuller Fabrics and other New York textile converters such as Arundell Clarke Ltd.

Little is currently known of Warhol's initial involvement with textile design, but it apparently began in about 1954, more or less at the time of Fuller Fabric's collaboration with Picasso and other well-known artists. Especially in the later 1950s, Warhol's career, principally as an illustrator, was beginning to be adversely affected by both photography – namely the seductive grasp of photographic illustration that meant even the most prestigious of illustrators was receiving far less commitment from major magazines and journals – and television, which underwent an overwhelming rise in home ownership during the decade. In 1960 Warhol's annual earnings were $70,000 but in 1961 only $57,000, and even then, among other activities, by undertaking window displays for Bonwit Teller.[4] He thus may have chosen to make textile design another useful string to his bow.

However, Warhol's work with commercial textiles may have taken on a much more prominent role in his early career had the textiles, which he tended to 'throw off', been treated as a more serious aspect of his working life. Professionally, his work then received official payment from the buyers, but his textile designs did not necessarily in the same way. Instead, they were mainly dealt with by agents selling directly to textile manufacturers, who rarely, if ever, asked for a designer's name to be attached to a selvedge.

With particular reference to the commercial textiles, the Warhol Museum's former chief archivist, the late Matt Wrbican, has written that 'Typically, Warhol's business records do not clearly indicate what he was doing for a client ... they are extremely vague and very much of the moment'.[5] As a result, it is often necessary to use stylistic evidence to identify textiles by Warhol's hand. Moreover, an absence of documentary evidence is not necessarily due to any absent-mindedness, hurry or confusion on Warhol's part. He could be, at least in commercial practice, extremely secretive, never willingly letting his right hand know what his left was doing. For instance, he was always trying to ensure that art directors and other clients were kept away from his studio assistants and vice versa. His assistants rarely knew for what or for whom a piece of work was eventually intended.[6]

In the 1950s Warhol's good friend Stephen Bruce, proprietor of the well-known New York café-bistro Serendipity 3, sold examples of rejected advertising work by Warhol as 'framed' wall art and also held informal exhibitions of Warhol's decorative prints at the café. Bruce has recalled how, during afternoons at the time, 'Andy and his somewhat exotic entourage would sit around tables in the café applying colour to his prints of "bugs" or "shoes", using brilliantly coloured Indian inks – Dr Martin's Aniline Watercolor Dyes'.[7] Apparently, the colours were chosen and applied in a somewhat random fashion, the end result being more down to the individual and chance than to design. Typically, Warhol's commercial textile designs, mostly making use of the 'blotted broken line', were nearly all vibrantly coloured with Dr Martin's dyes.

The work setup described by Bruce is very much a precursor of Warhol's Silver Factory in the 1960s. During the 1950s Warhol developed several design traits within his commercial work which not only formed a distinctive Warholian style but also enabled him to achieve a good deal of work through the use of assistants. This was something he subsequently continued throughout his life and which has set a precedent for the work of artists such as Jeff Koons and Damien Hurst.

Although sometimes used by other designers and artists, such as Ben Shahn, the well-known blotted, broken line became a signature trait of Warhol's in the 1950s. It was the result of a simple printing process which consisted of the designer's original drawing of an image being traced over with ink, section by section. While still wet, the inked tracing was pressed onto a sheet of absorbent paper, which resulted in a blotted, broken line impression of the original drawing. This method allowed an image to be reproduced a number of times, although each impression was a slight variation of the original. Warhol was apparently very happy with the result, which, combined with other carefully developed design traits, enabled his assistants to work in what became a Warholian house style.[8]

Another distinguishing trait, which later became an integral part of Warhol's Pop art, was the occurrence of individuality within a series of repetitions. Exemplary here is his exploration in a textile design of continuous rows of near identical buttons. The rhythmic nature of pattern making by repetition is closely analogous to that of mass production, and is something Warhol explored more exhaustively in paintings of near identical Coca-Cola bottles and Campbell's soup cans that he showed in early exhibitions of Pop art in Los Angeles and New York in 1962.

Tina Fredericks has written that even in Warhol's first work for *Glamour* magazine in 1949,

> His ink lines were electrifying. Fragmented, broken and intriguing, they grabbed at you with their spontaneous intensity. There was something wallpaperish about the way the drawing covered the space. Much later, of course, we could see these as the precursors to the multiple coke bottles, the cow heads, the infinite, repetitive silk-screens of Marilyn and Mao.[9]

The various designs Warhol used for his textiles are, often, variations or combinations of favoured patterns or motifs, such as 'Happy Butterfly Day'. Like many other professional designers, both before and since, Warhol would often recycle a particularly successful design, using it, somewhat indiscriminately, on large decorative screens created as part of window displays for upmarket New York stores, or for gift-wrapping, greetings cards or textiles. As Matt Wrbican has written, 'Some of Warhol's pattern designs may have been created for gift-wrap, rather than fabrics. They may also have been used for both these end products. The artist was always happy to oblige a paying client.'[10]

Warhol's textile designs, mainly produced on fabrics intended for clothing, were among those loosely termed 'novelty' or 'conversational' prints by the fashion and textile trades of the time. The subjects of such prints were largely derived from everyday objects and activities rather than the floral and geometric patterns that had traditionally been used on printed silk, cotton or linen.

The use of so-called novelty textiles, especially for summer clothes, had steadily increased over the course of the twentieth century, particularly in the United States. Between 1925 and 1927, Kneeland Green, then artistic director of the Stehli Silks Corporation, New York, had introduced a series of textiles known as the 'Americana Prints'. Green chose to only commission American artists, illustrators and so-called star personalities as designers of the series, and the result was a triumph of 'silk designs that tell a story' and 'reflect the modern American scene and temper'.[11]

Given this earlier history, it seems appropriate that Stehli Silks would later produce, between 1962 and 1963, what appear to be

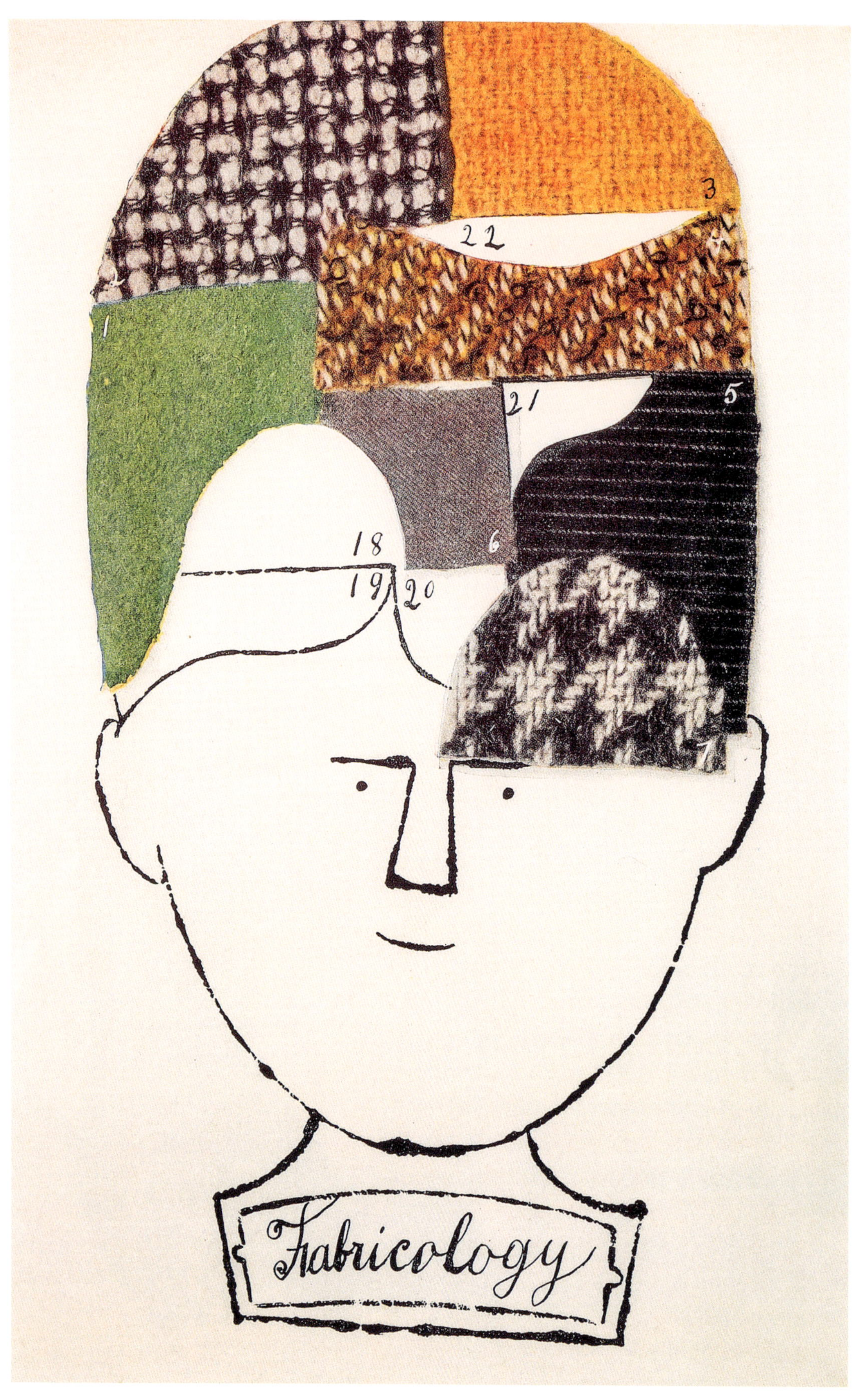

'Fabricology' illustrations by Warhol for *Harper's Bazaar* (July 1960) showing two drawings of collaged heads.

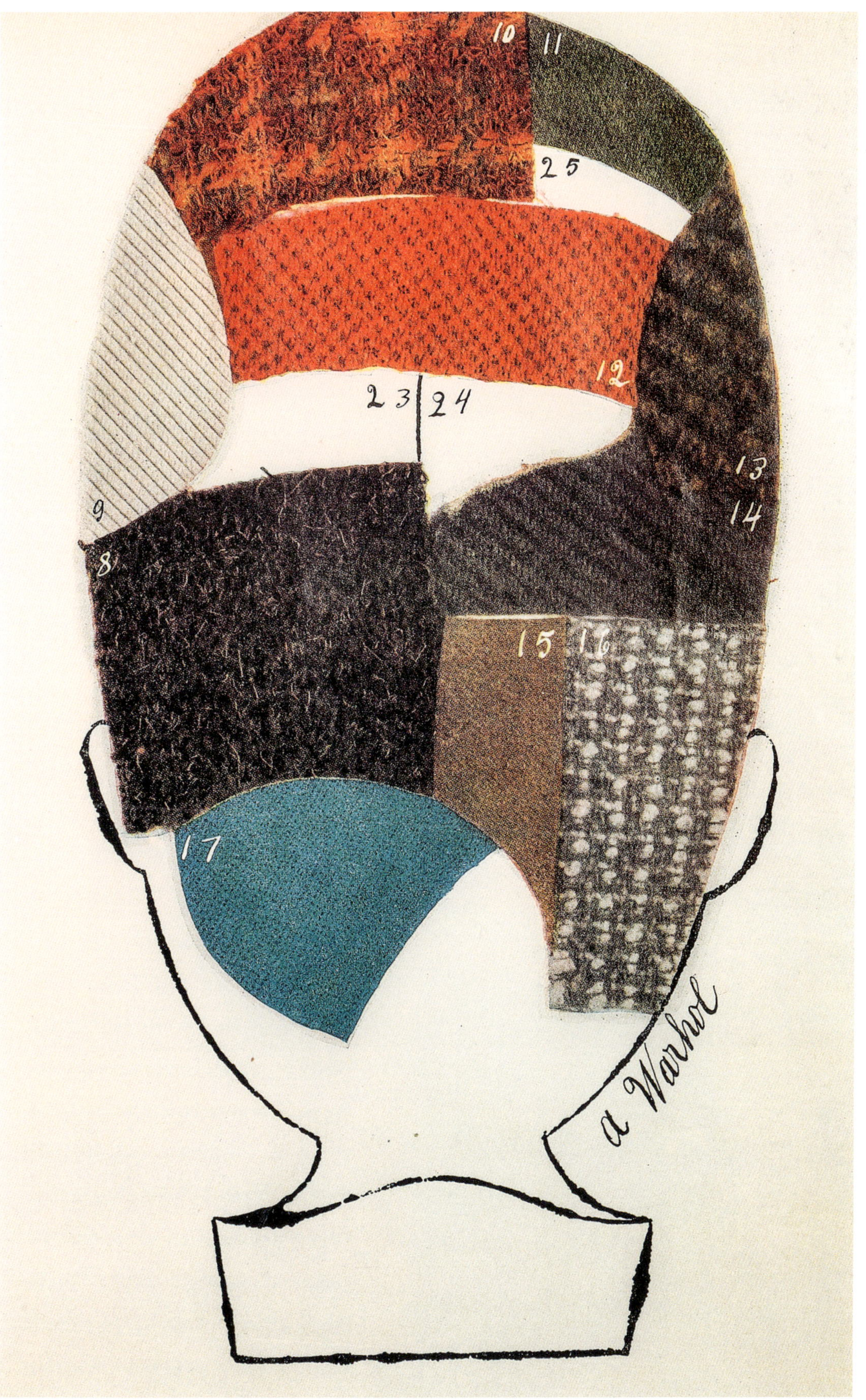

10
11
25
12
23
24
9
8
13
14
15
16
17
a Warhol

Warhol's last commercial textile designs. Like most large successful textile companies, the Stehli Corporation not only printed on silk but also on cotton or linen and, especially, new man-made fibres such as polyester. Stehli produced Warhol's last-known commercial textile designs on most of these fabrics. All are in a high Pop vein and are closely related to the artist's early Pop art paintings and prints of Campbell's soup cans and Coca-Cola bottles, which were first shown in exhibitions in Los Angeles and New York in 1962.

However, around 1963 Warhol ceased working on his commercial textile designs, and they duly became as redundant as the rest of his pre-Pop art work as an illustrator and graphic designer. The only later exceptions are projects that occasionally sparked his interest, such as a record sleeve or magazine cover.

Since Warhol's relatively early death, aged fifty-eight, in February 1987, there has been a considerable renewal of interest in his early pre-Pop art designs from the 1950s and early 1960s. Although he claimed there was little of interest for others here, everything from the advertisements for I. Miller Shoes to window displays for Bonwit Teller and cookery books like *Wild Raspberries* is now cherished like gold. There has been a succession of books on his decorative style and aesthetic at this time, especially his use of a distinctive *faux-naïf* style of drawing and a seductively droll sense of humour. The commercial textiles that are the subject of this book are probably the last remaining unexplored area of his pre-Pop work. As such, they are a pleasure to explore and work with.

Notes

1. Geoffrey Rayner, Richard Chamberlain and Annamarie Stapleton, *Artists' Textiles, 1940–1976* (Woodbridge, Suffolk: Antique Collectors Club, 2012), p. 229.
2. Ibid., p. 9.
3. Ibid., p. 231.
4. Paul Maréchal, *Andy Warhol, The Complete Commissioned Magazine Work, 1948–1987,* catalogue raisonné (Munich, London, New York: Prestel, 2014), p. 13.
5. Email correspondence between Richard Chamberlain and the late Matt Wrbican, then the chief archivist of the Andy Warhol Museum, Pittsburgh, 24 January 2010.
6. Andy Warhol, *Andy Warhol: Drawings and Illustrations of the 1950s* (Tokyo: Goliga Books and New York: Distributed Art Publishers, 2000), p. 107.
7. Rayner, Chamberlain and Stapleton, *Artists' Textiles, 1940–1976,* p. 228.
8. *Andy Warhol: Drawings and Illustrations of the 1950s,* p. 100.
9. Tina S. Fredericks, 'Remembering Andy', in Jesse Kornbluth, *Pre-Pop Warhol* (New York: Panache Press at Random House, 1988), p. 11.
10. Chamberlain and Wrbican, email correspondence, 24 January 2010.
11. Valerie Mendes, 'Introduction' to *Novelty Fabrics*, Victoria and Albert Museum colour books series (Exeter: Webb & Bower, 1988), pp. 7 and 8.

NOTE ON THE CATALOGUE OF TEXTILES

The identification of Andy Warhol's commercial textile designs is a relatively new and ongoing project. In the catalogue that follows each of his currently known textile designs is, as far as is possible, given an approximate date, together with some associated drawings and relevant printed material. Also shown are the various colourways in which they survive. Some of the designs were printed on a variety of fabrics, and were sometimes rescaled to suit the needs of a particular market. This was particularly the case with the synthetics used by the Stehli Silks Corporation for what are probably Warhol's last commercial designs, dating from 1962–3.

Pinpointing the dates of most of his pre-Pop art textile designs is often difficult as Warhol kept few, if any, actual records. Fortunately, many of the designs are related to groups of his drawings with particular themes, which tended to coincide with advertising campaigns and other commercial projects he was engaged in at a particular time. By chance, the date of apparently his last commercial textile designs is known as 1962–3. This particular group of textiles was subsequently used for a Spring 1964 fashion collection by his close friend Stephen Bruce, owner of the well-known Manhattan café-bistro Serendipity 3. Similarly, Warhol's 'Bright Butterflies' design – produced by the textile converter Nat Wager and used for a fashion collection designed by Sylvia de Gay for Robert Sloan of New York – was prominently featured in the December 1960 edition of *Glamour* magazine, a publication which had continued to support Warhol's work since he first arrived in New York in 1949.

Only a few of the converters who produced Warhol's textile designs printed their name or logo on a selvedge, and most large retailers in the mass market, such as J. C. Penny, were reluctant to have a name or logo, other than their own, on any of the products they sold. In a few cases, however, a retailer's label has survived attached to a length of cloth, which at least gives one an idea of the market the fabric was originally intended for. This was equally true of the more exclusive upmarket stores in the United States, which wished to guard the exclusivity associated with their name.

While some of the textiles included here have archival links with Warhol, others have until now remained unknown. Hardly any research has been given to these textiles, and the evidence in the present book is probably the first to explore their origins.

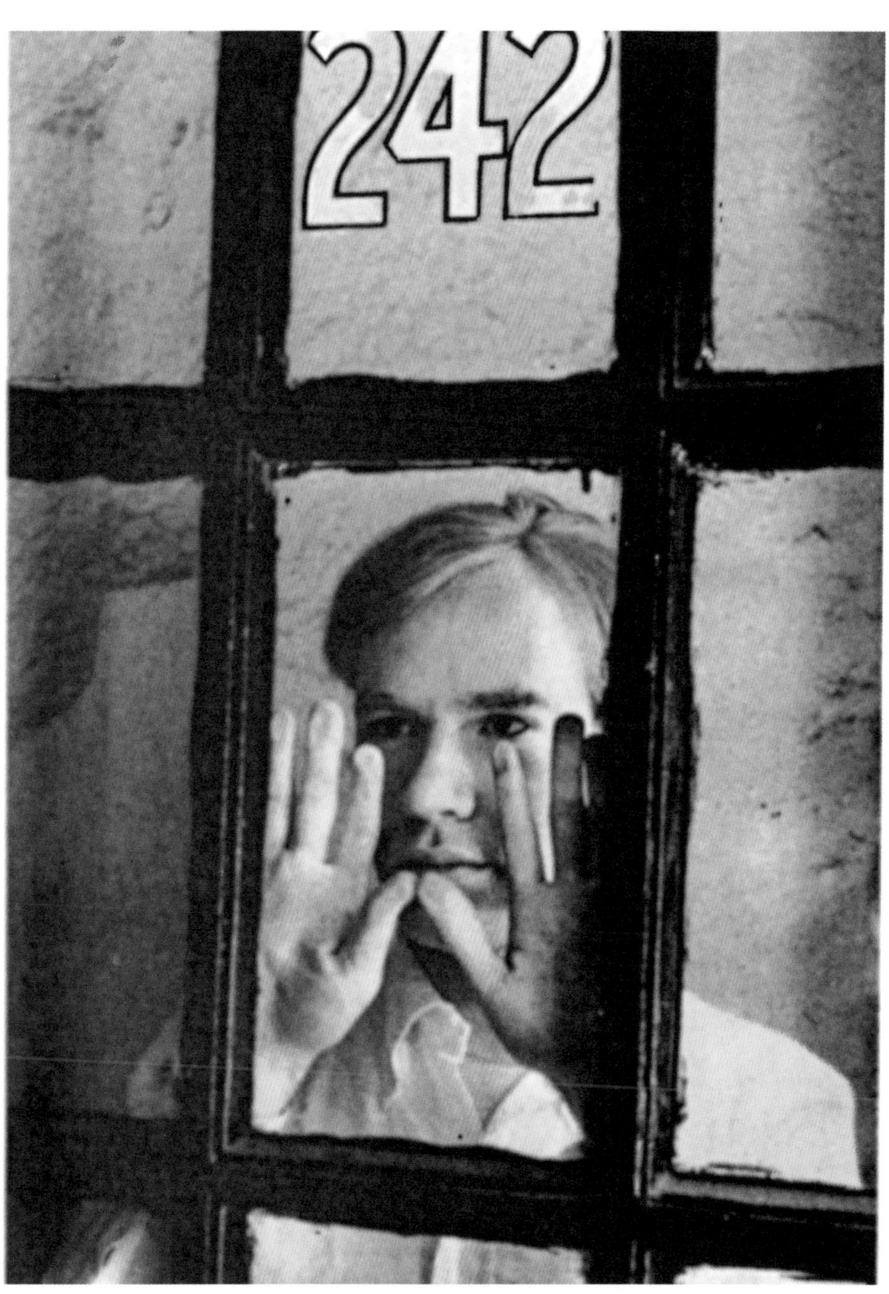

Warhol in his apartment, 242 Lexington Avenue, New York, 1958.
Photographer: Duane Michals.

CATALOGUE OF TEXTILES

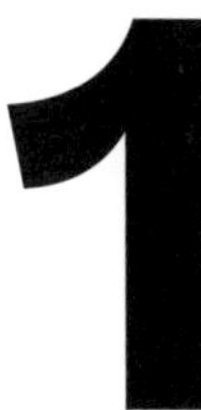

THREE DESIGNS FOR TEXTILES WITH
BIRDS AND BEES

Collage, ink and gouache on paper, *circa* 1953–1955

These three repeating patterns of birds and bees are thought to be some of the earliest textile designs created by Warhol. They are the result of printed stamps made by Warhol and his assistants from gum erasers, which were then used with ink, gouache and collage. The actual textiles from these designs do not appear to exist, nor do we know who produced them.

Opposite and following spread (a, b and c) Three early textile designs.

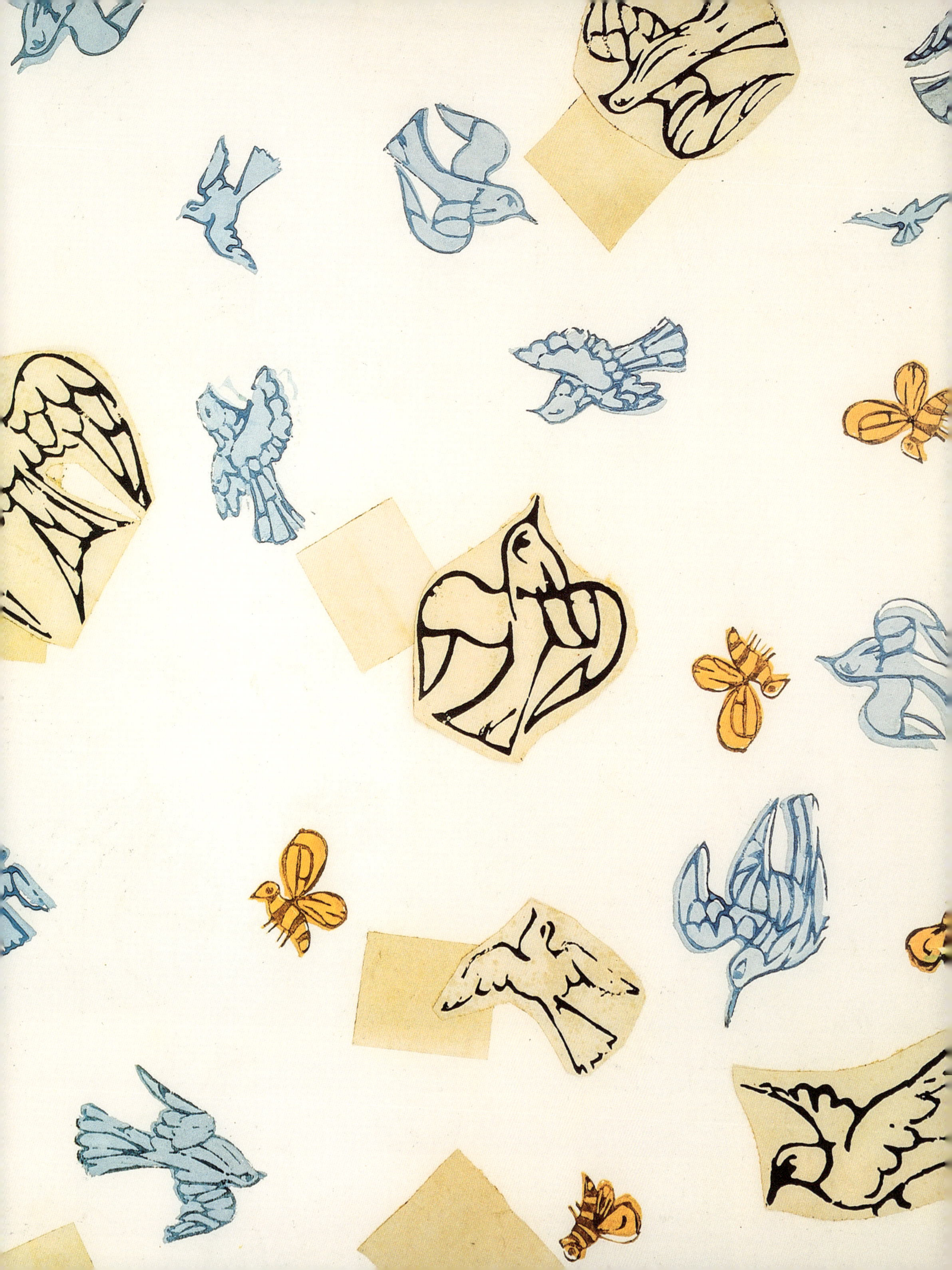

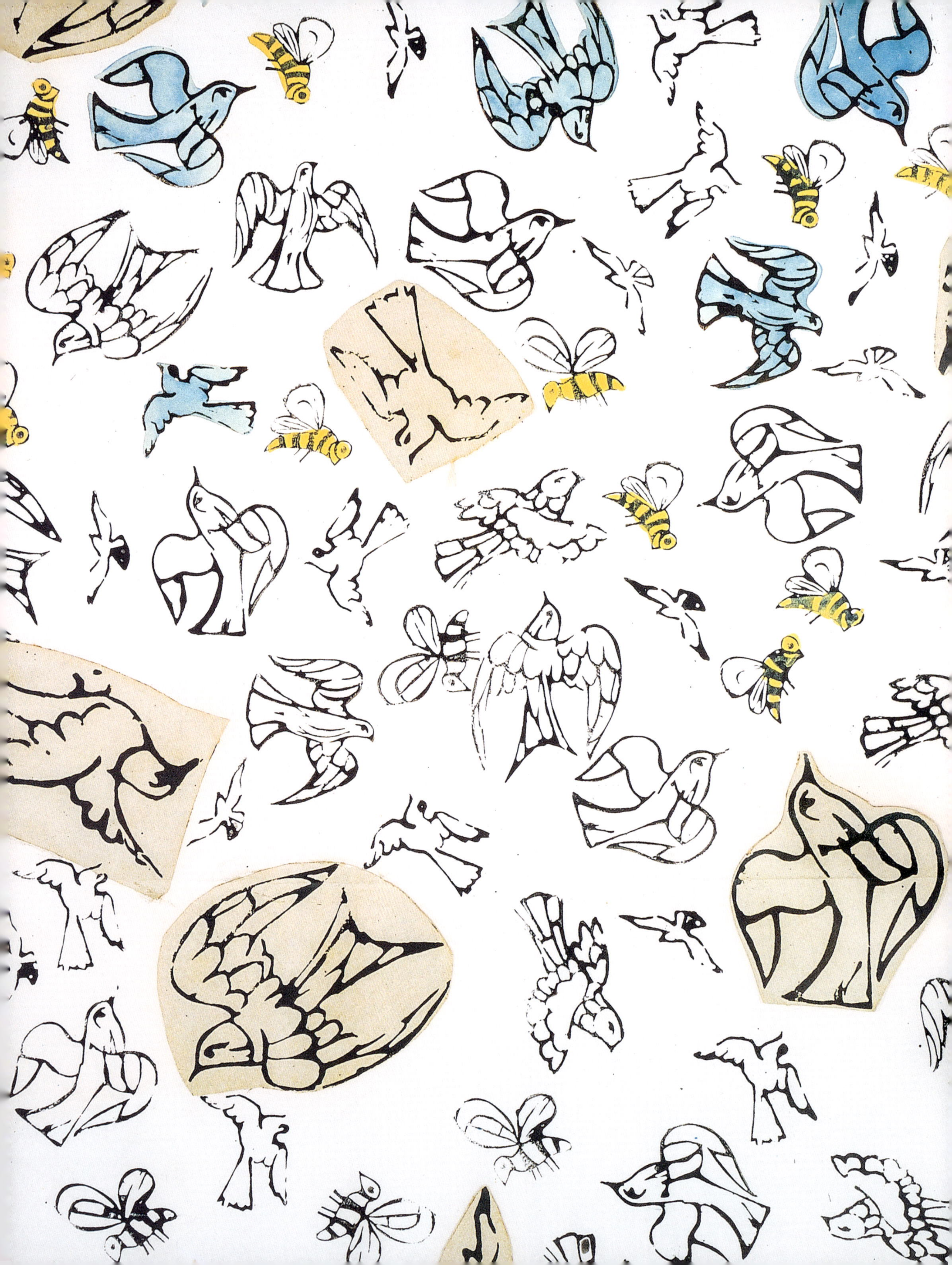

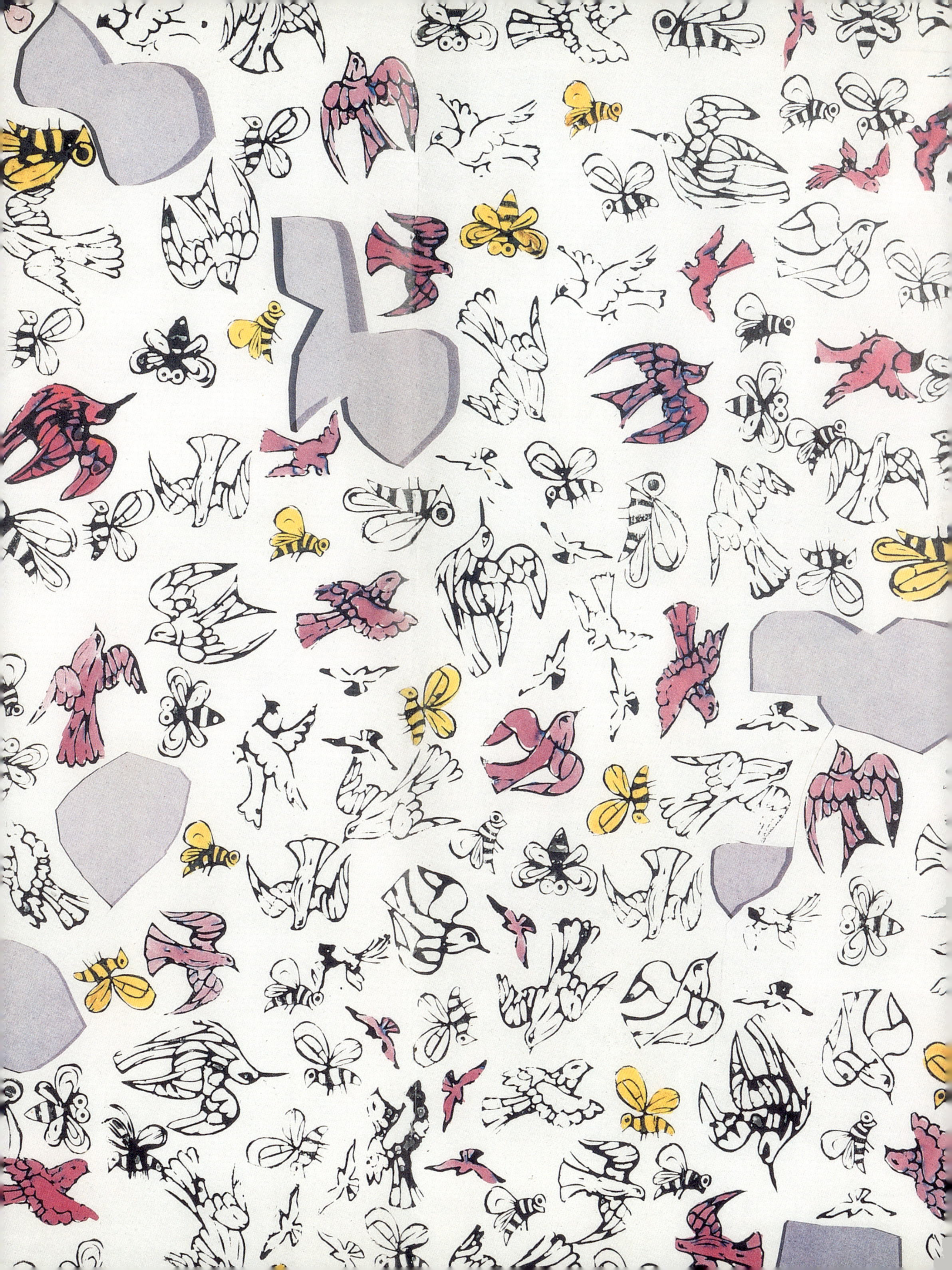

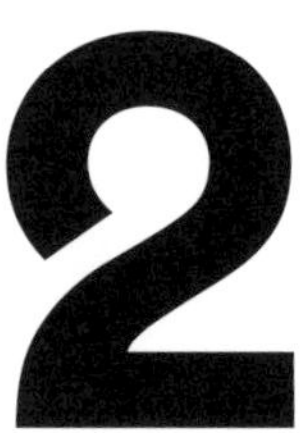

HAPPY BUG DAY

Printed cotton, *circa* 1955–1956
D. B. Fuller & Co., Inc. (Fuller Fabrics, Inc.)

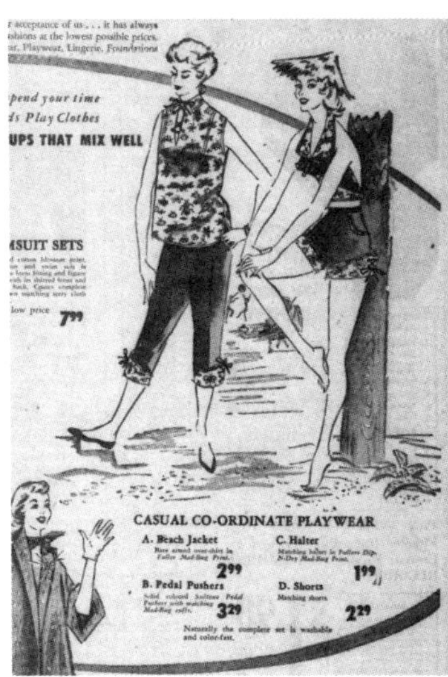

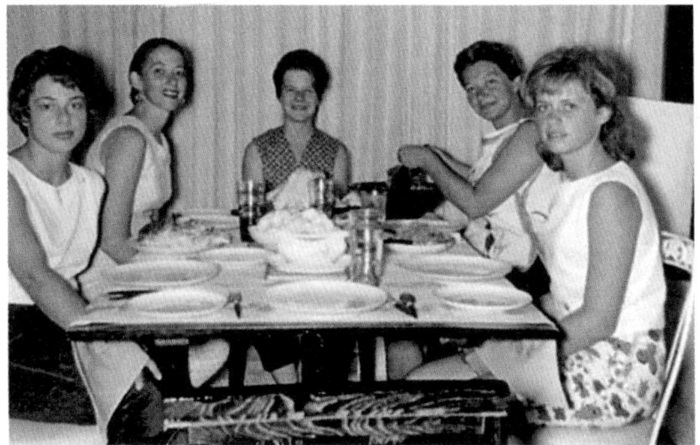

'Happy Bug Day', manufactured by Fuller Fabrics, is probably one of Warhol's most commercially successful textile designs. It appears to have been derived from eighteenth- and nineteenth-century mounted displays of arthropods such as spiders, butterflies and moths, a ludicrous gathering of creepy bugs.

The design, which was also used by Warhol on greetings cards, stationery and wrapping paper, is proof of the popularity of 'mad bug' images in the United States at the time. Although sold by many other stores, the company J. C. Penny, one of the biggest of the American commercial chains, sold this textile as both 'off-the-peg' clothing and as yardage for the home dress-making market. A newspaper advertisement from 1956 exists which shows garments using Fuller's 'Mad Bug Print' for accessories and other items of clothing. Clothing using the 'Happy Bug Day' design printed on a green background is also known. A further colourway in pink and red is in the collection of MoMA, New York.

An old friend of Warhol's, the artist, illustrator and window display designer Dudley Huppler, possessed an envelope, originally addressed to Warhol, containing lengths of 'Happy Bug Day' and the textile with large butterflies (no. 3). Warhol's address on the envelope, from Tiffany & Co. of New York, is postmarked 'April 24th, 1956'.

Warhol first met Huppler in 1954. According to the late Matt Wrbican, the two men became very good friends, corresponded frequently and collaborated on window displays for Bonwit Teller and I. Miller Shoes. Huppler, probably through his relationship with Warhol, also sold postcards and examples of his artwork at the New York café Serendipity 3. The envelope from Warhol with these two textile samples was sold when Huppler's artistic estate was auctioned by Ripley Auctioneers on 24 August 2011.

Above left (a) Advertisement for beachwear made from Fuller's 'Happy Bug Day' textile, *Honolulu Advertiser*, 22 April 1956.
Above right (b) Family snapshot of the singer Janis Joplin with friends and family, *c.*1960. The girl in front wears a skirt in Fuller's 'Happy Bug Day' textile. **Opposite (c)** Blue and green colourway.

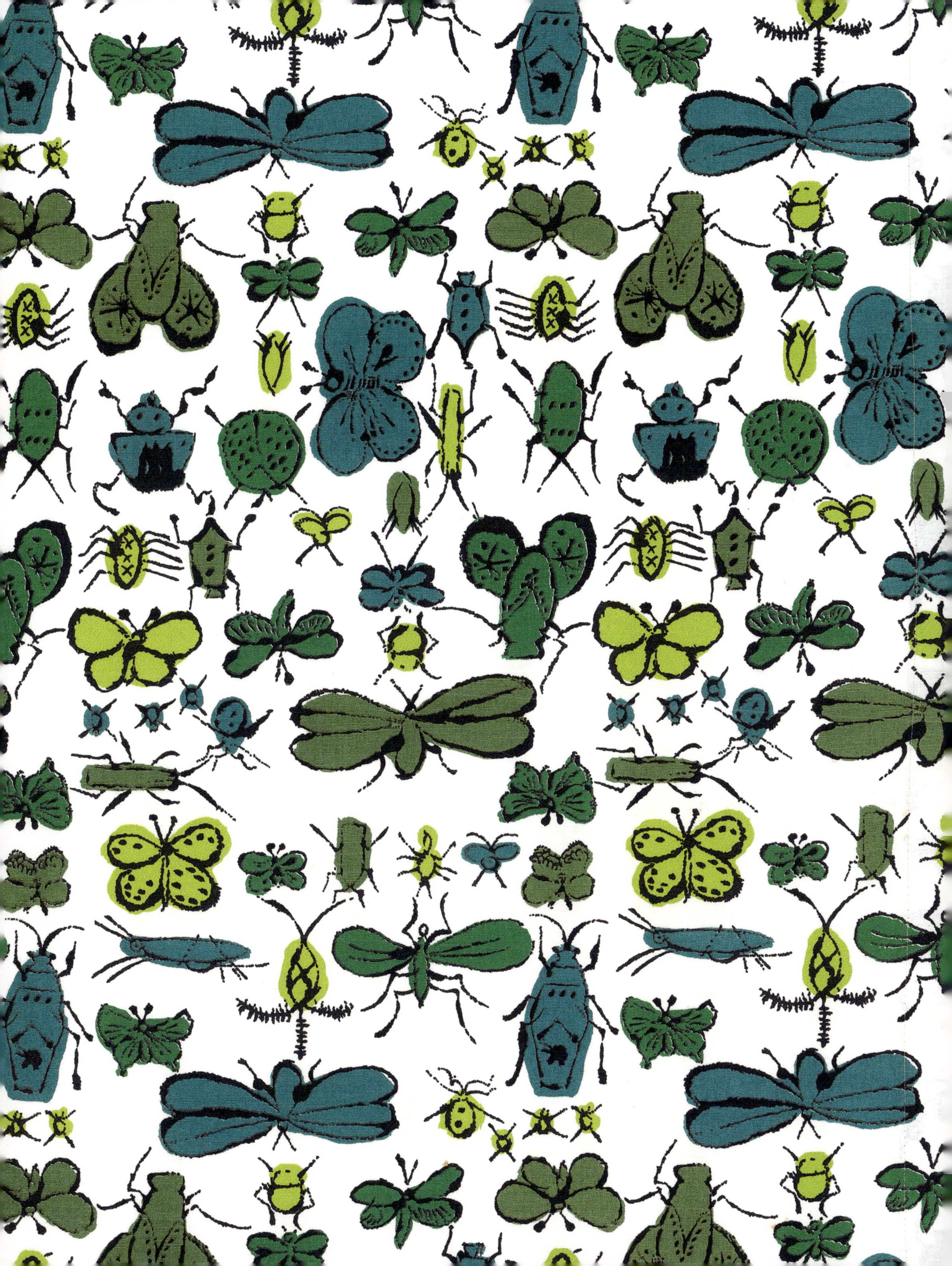

(d) Lilac and blue colourway.

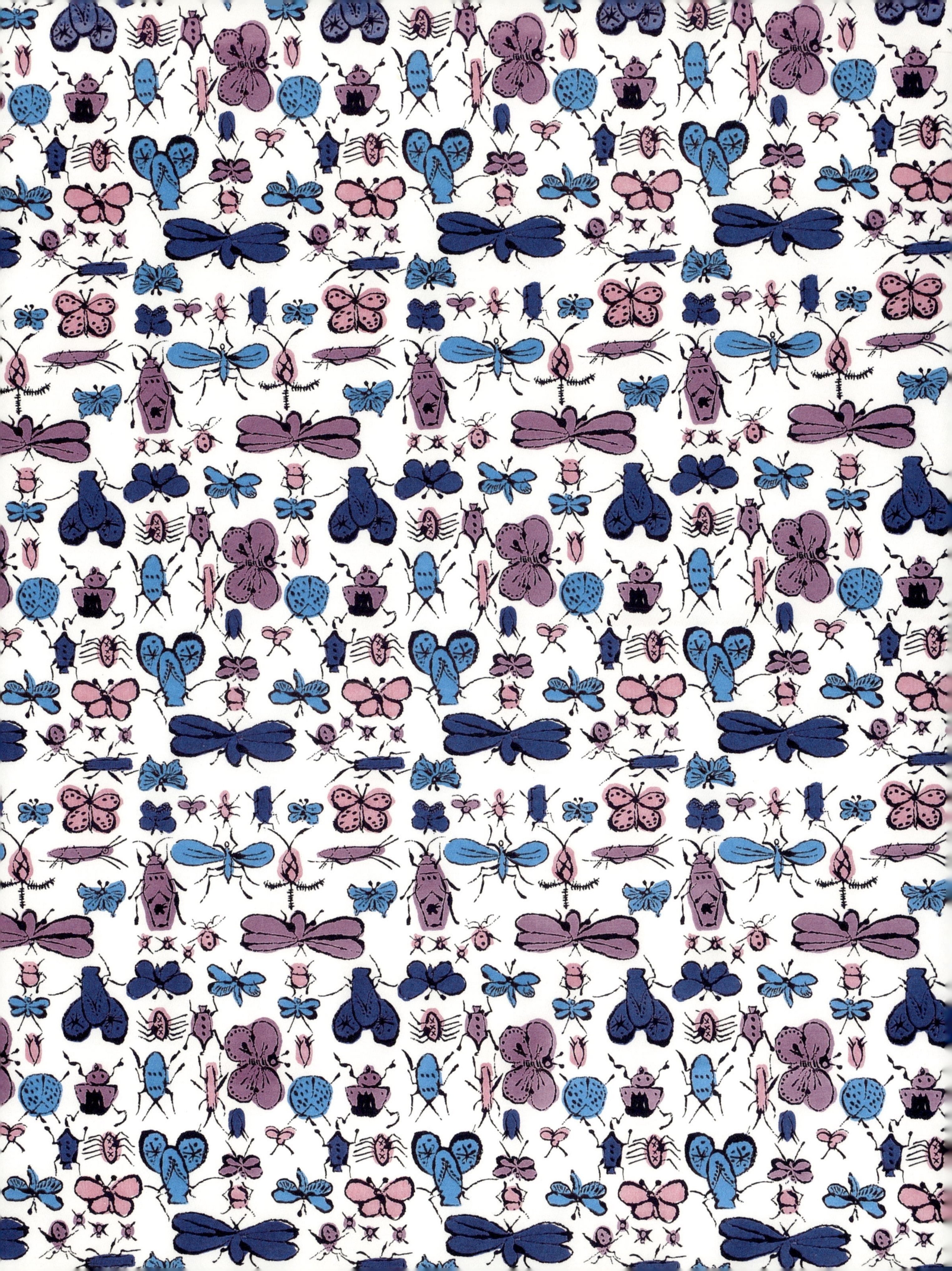

(e) Brown, orange and yellow colourway.

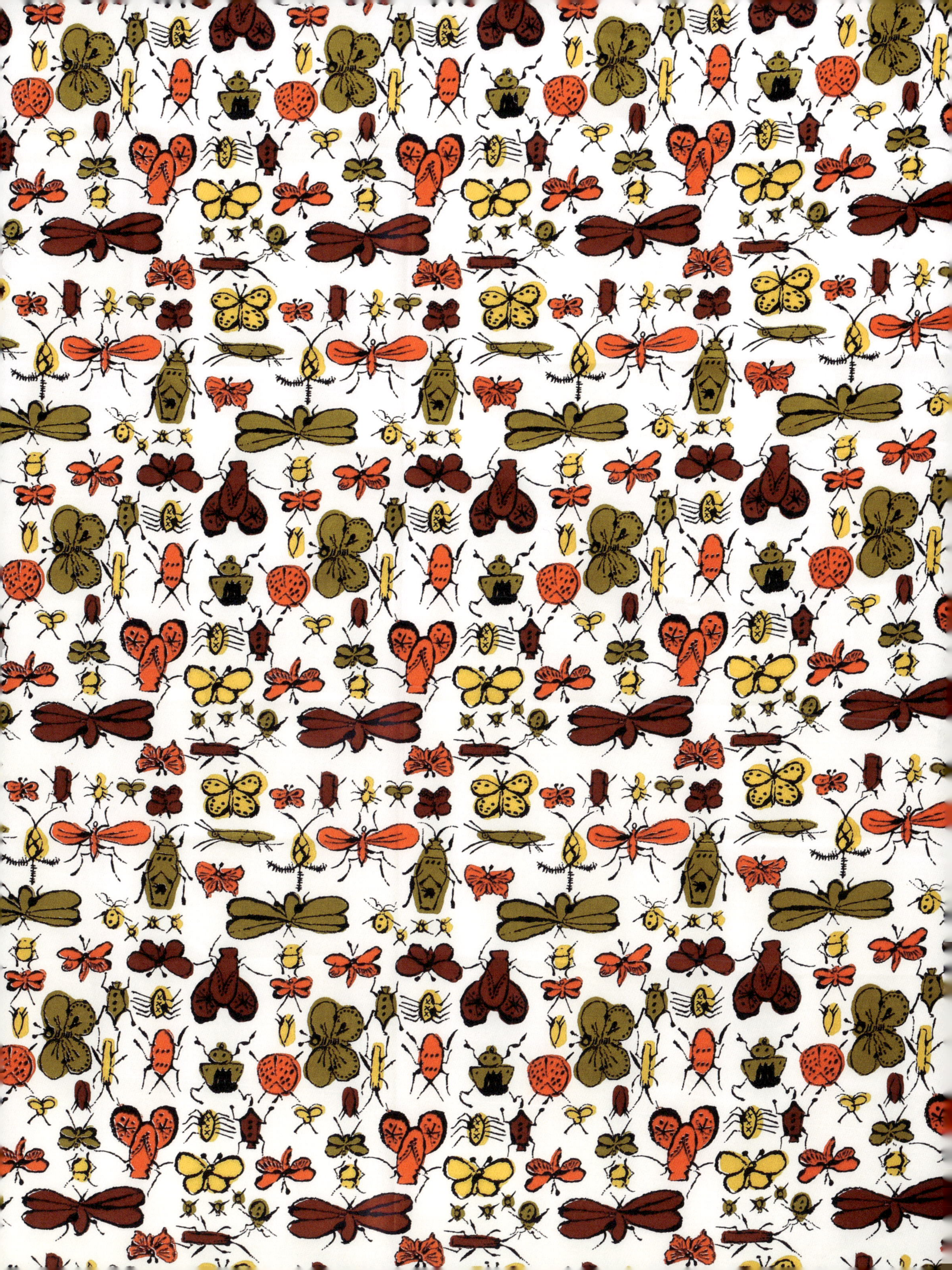

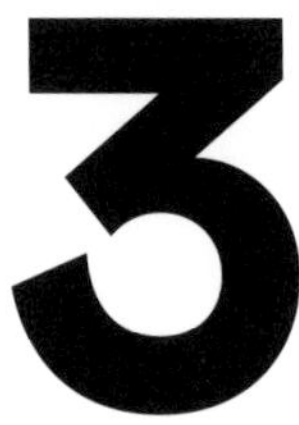

TEXTILE WITH
LARGE BUTTERFLIES

Printed cotton, *circa* 1955–1956
D. B. Fuller & Co., Inc.

This textile decorated with large butterflies is one of the fabrics designed by Warhol which demonstrates his great interest in the species. He chose various permutations of them, but this one with large butterflies is the most dominant in terms of scale and colour.

The pattern is a large-scale print in which butterflies dramatically fly around. This version of butterflies, enlarged and freely spaced, is very much in keeping with Warhol's later Pop art ethos from the 1960s.

An example of this textile was in the envelope Warhol gave to his friend Dudley Huppler in 1956. It accompanied a piece of 'Happy Bug Day' (no. 2), both of which were manufactured by Fuller Fabrics, Inc.

Opposite (a) Red, pink and orange colourway. **Following spread (b)** Skirt in brown, orange and yellow colourway by Paddle and Saddle, Oregon. **(c)** Skirt in green and blue colourway, maker unknown.

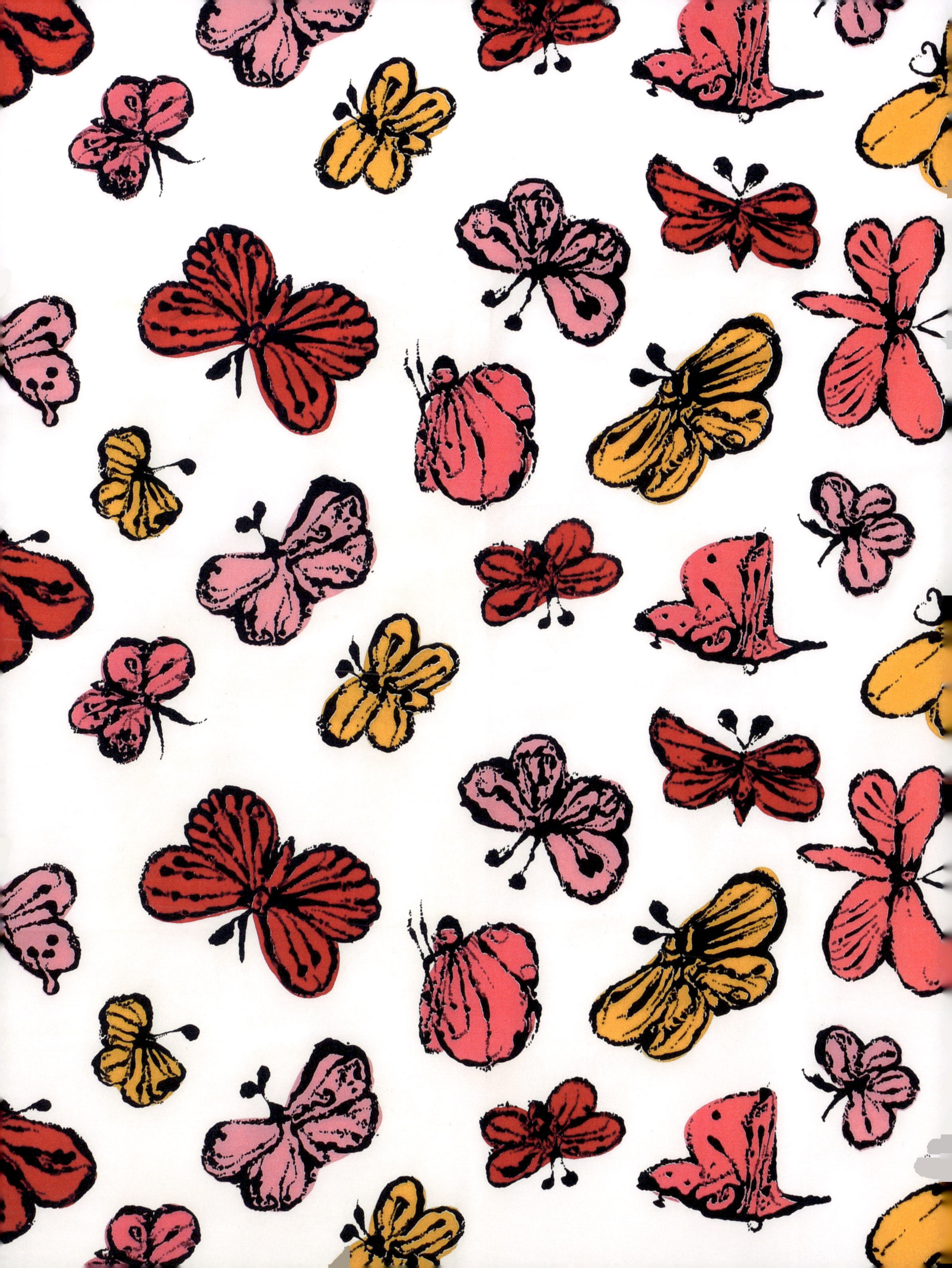

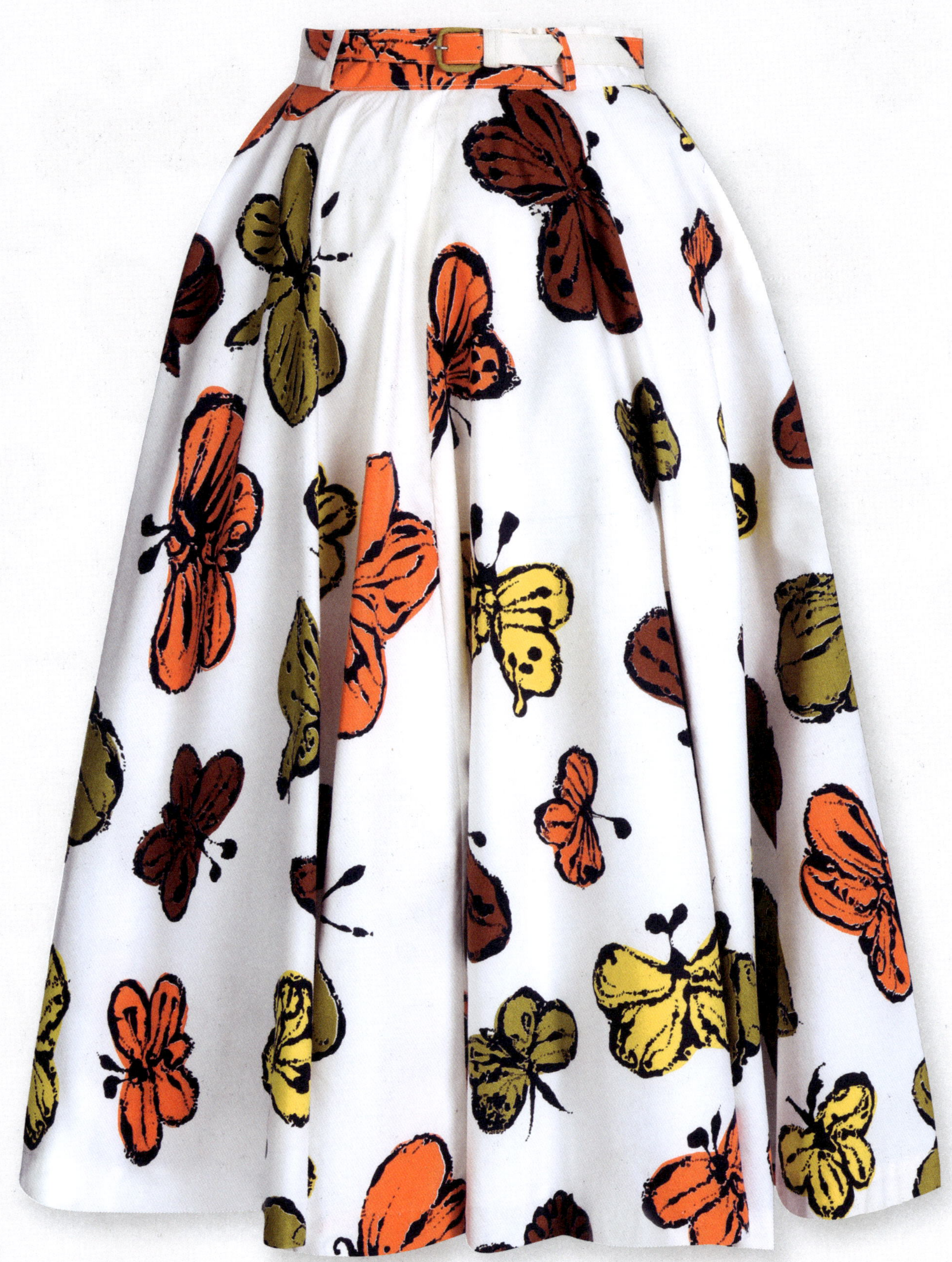

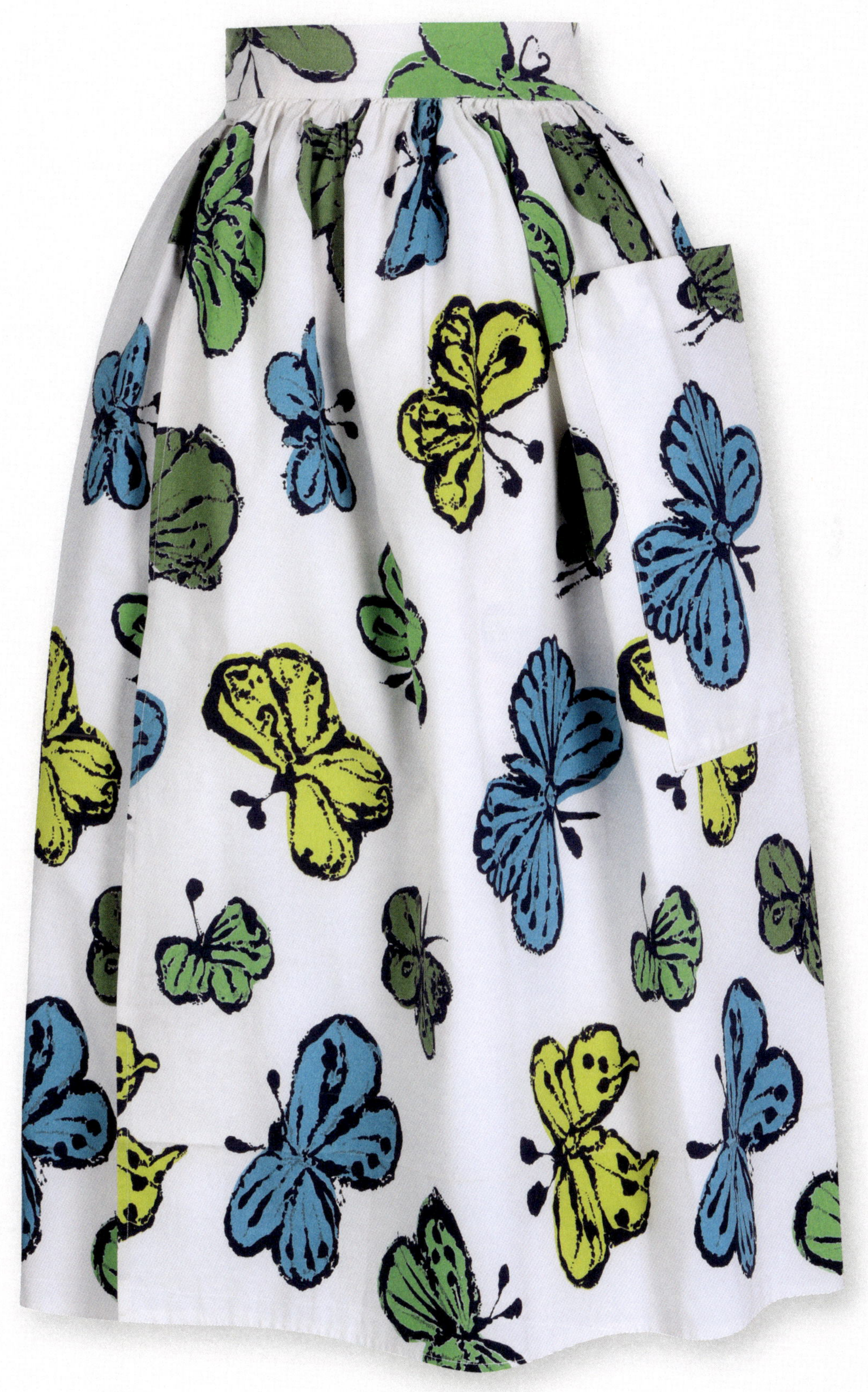

(d) Blue and lilac colourway.

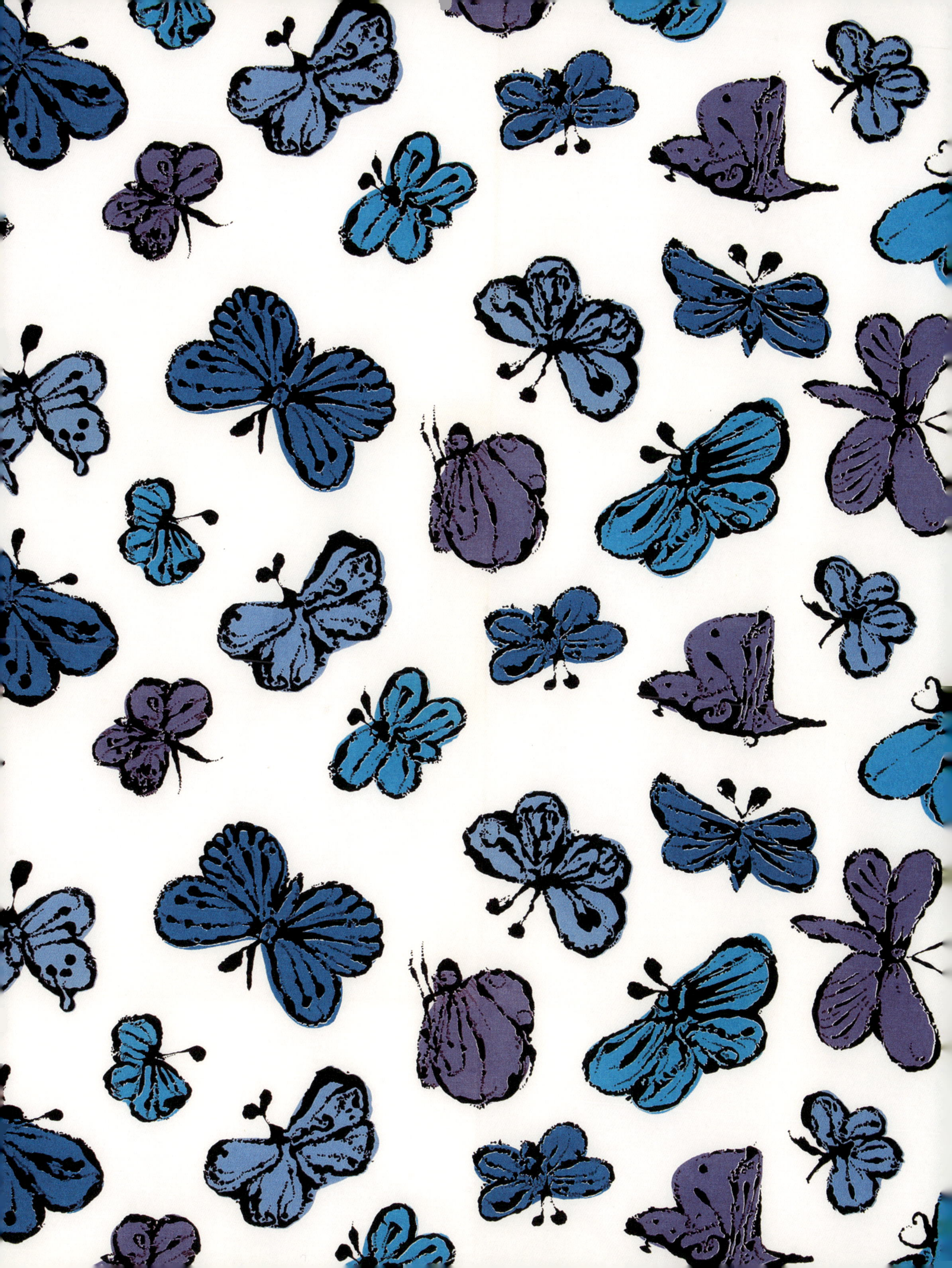

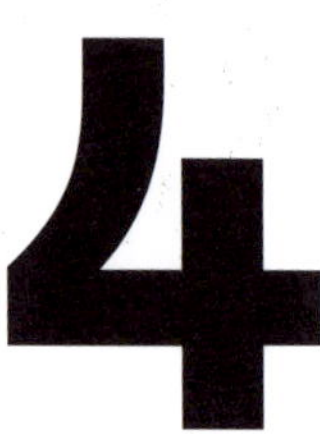

HAPPY BUTTERFLY DAY

Printed silk, *circa* 1955–1956
Manufacturer unknown

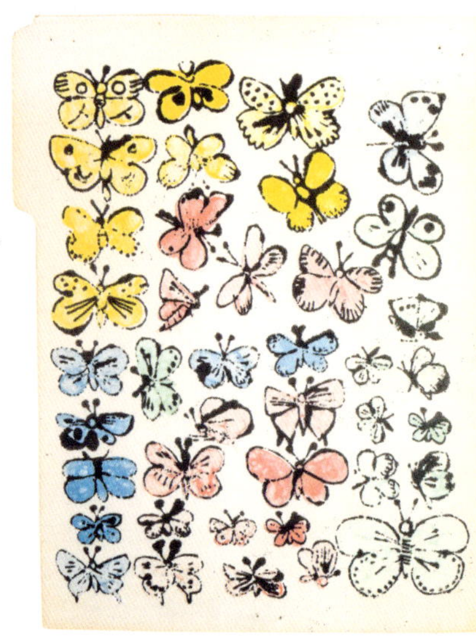

'Happy Butterfly Day' is almost certainly based on eighteenth- and nineteenth-century displays of mounted butterflies. The butterfly motif seems to have been a particularly happy expression of well-being for Warhol. Similar designs were also created by him at that time for greetings cards and stationery. The textile is realised in subtle pastel colours, in contrast to Warhol's more usual palette of brilliant primaries and secondaries.

Although the manufacturer of this textile is still unknown, among the makers and retailers using it was The Needlecraft, an upmarket fashion retailer located on the Boardwalk in Atlantic City, New Jersey. (Whenever the film star Liz Taylor visited Atlantic City, she always made a special visit to this store.) Another retailer was the New York department store Lord & Taylor, who also retailed dresses made from the textile. Like The Needlecraft, Lord & Taylor were also somewhat exclusive.

Above (a) Promotional folder for Vanity Fair Lingerie. Offset lithography painted with Dr Martin's watercolour inks, c.1955.
Opposite (b) Textile (detail of dress overleaf).

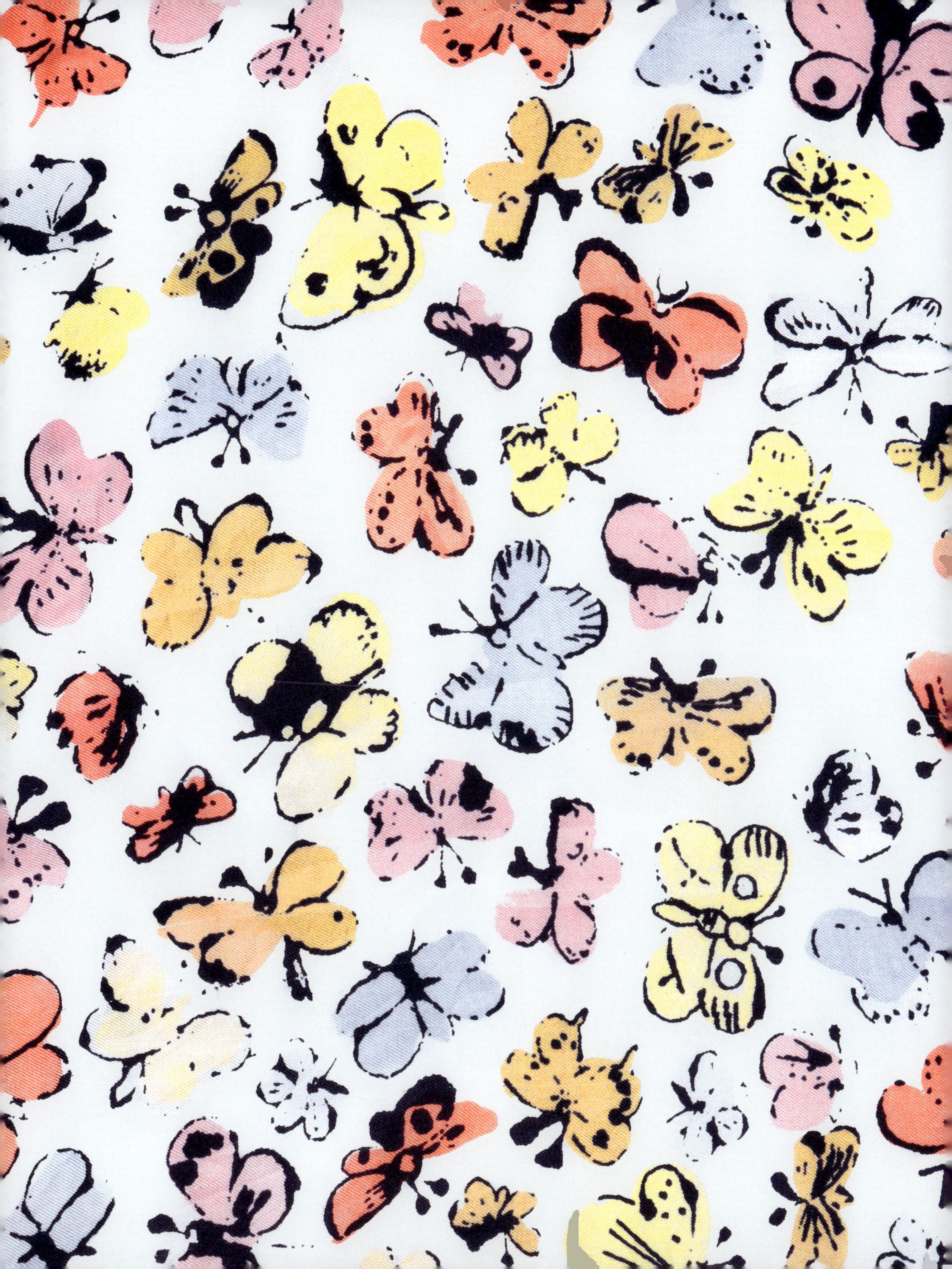

(c) Silk dress by The Needlecraft, Boardwalk, Atlantic City, c.1955–6.

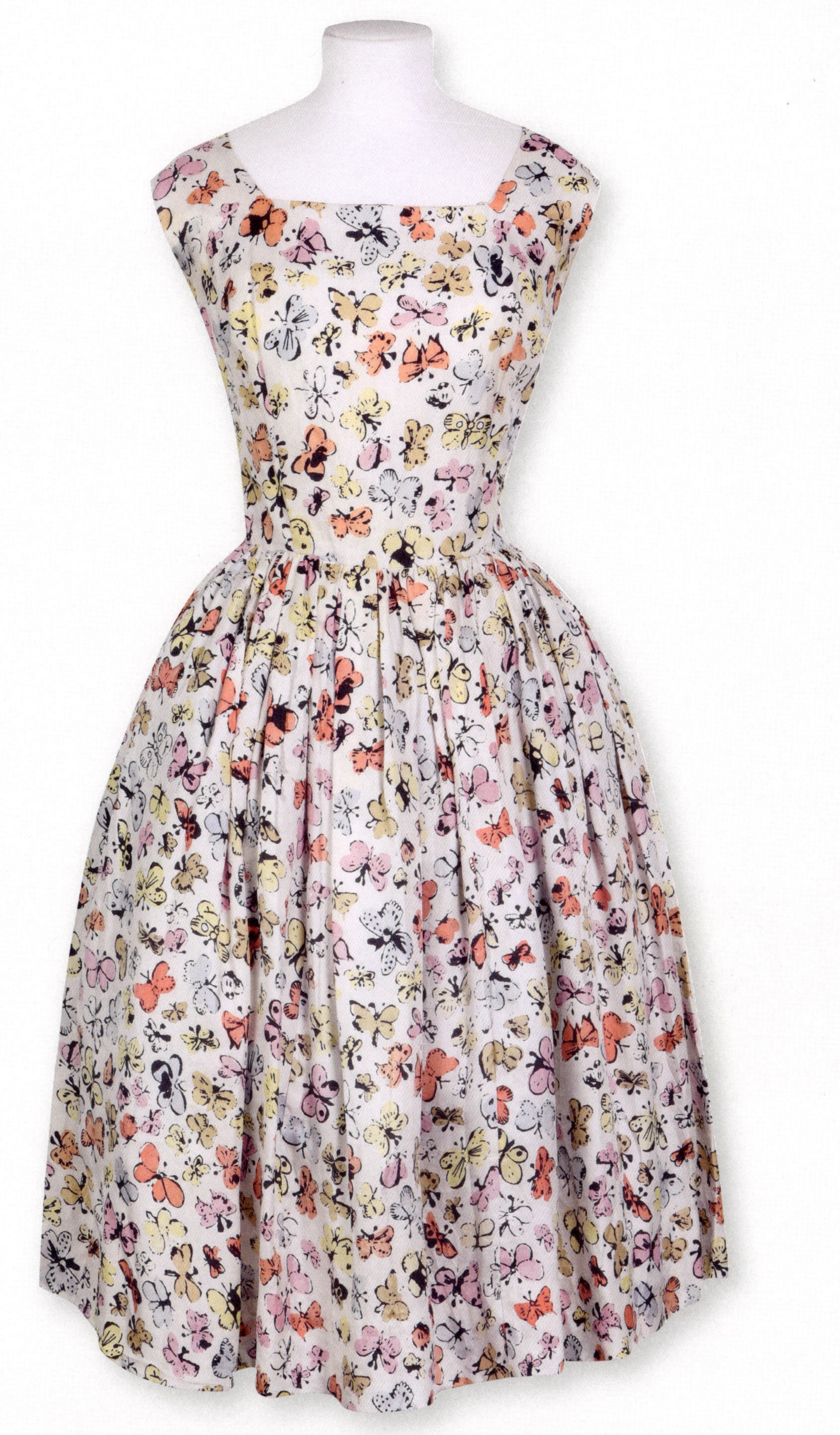

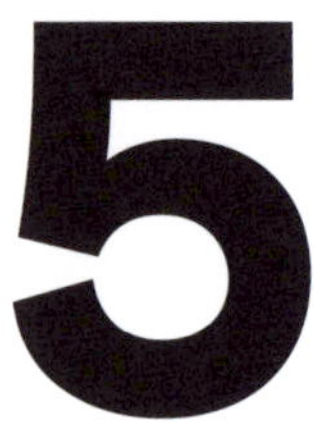

TEXTILE WITH
BOLDLY COLOURED BUTTERFLIES

Printed silk, *circa* 1955–1956
Manufacturer unknown

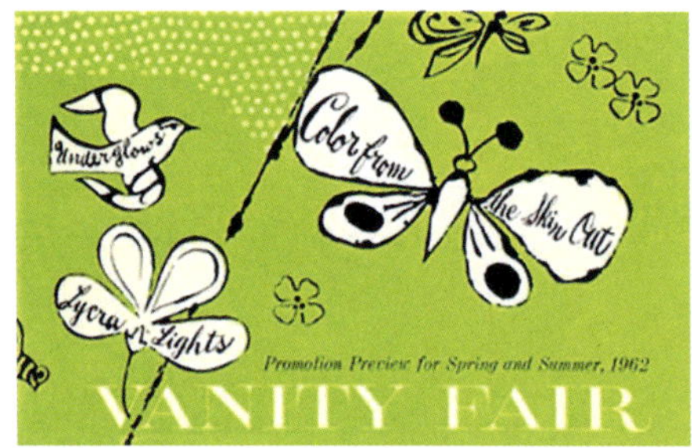

Unlike the softer palette shown on ‘Happy Butterfly Day’ (no. 4), a riot of bright colour is displayed here. Butterflies, boldly drawn, float freely in space, unrestricted by the limitations of the cloth. The textile is closer in design to Warhol’s later 1962 cover for the spring and summer promotional preview of *Vanity Fair*, an exercise in strong colour and much more powerful drawing.

Above (a) *Vanity Fair* promotion preview for Spring and Summer 1962 (detail). **Opposite (b)** Textile (detail of blouse overleaf).

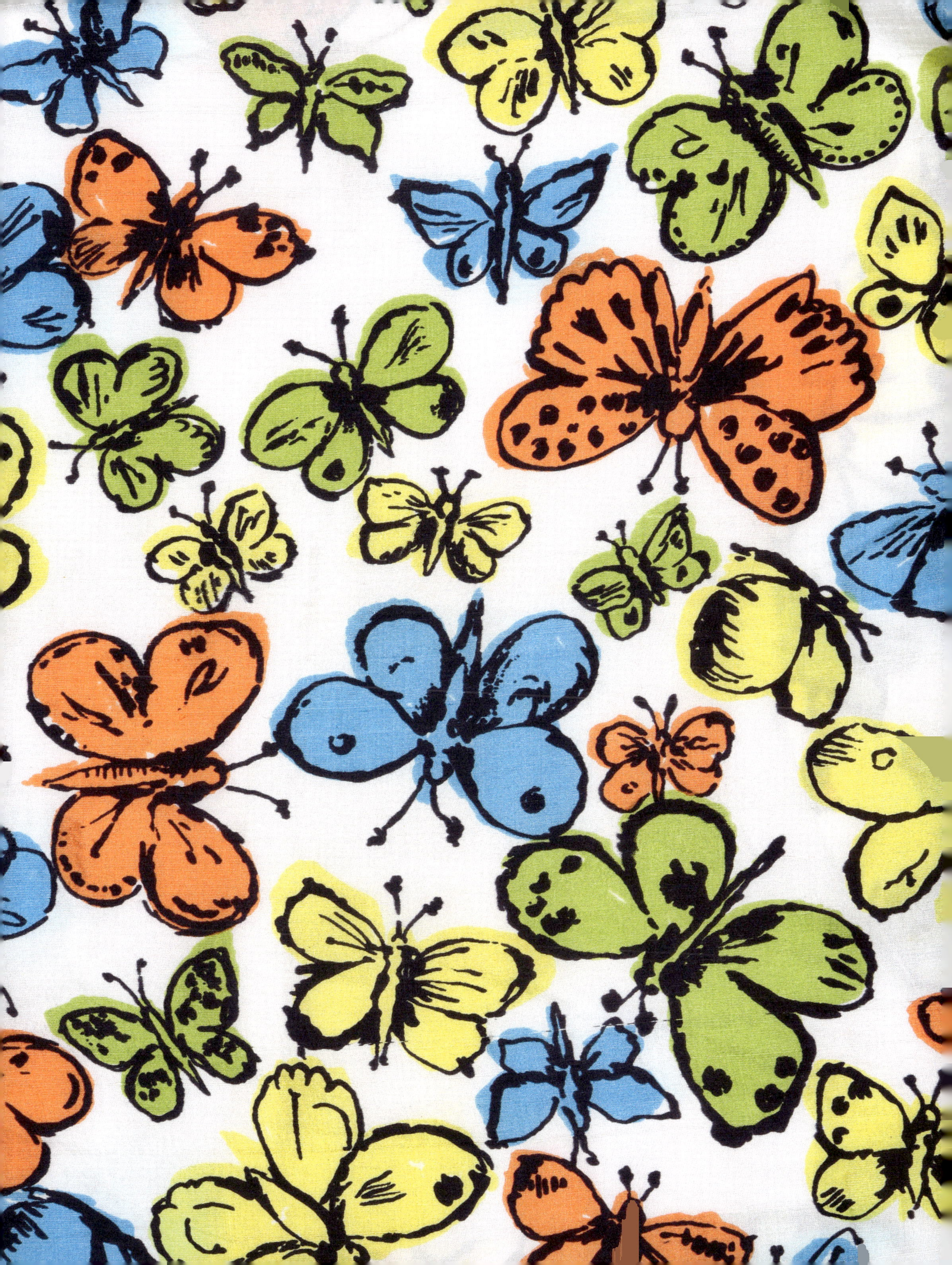

(c) Silk blouse by Pantino, New York and Rome, *c.*1956.

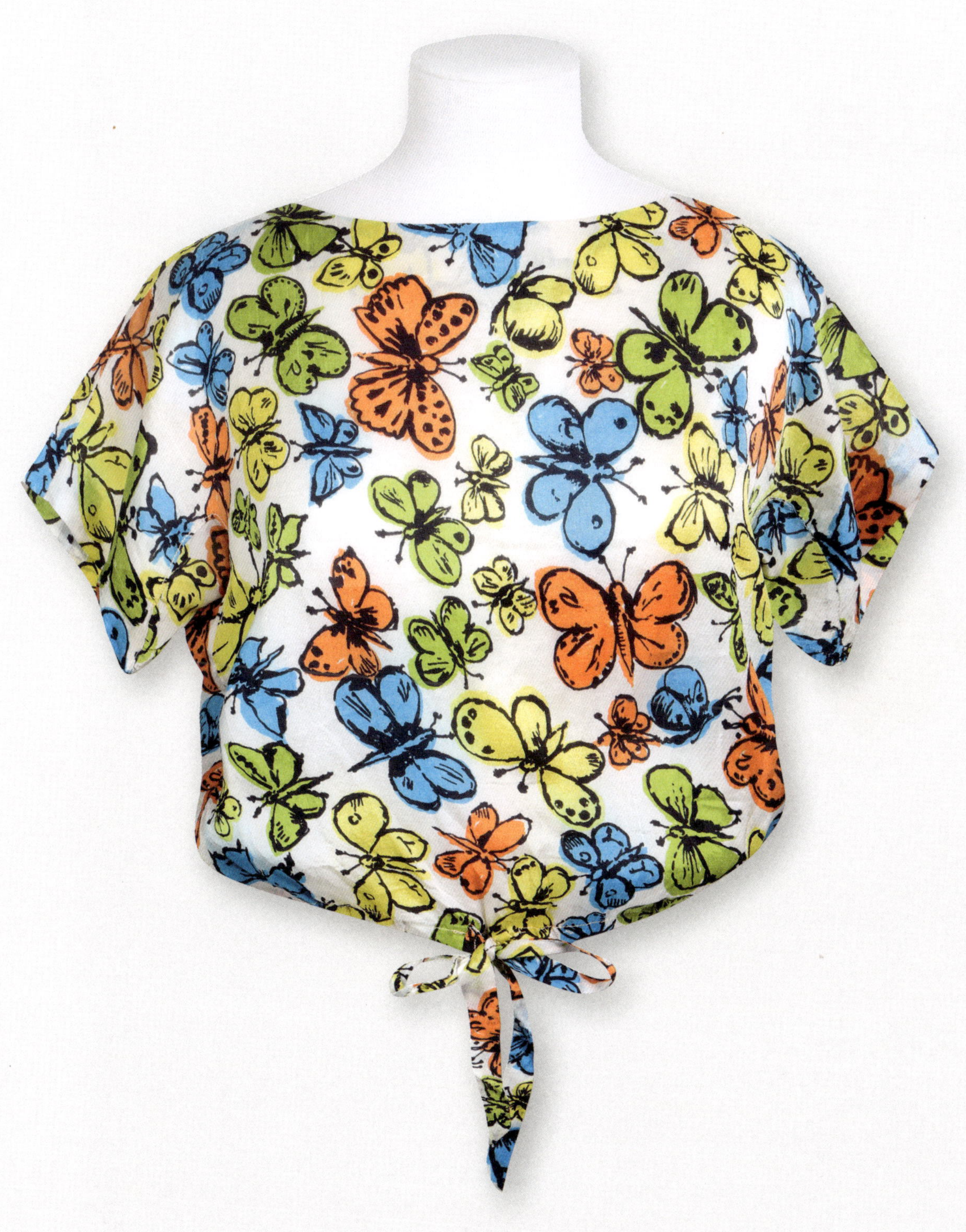

TEXTILE WITH APPLES

Printed cotton, *circa* 1955–1956
Attributed to M. Lowenstein & Sons, Inc.

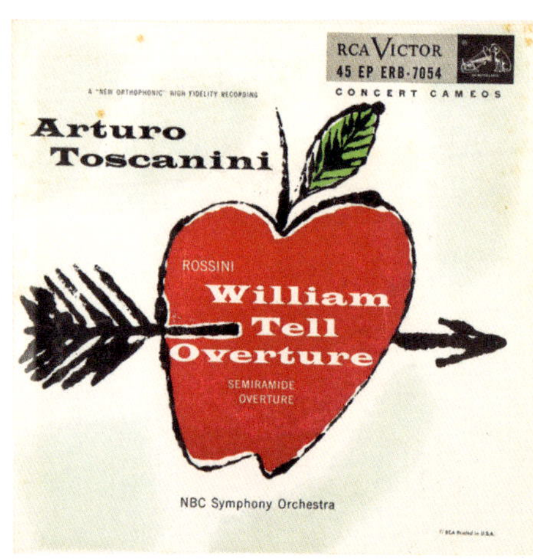

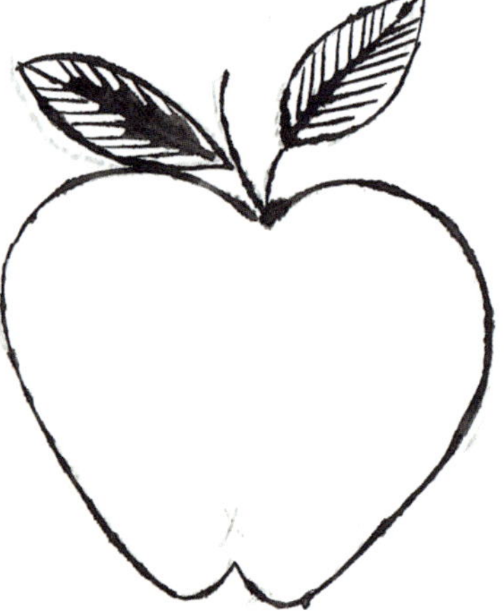

Many apple-related drawings by Warhol are in existence. Among them is a preparatory artwork for a record sleeve design for the RCA Victor recording of Gioachino Rossini's William Tell Overture, conducted by Arturo Toscanini and released in 1954.

Warhol's drawing for the extended play (EP) record is, more or less, the same for this textile, although the leaf of the apple in the textile is reversed and the arrow is not present. The textile is a border print with apples drawn on a large scale, akin to the repetitions of Coke bottles and soup cans in Warhol's Pop art of the early 1960s.

Given the particular weave of the cloth and the general style of the printing, the manufacturer is probably M. Lowenstein & Sons, Inc.

Above left (a) William Tell Overture, EP cover. RCA Victor Records, 1954. **Above right (b)** Drawing of an apple, c.1954. Ink on paper. **Opposite (c)** Skirt in blue colourway, maker unknown. **Following spread (d)** Yellow colourway.

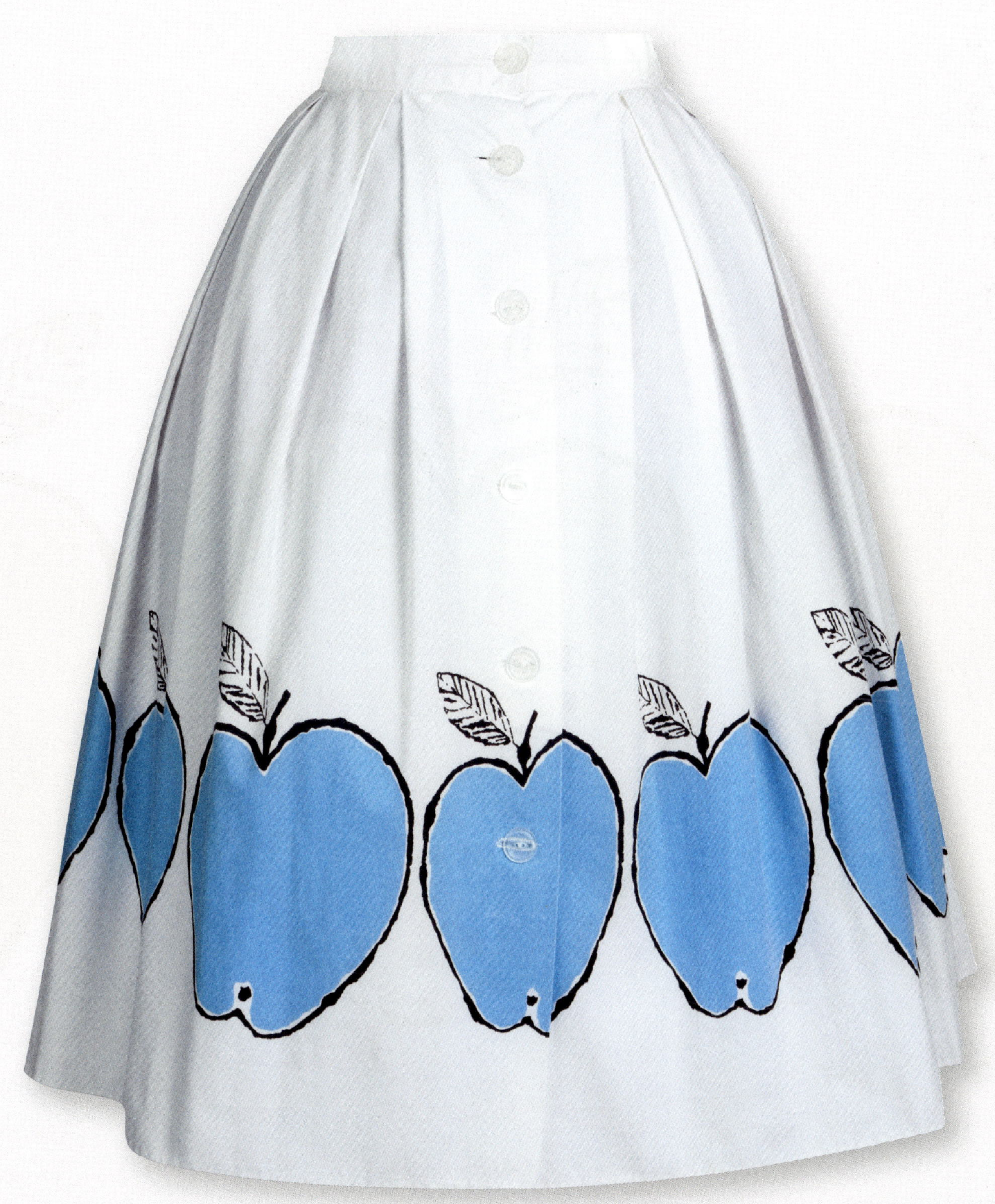

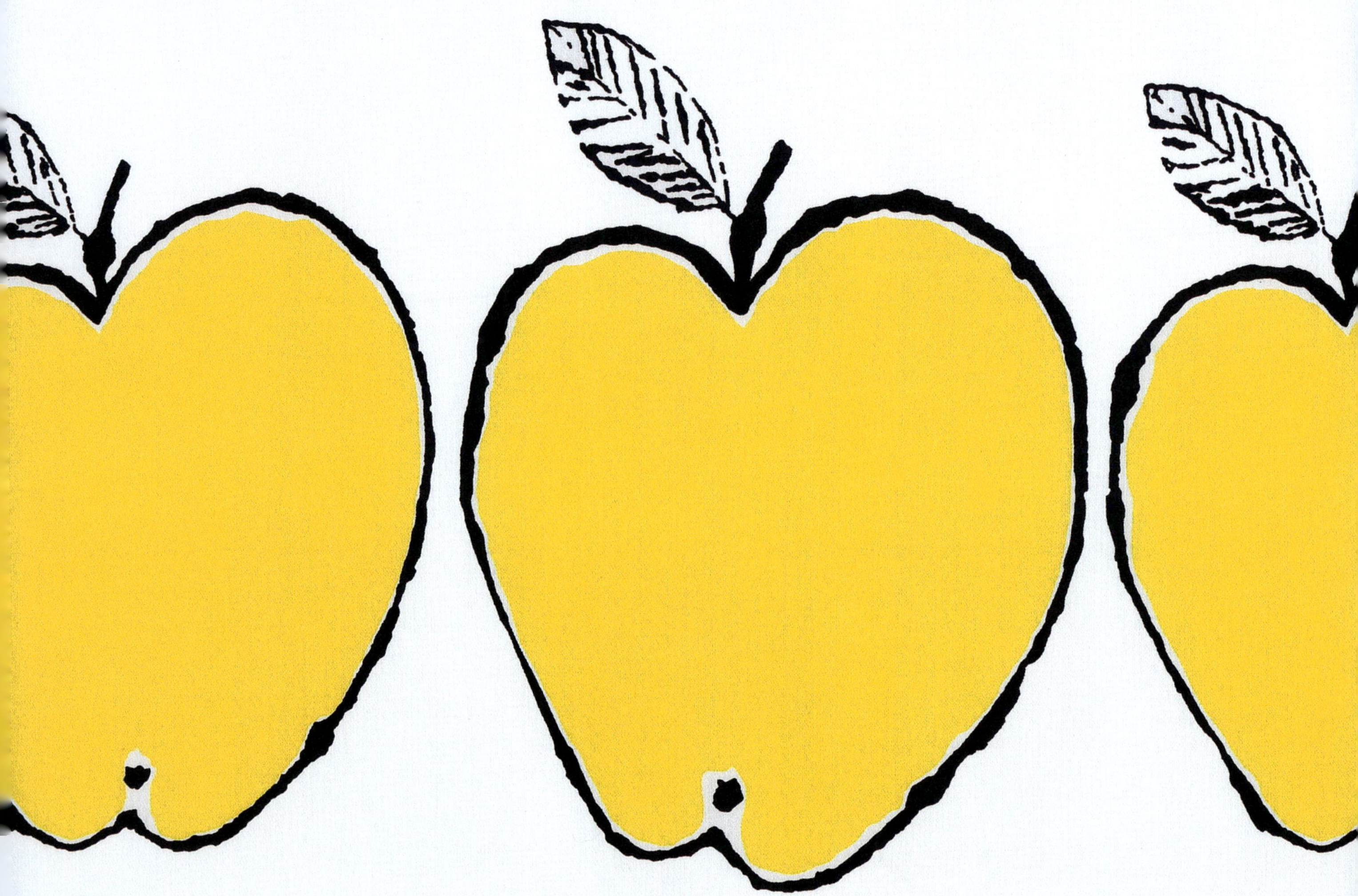

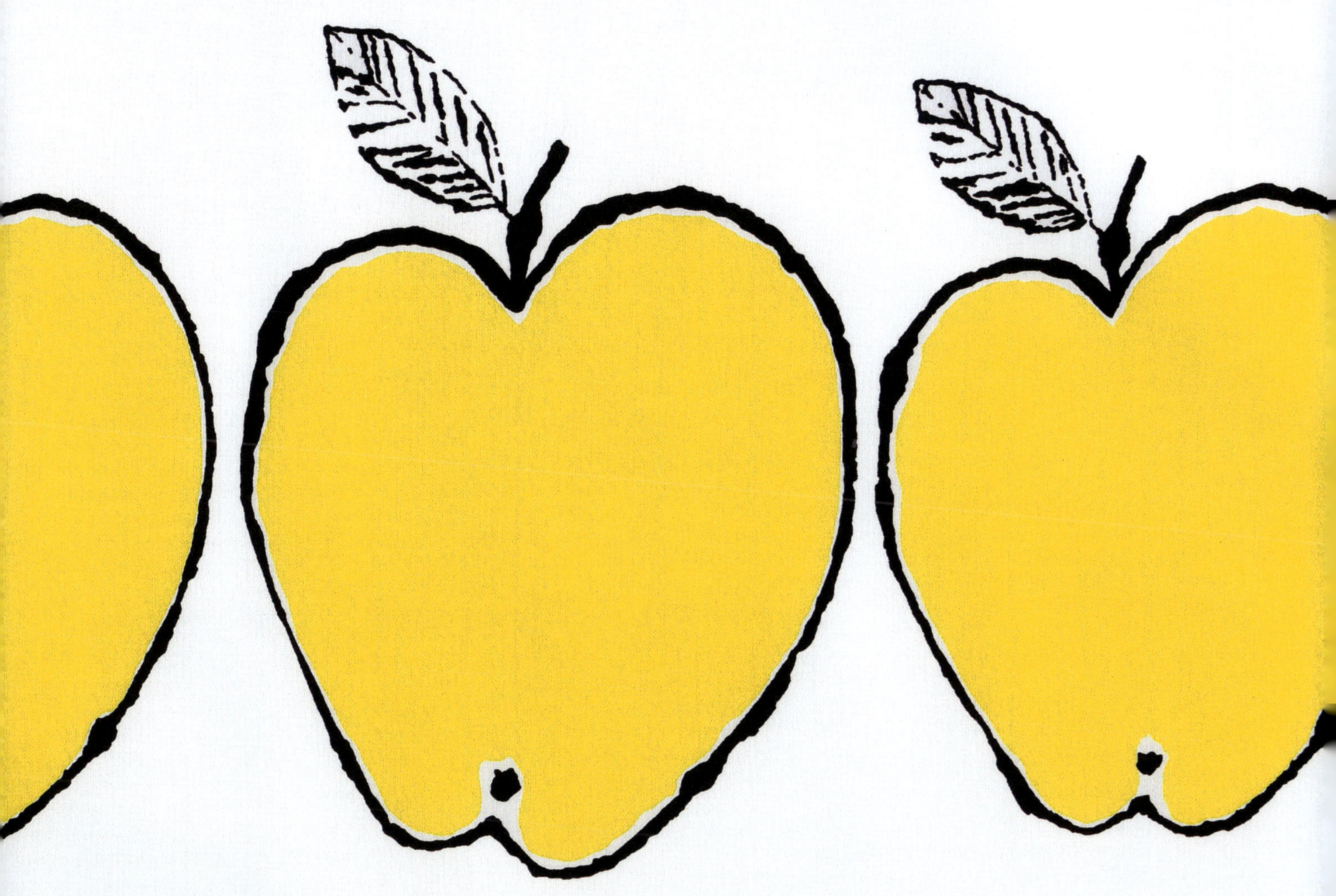

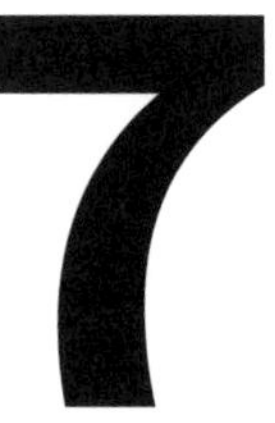

TEXTILE WITH
ACROBATIC CLOWNS AND HORSES

Printed cotton, 1955–1956
Attributed to M. Lowenstein & Sons, Inc.

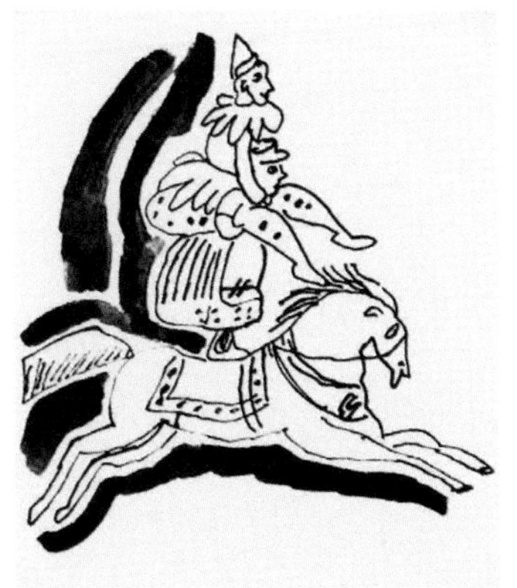

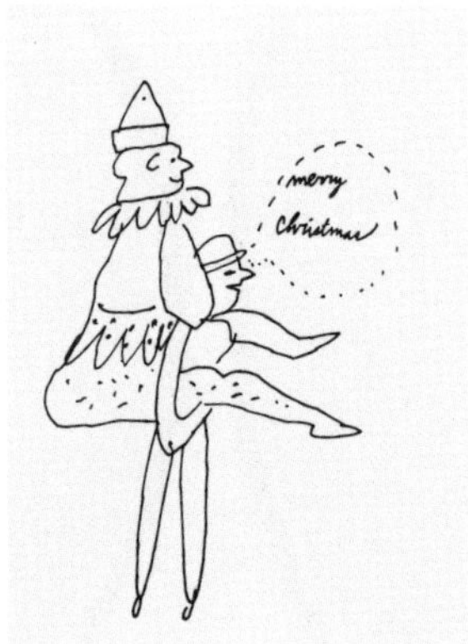

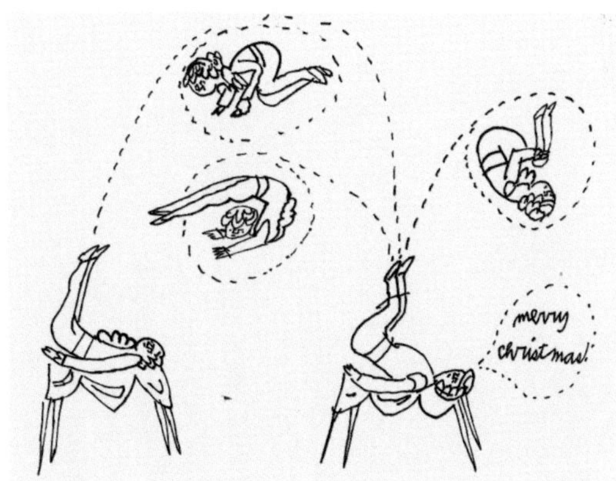

The origins of this pattern can be traced back to a group of Christmas cards Warhol designed for Robert MacGregor of New Directions Publishing in 1951. A group of related drawings by Warhol survive which give several versions of the design for the textile.

The drawings range from studies of figures in acrobatic motion to repeat versions of the clown taken from this textile. Like many of Warhol's textiles, the design is a border print that is supposed to be read in a sequence. In this case, the clown somersaults in circles from horse to horse around the circle of the skirt.

Above, left to right (a) Drawing, possibly a preparatory design for the textile. Ink on paper, early to mid 1950s; **(b)** Drawing for a proposed Christmas card for Robert MacGregor of New Directions Publishing. Ink on paper, c.1951; **(c)** 'Three Twirling Sprite Acrobats'. Ink on paper, early to mid 1950s. **Opposite (d)** Blue and green colourway. **Following spreads (e)** Pink and orange colourway; **(f)** Yellow and lime green colourway.

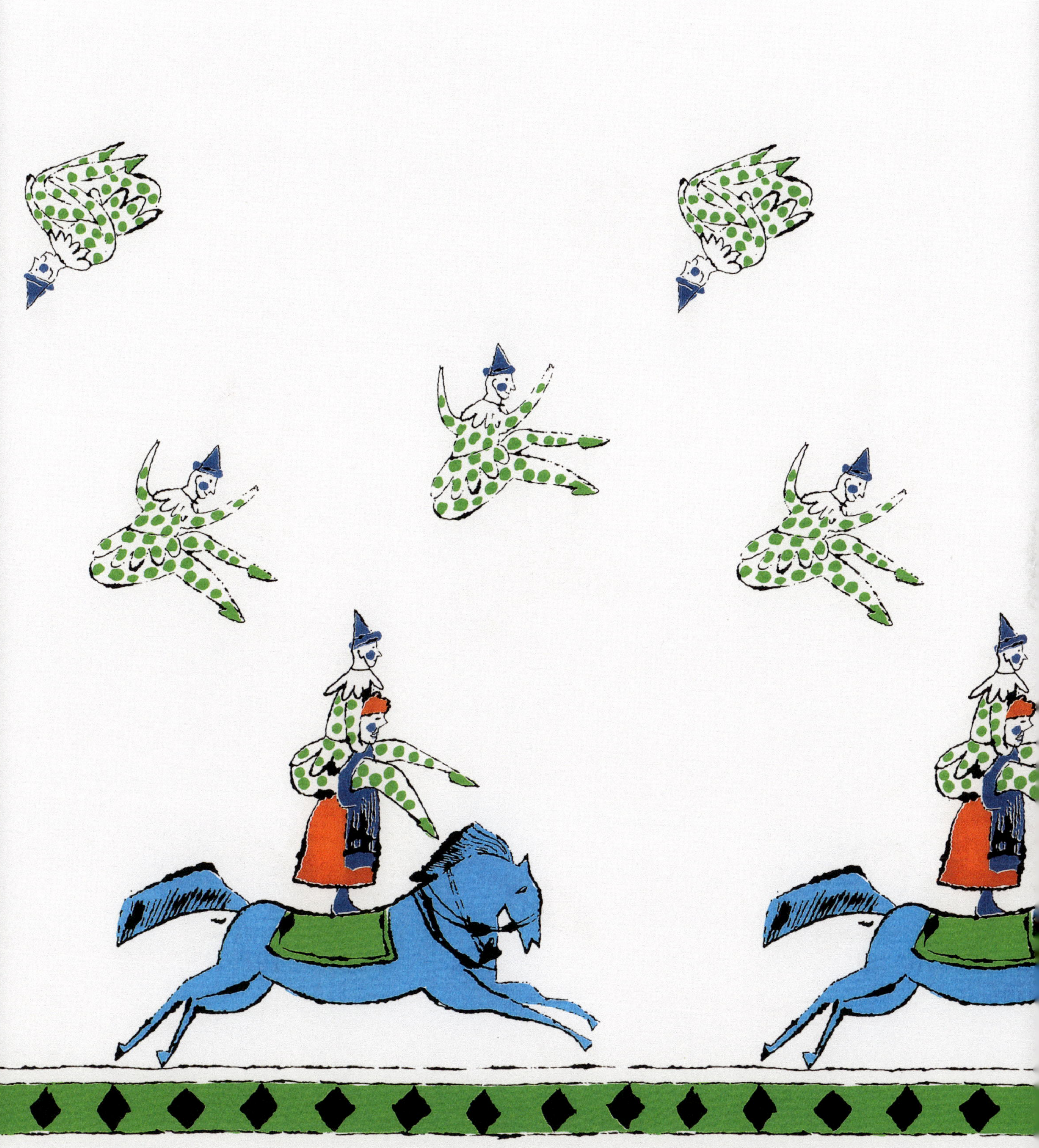

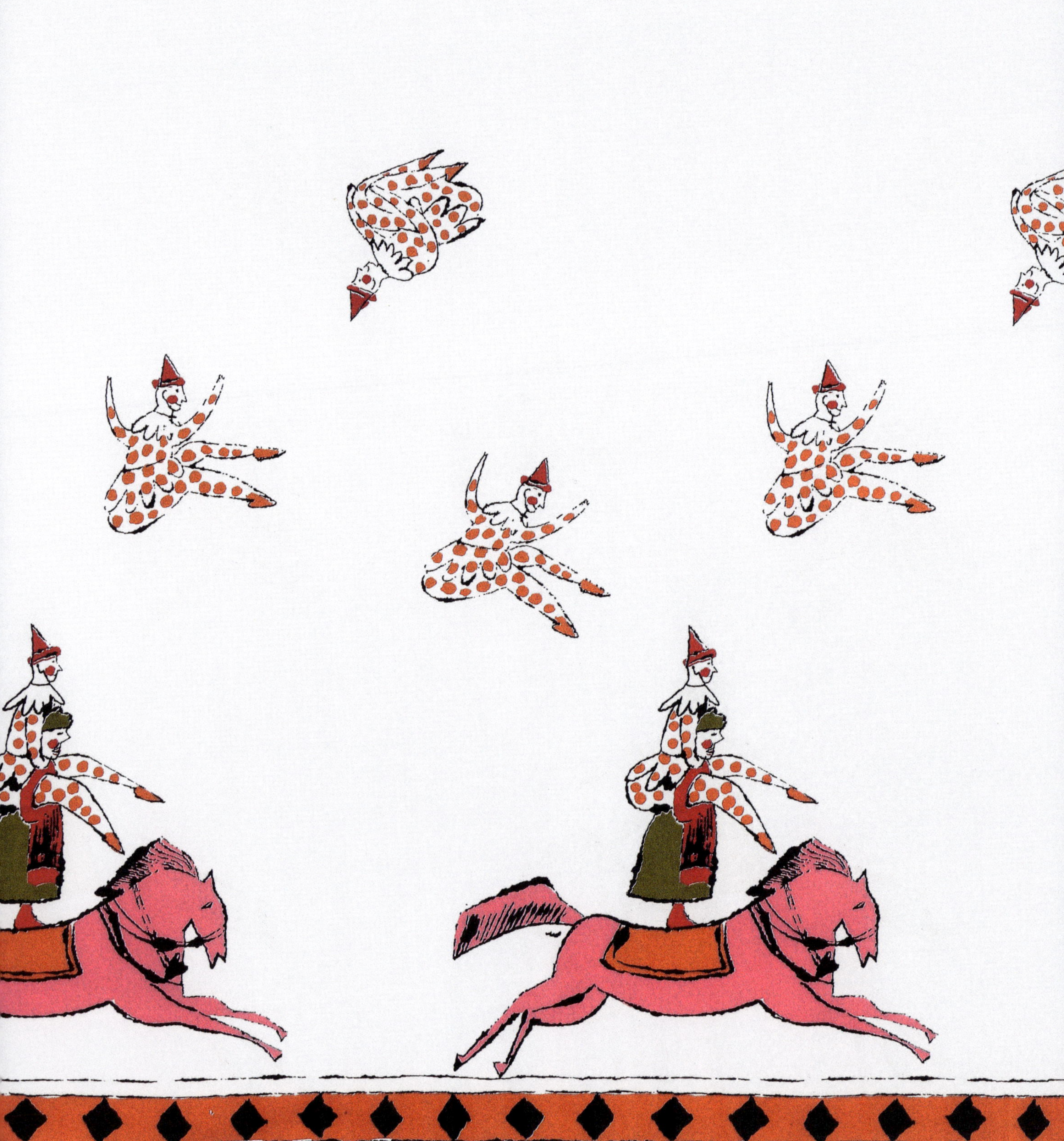

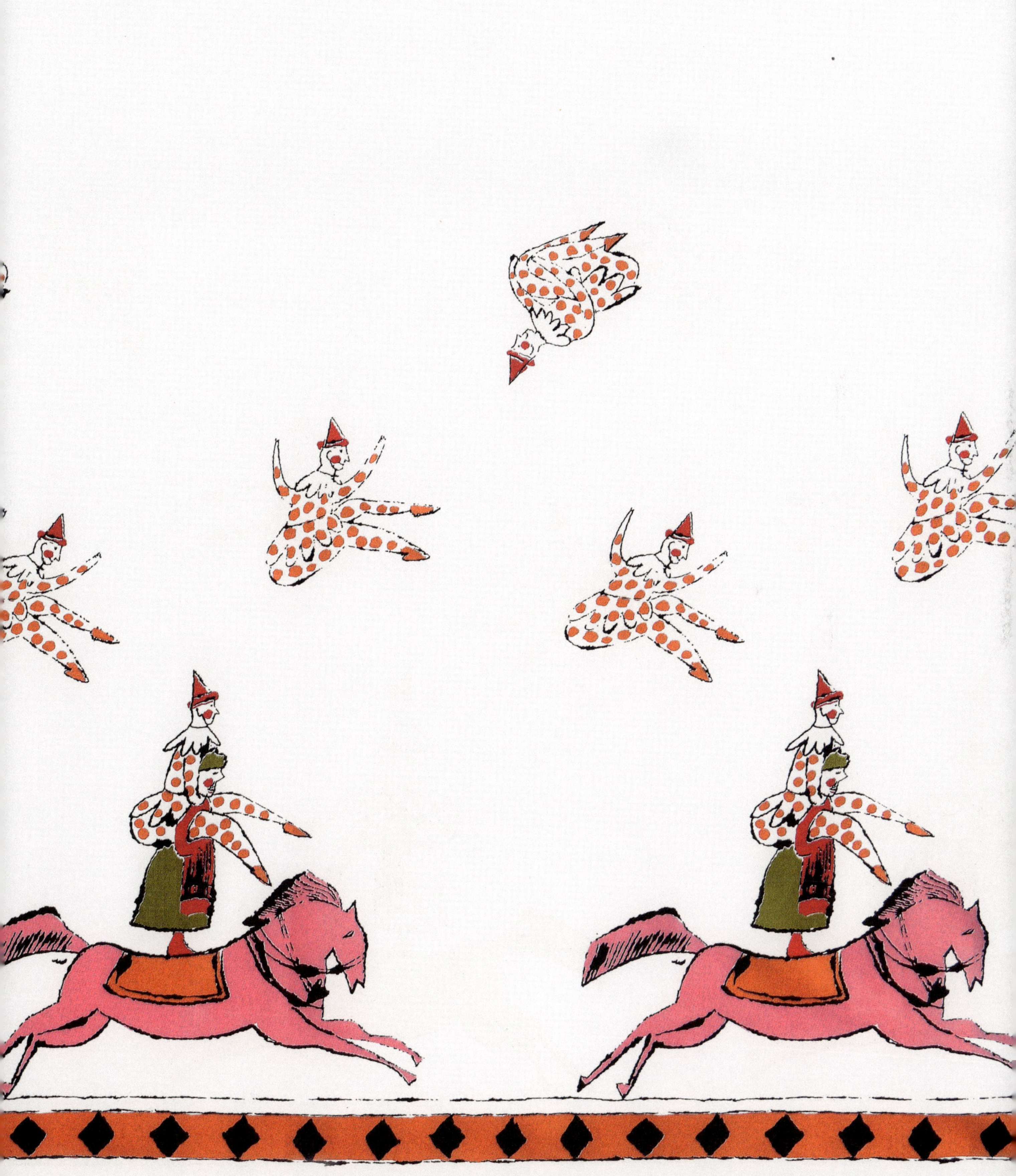

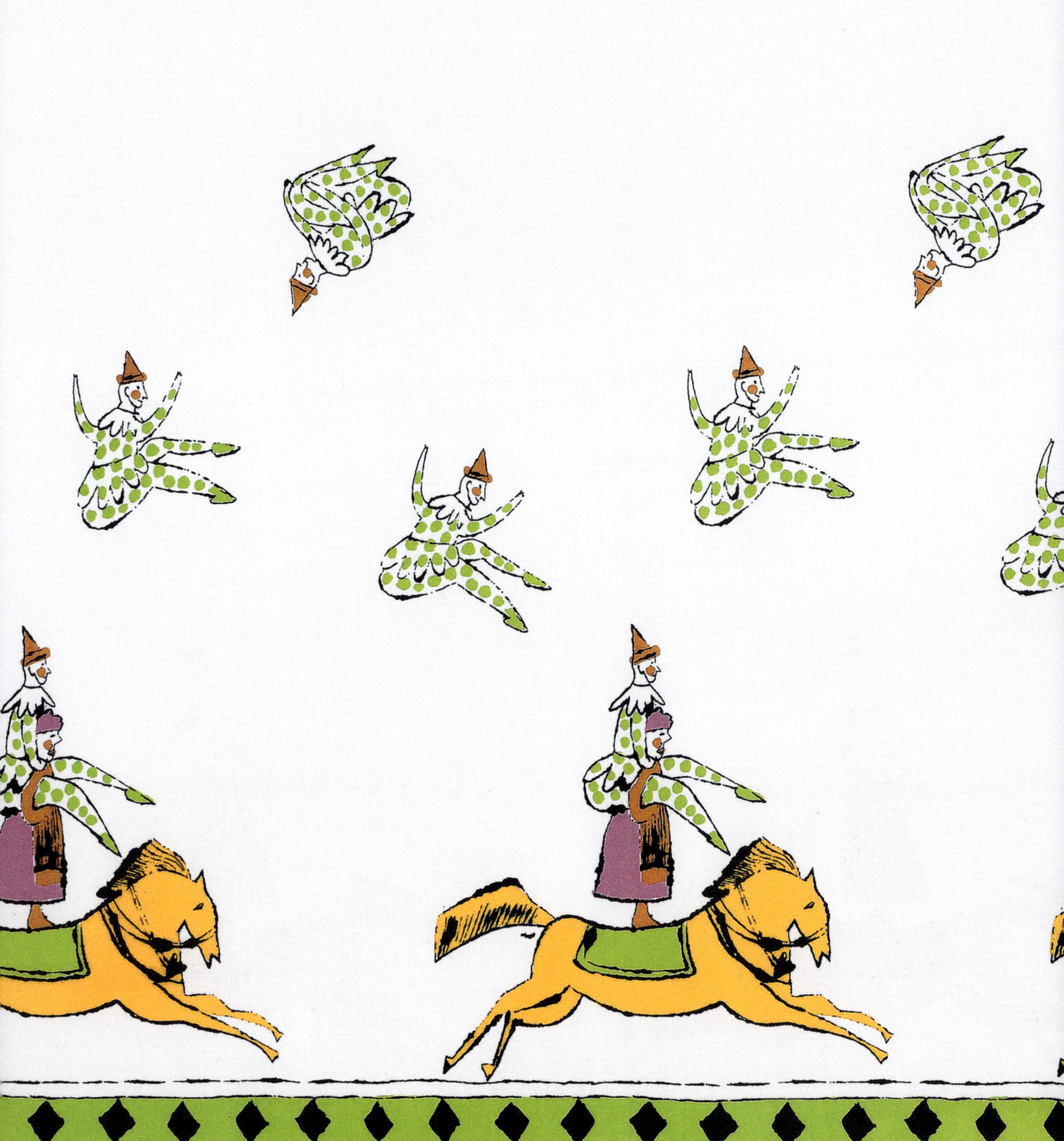

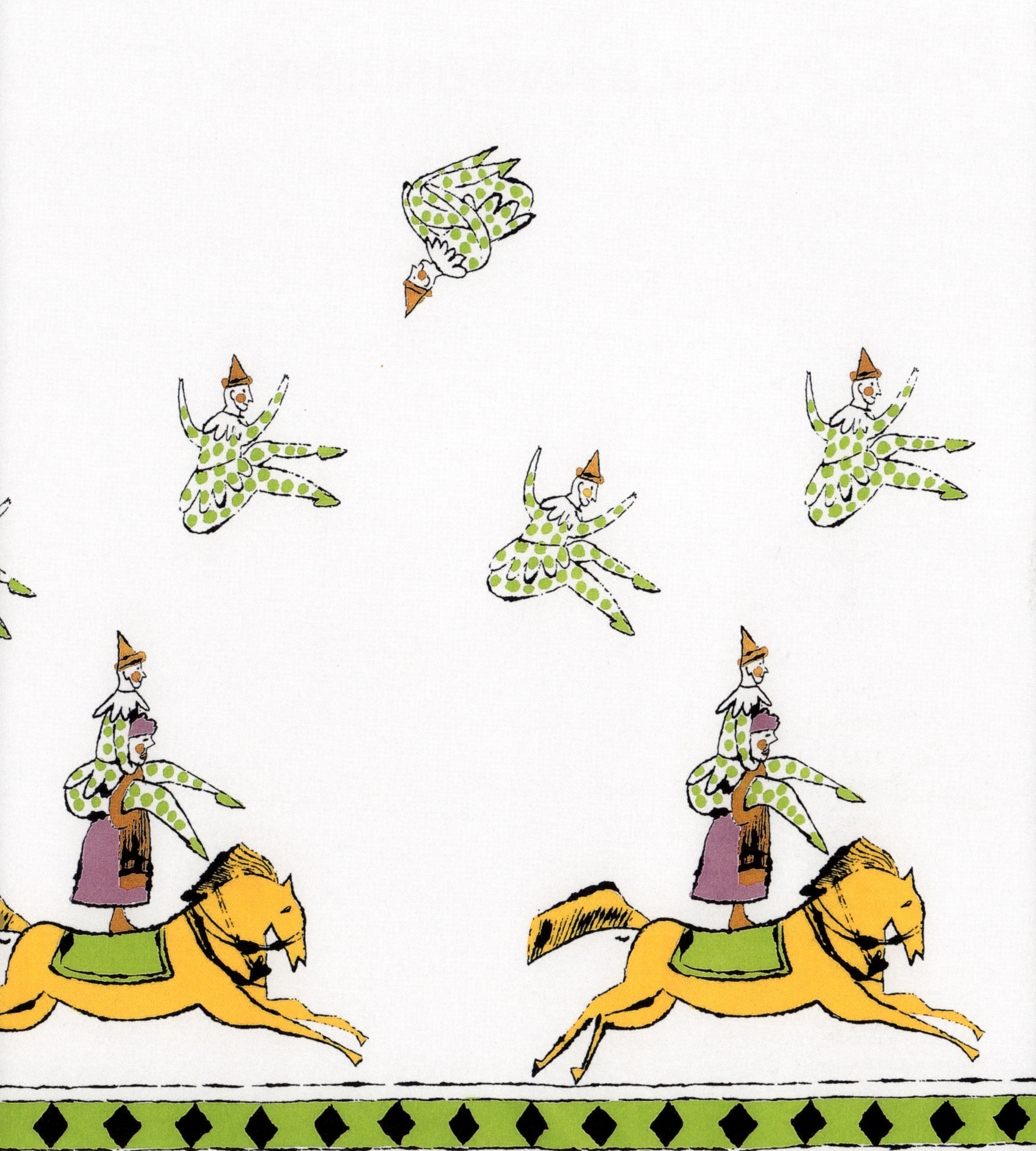

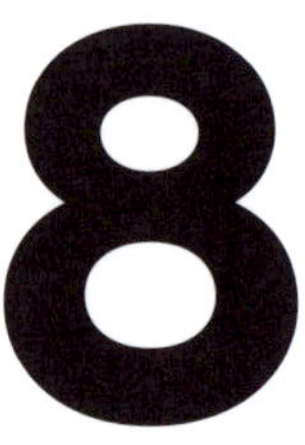

TEXTILE WITH

PENS, PENCILS AND BRUSHES

Printed cotton, *circa* 1956
Attributed to D. B. Fuller & Co., Inc.

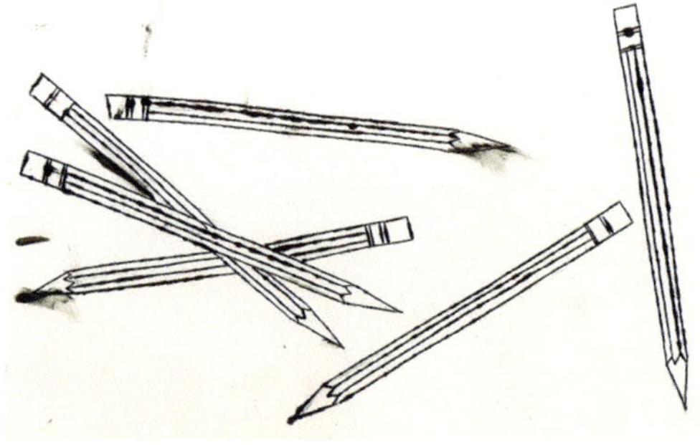

Realised in Warhol's blotted, broken line technique, this design showcases the tools of his trade as a commercial designer. He explored the same theme a number of times: several pen and pencil designs exist, some of them also incorporating paper clips and pen nibs.

Above (a) Drawing of pencils. Ink on paper, c.1956. **Opposite (b)** Textile (detail of skirt, maker unknown).

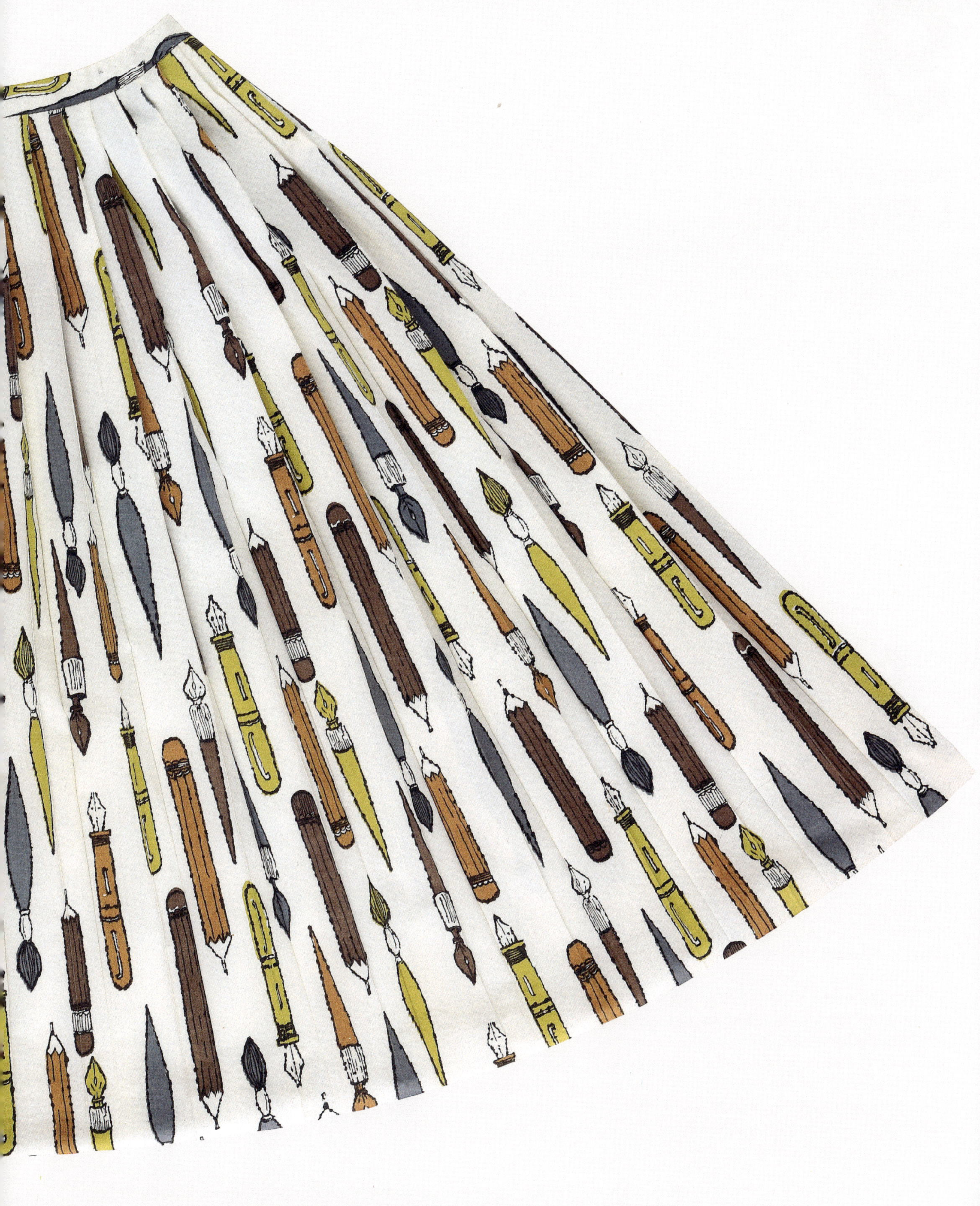

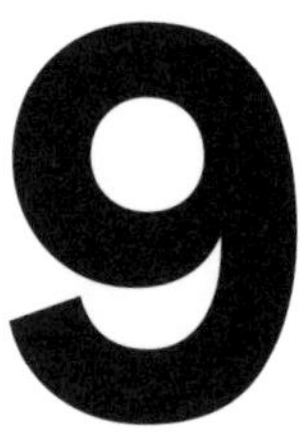

TEXTILE WITH LEMONS

Printed cotton, *circa* 1956—1957
Crompton Richmond Inc.

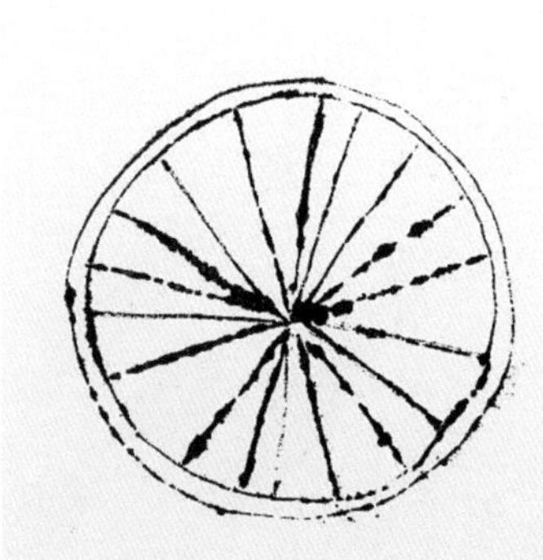

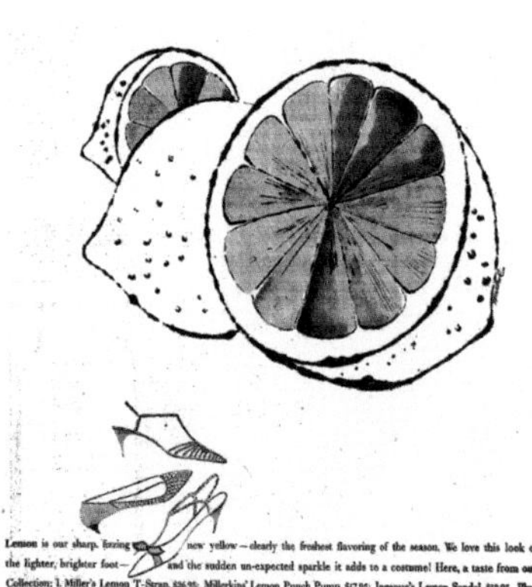

The subject of lemons features in much of Warhol's commercial art work, his depiction of fruit being always in demand for magazine illustrations and advertisements.

This design was selected to create a tightly grouped repeat of lemons and was set against a coloured ground, something Warhol would not usually do unless particularly requested by the manufacturer. As Stephen Bruce recalls, most of Warhol's work was then mainly on a white background, including his textile designs.

A very close version of this particular design was used by the shoe manufacturer I. Miller in their newspaper advertisement for lemon-coloured shoes of 1956. Slices of lemons also feature in a wide variety of his drawings; for instance, in the satirical cookery book *Wild Raspberries* from 1959, which he co-wrote with his lifelong friend, the New York interior designer Suzie Frankfurt. Here, segments of lemons, together with apples and cherries, decorate a roast suckling piglet.

Above left (a) Drawing of a lemon. Ink on paper, *c.*1959. **Above right (b)** Newspaper advertisement for I. Miller Shoes, featuring two lemons. *New York Times*, 15 April 1956. **Opposite (c)** Textile. **Following spread (d)** Suckling 'Piglet' from *Wild Raspberries*, by Suzie Frankfurt and Andy Warhol (New York: Seymour Berlin, 1959).

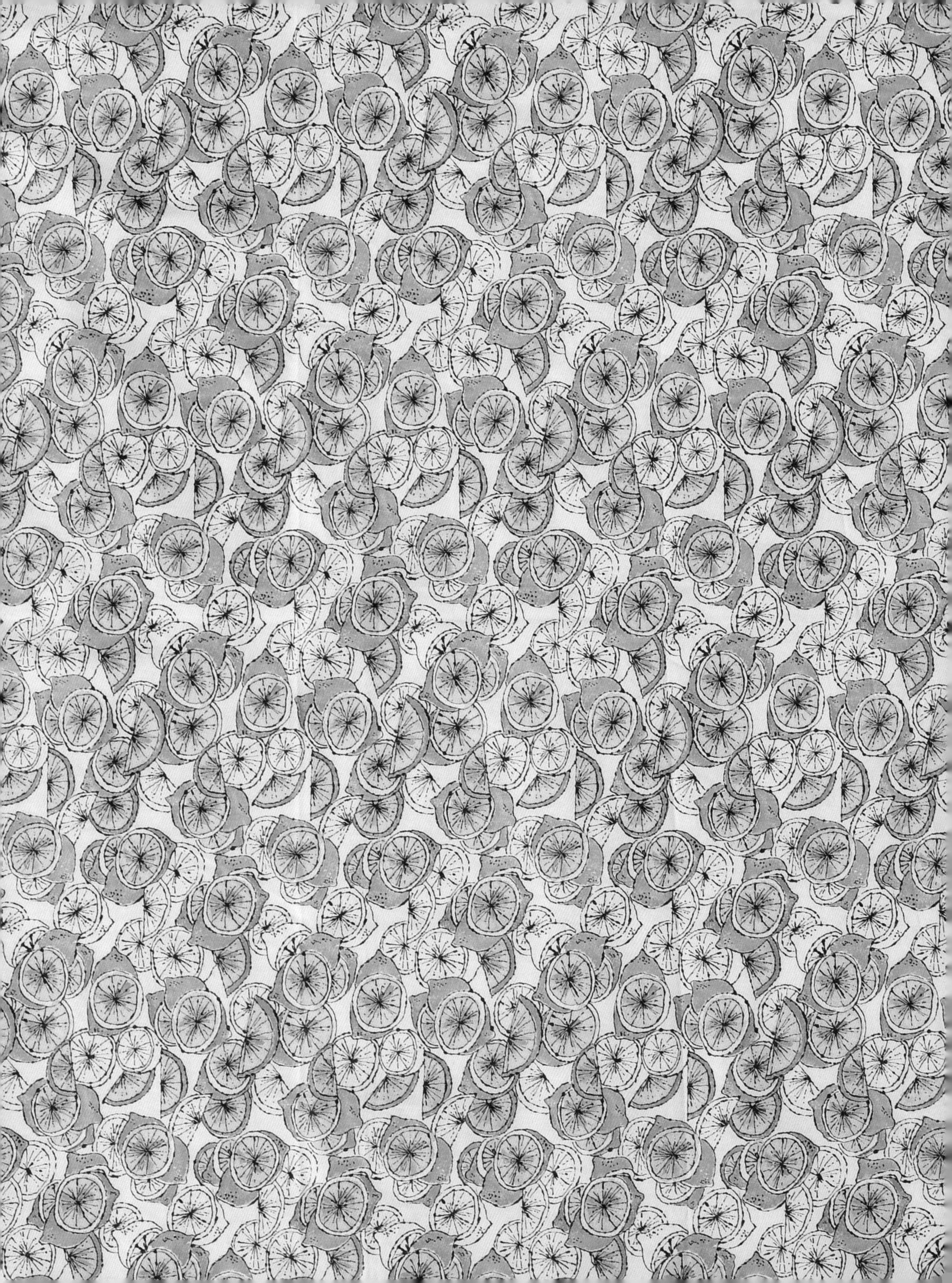

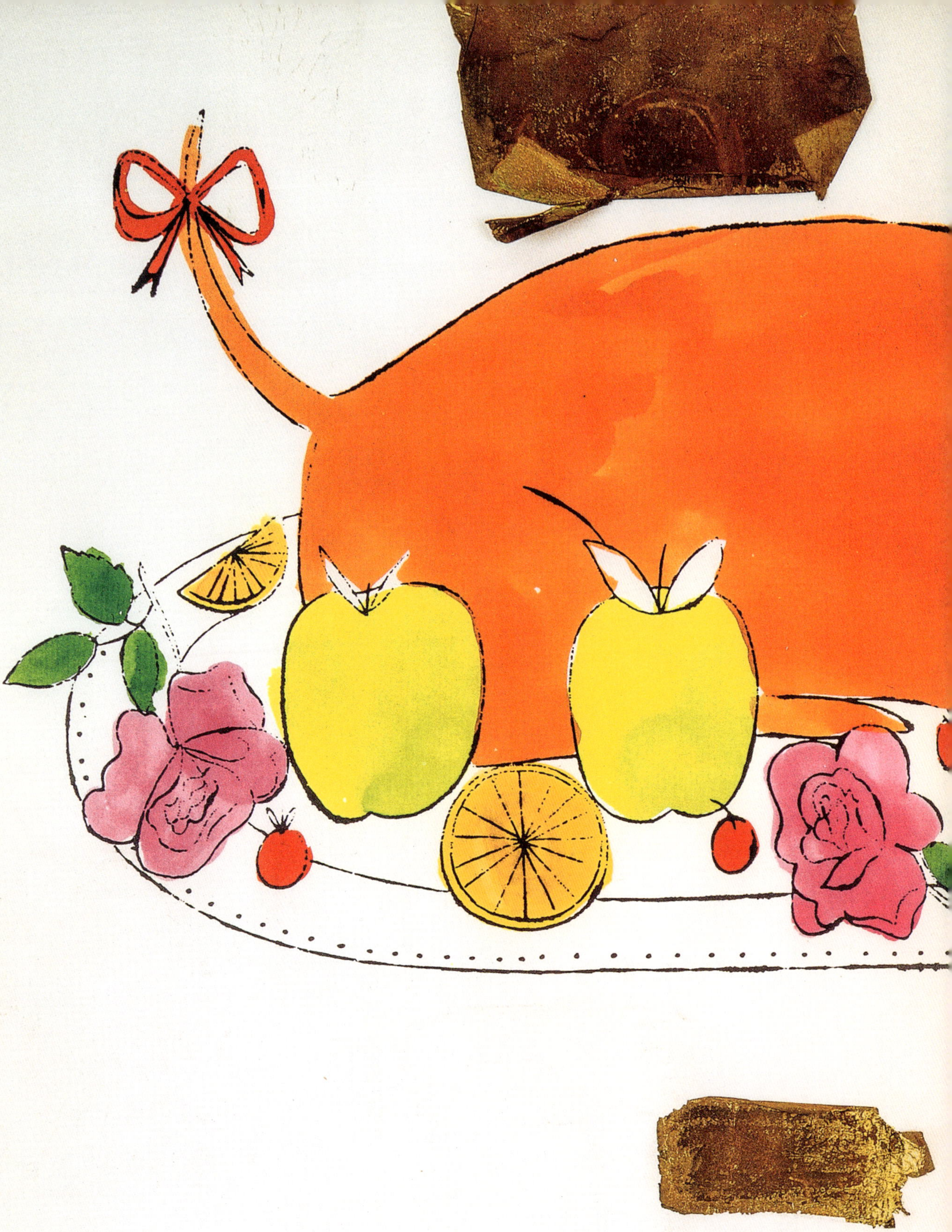

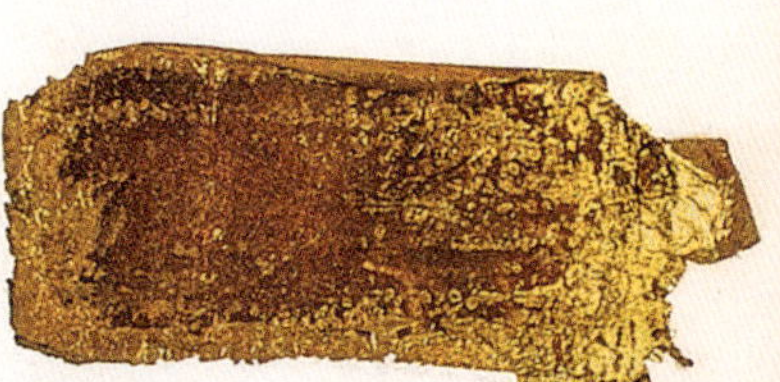

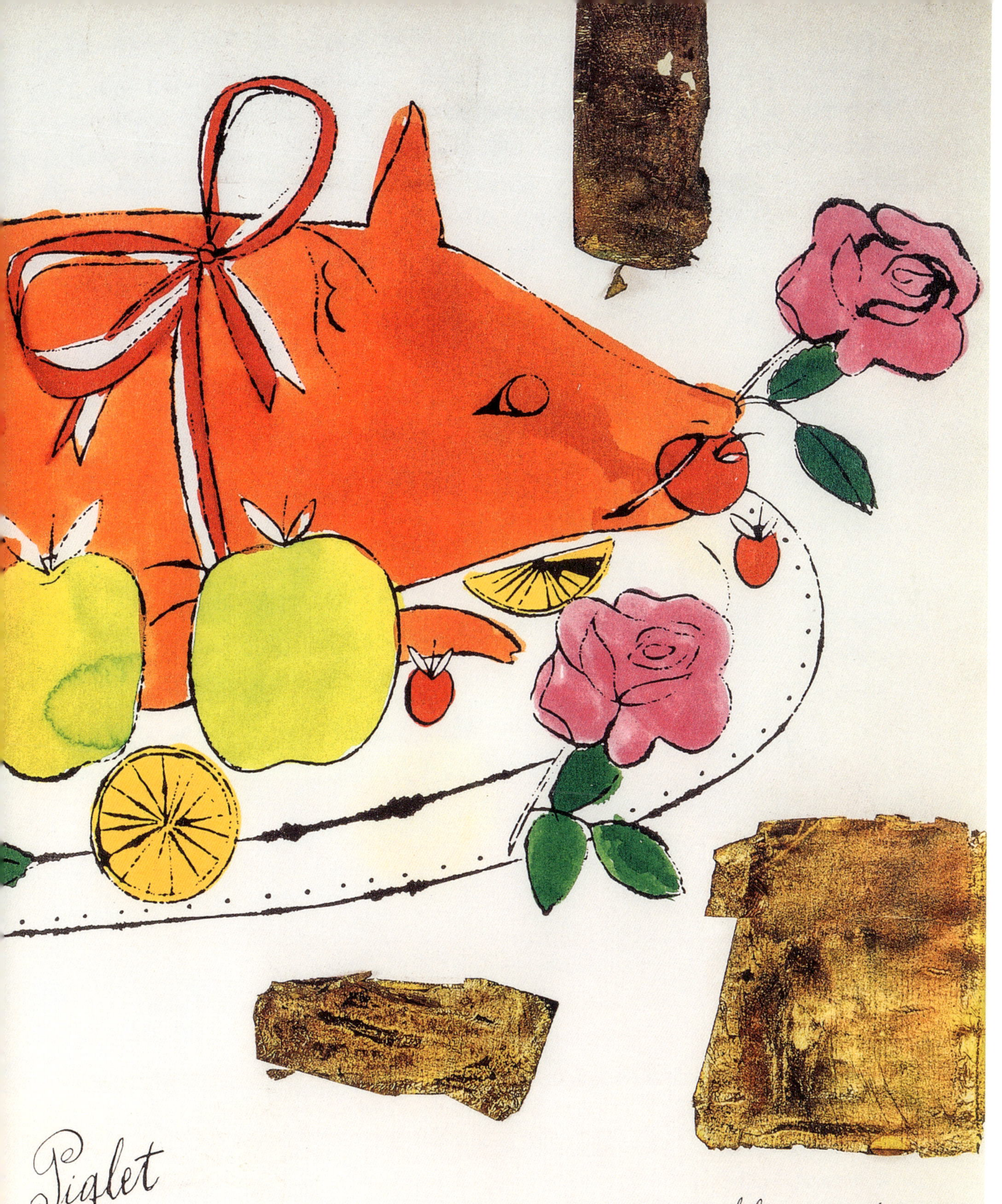

Piglet

Contact Trader Vic's and order a 40 pound suckling pig to serve 15. Have Hanley take the Carey Cadillac to the side entrance and receive the pig at exactly 6:45. Rush home immediately and Place on the open spit for 50 minutes. Remove and garnish with fresh crabapples.

10

TEXTILE WITH
MELONS

Printed cotton, *circa* 1956–1957
D. B. Fuller & Co., Inc.

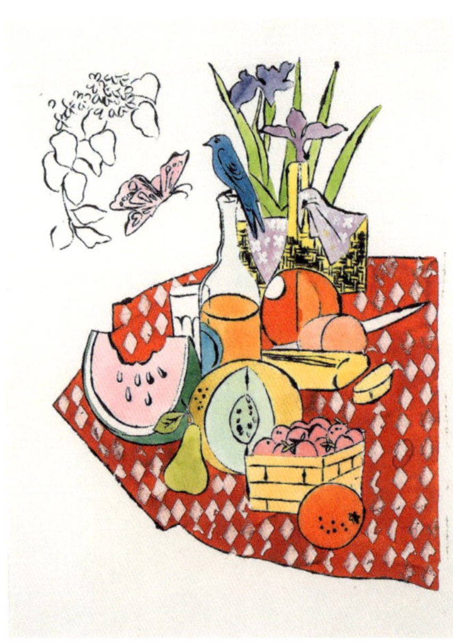

This textile was produced by one of New York's most progressive textile manufacturers. Fuller Fabrics, established in 1933, was to break new ground from the mid 1950s onwards with its Modern Masters and Scanlandia ranges of clothing and furnishing textiles. In about 1957, the New York artist and illustrator John Rombola distinctly remembers his close friend Warhol saying that he had designed dress textiles, particularly 'some three or four for Fuller's, in 1956 or 1957'.

Melons were a theme of Warhol's throughout the 1950s. In this instance, as a textile, it was used both as an all-over design in purple and green on a white background and also as a larger patterned border print, realised against a light blue chambray.

The design features a star-like motif created from slices of melon, a clever compositional device Warhol was able to use in other drawings, while slices of melon with a bite removed often appear in other examples of his design work from this period.

Above (a) Illustration of a picnic, featuring slices of melon. Ink on paper, 1950s. **Opposite (b)** Cotton sateen border-printed textile.

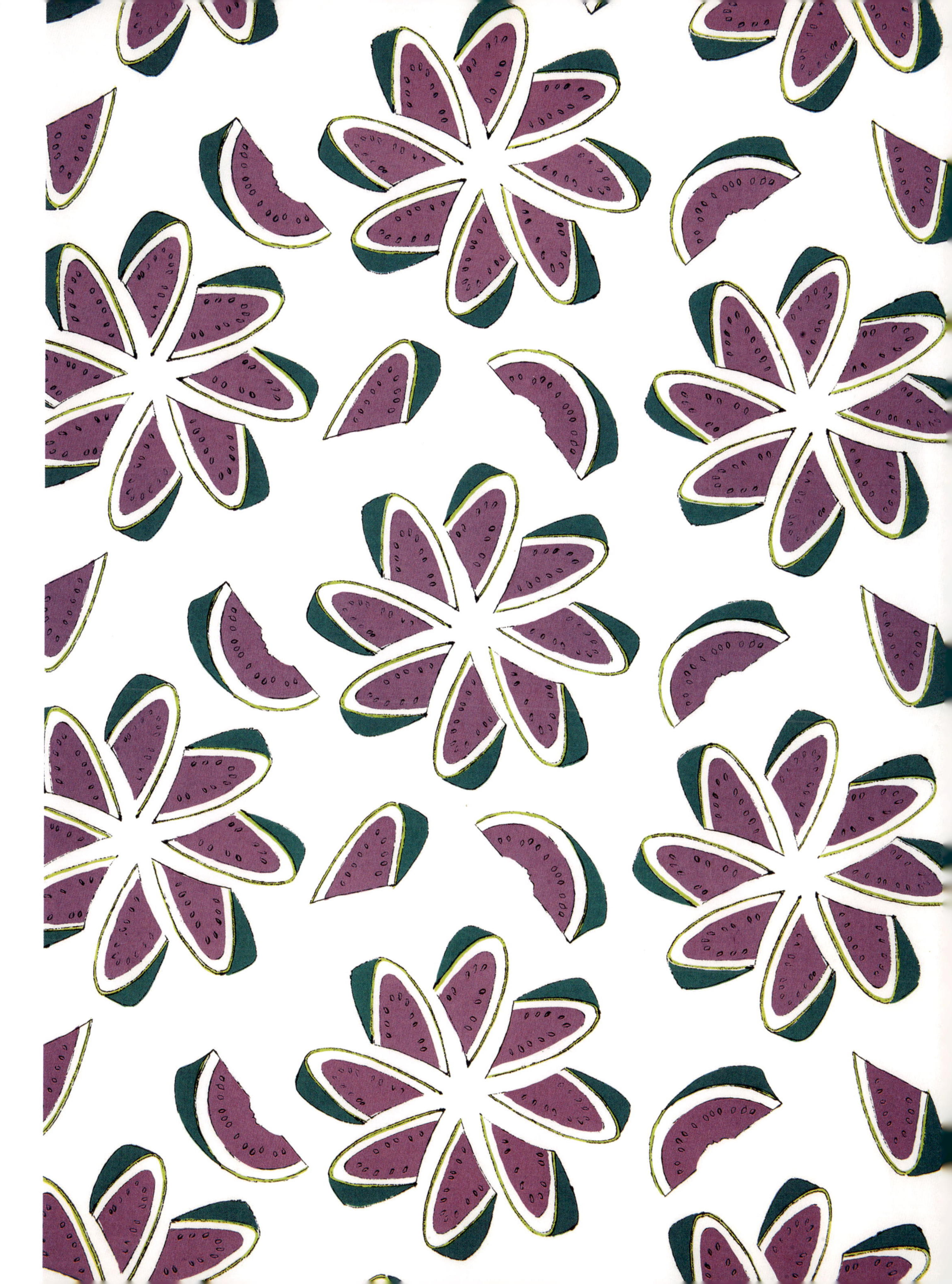

(c) Blue chambray dress with a pattern of single melon slices running round the skirt by Lorch of Dallas, *c.*1957.

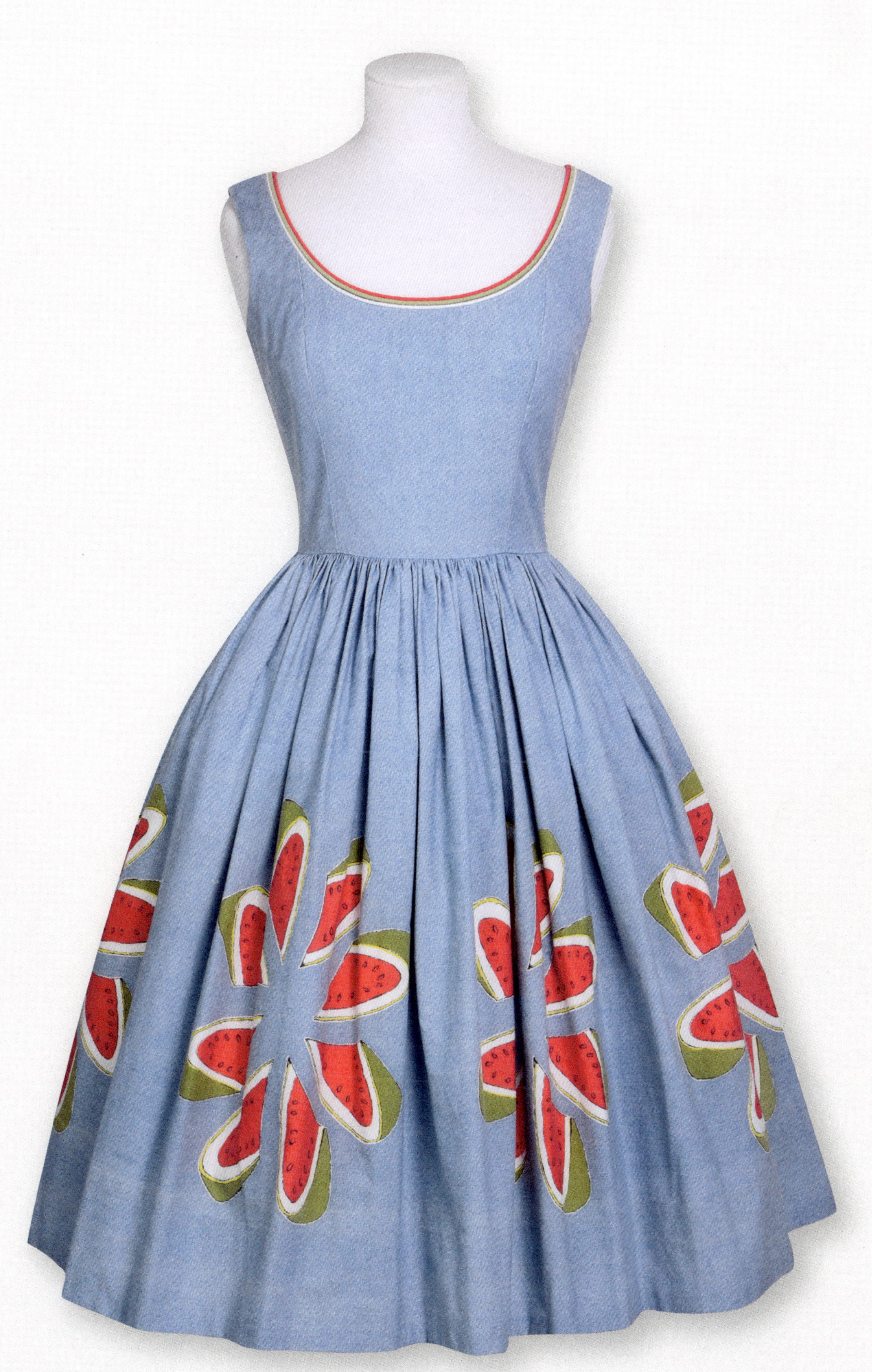

11

TEXTILE WITH
SEASHELLS

Printed cotton, *circa* 1956–1957
D. B. Fuller & Co., Inc.

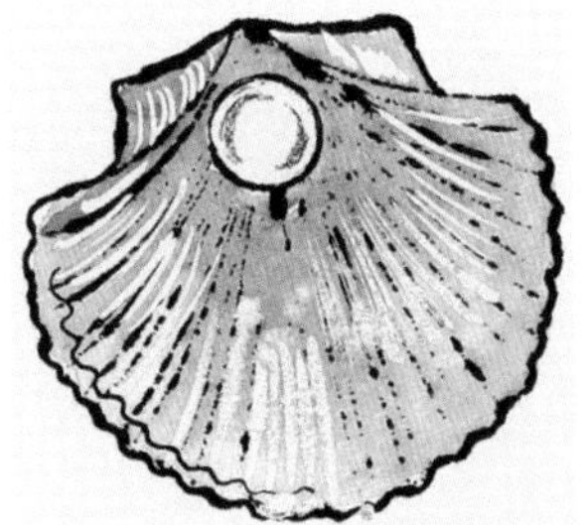
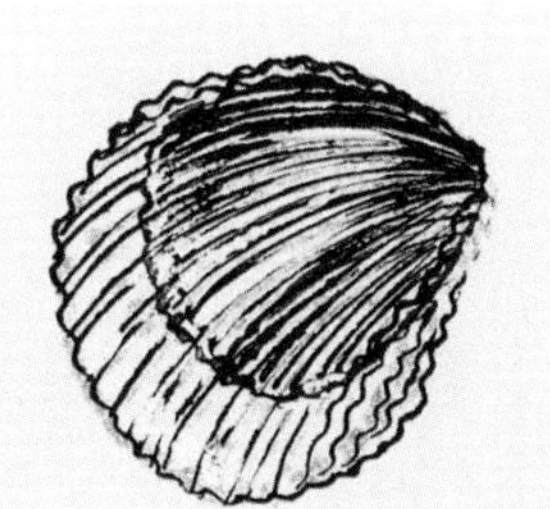
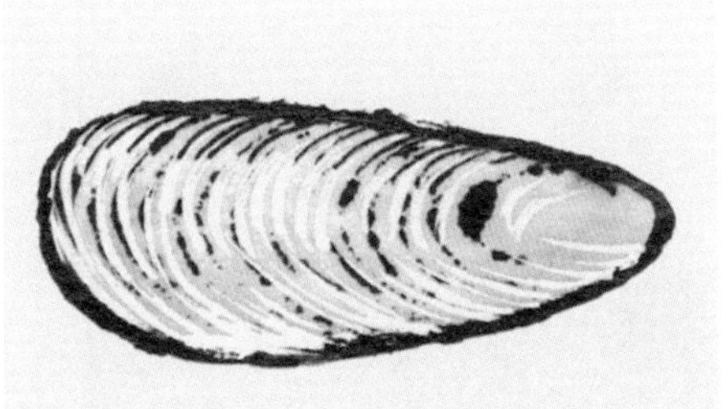

Seashells were very much part of Warhol's design repertoire, and he used them a great deal in his advertising work, often in association with perfumes and scents. Many of his preparatory drawings with razor clams, oysters, starfish and other denizens of the deep have survived.

Daniel B. Fuller, the president of Fuller's, was instrumental in the development of fine artists working with the American textile industry when he commissioned several of the world's most important living artists as designers for the company's Modern Masters project in 1954.

Above (a) Drawings of shells. Ink and gouache on paper, c.1956–7. **Opposite (b)** Textile (detail of dress, maker unknown).

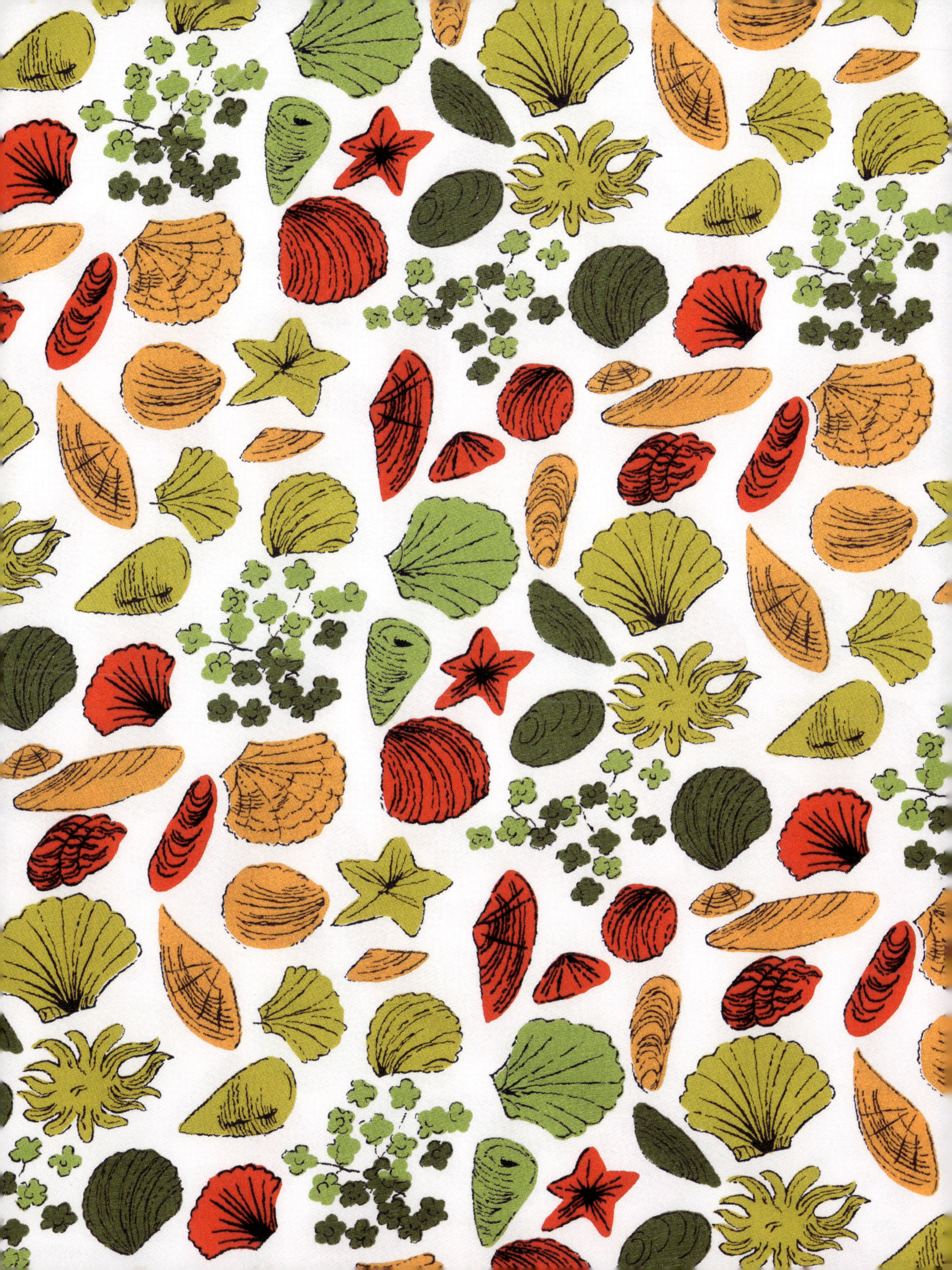

12

TEXTILE WITH SOCKS

Printed cotton, *circa* 1957–1958
Attributed to D. B. Fuller & Co., Inc.

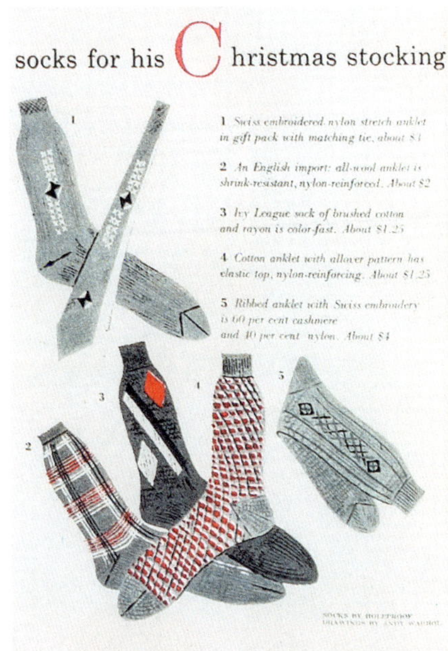

socks for his Christmas stocking

1 *Swiss embroidered nylon stretch anklet in gift pack with matching tie, about $*[illegible]

2 *An English import: all-wool anklet is shrink-resistant, nylon-reinforced. About $2*

3 *Ivy League sock of brushed cotton and rayon is color-fast. About $1.25*

4 *Cotton anklet with allover pattern has elastic top, nylon-reinforcing. About $1.25*

5 *Ribbed anklet with Swiss embroidery is 60 per cent cashmere and 40 per cent nylon. About $4*

In a similar vein to his many illustrations of shoes for I. Miller, Warhol explored the various permutations of hosiery, from muscular Argyles down to knitted baby booties, all with a sense of subtle sophistication and gentle irony.

In addition to hats and shoes, he regularly depicted socks for use in advertisements and editorial magazine commissions. In this textile he used a loose, blot-free broken line style to depict a world of socks – it was a way of drawing he also used successfully for illustrations in *Dance Magazine* in the 1950s as well as for a limited edition set of prints titled *Love Is a Pink Cake* (1953).

Above (a) 'Socks for His Christmas Stocking', *McCall's* magazine (December 1957). **Opposite (b)** Textile (detail of dress by Sis Originals).

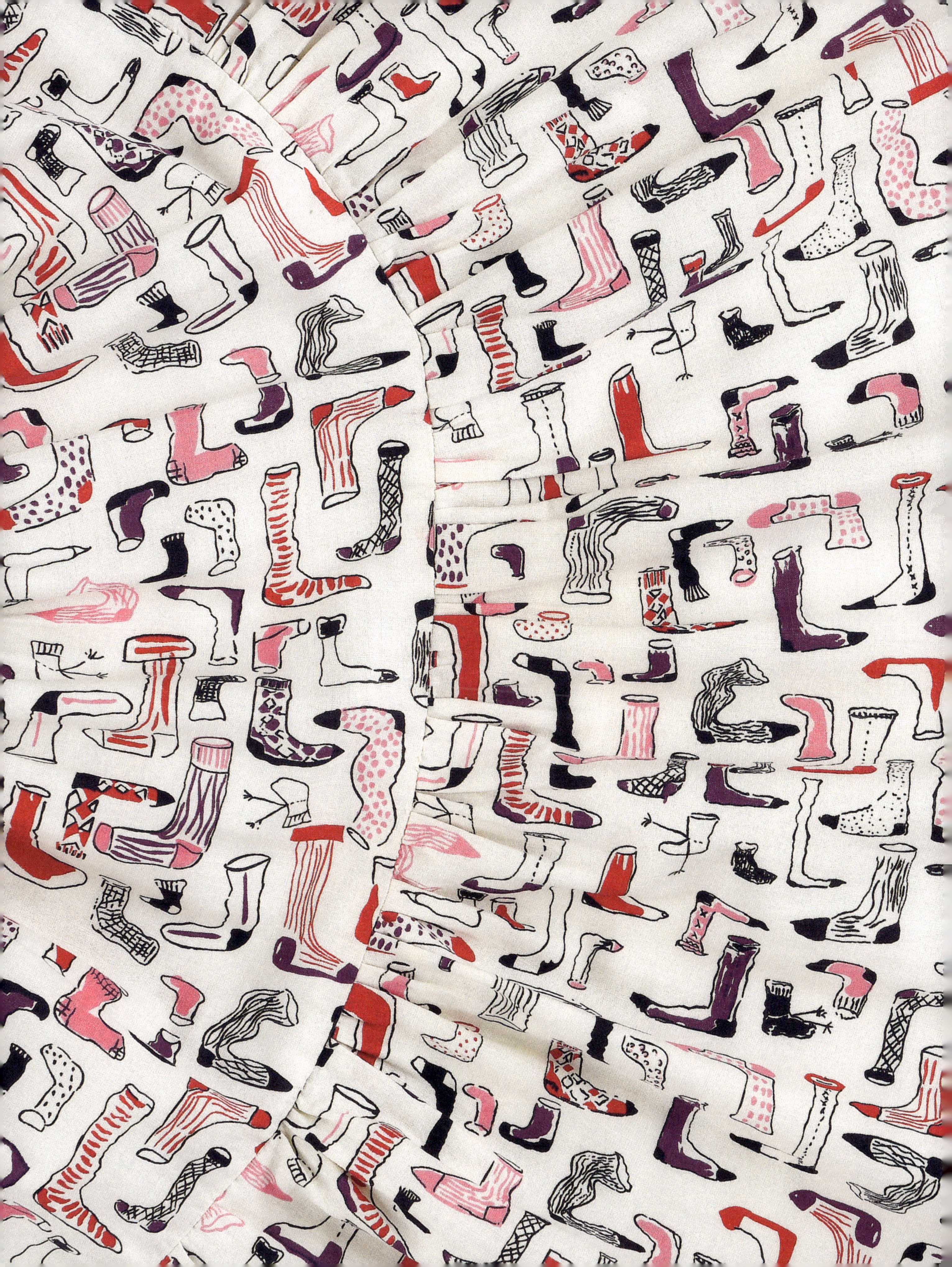

13

TEXTILE WITH
SHOES AND BOOTS

Printed cotton, *circa* 1957–1958
Attributed to Crompton-Richmond Company, Inc.

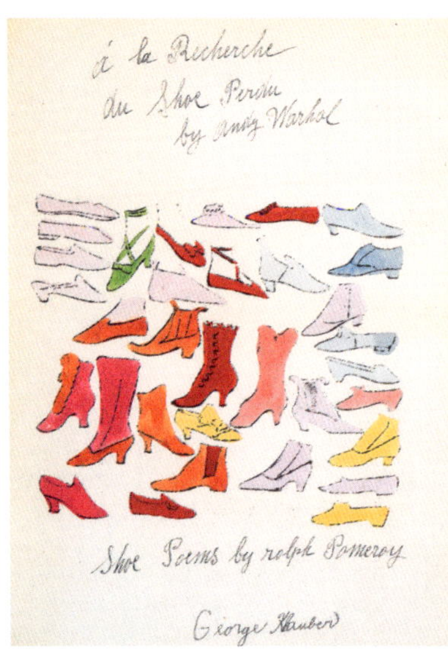

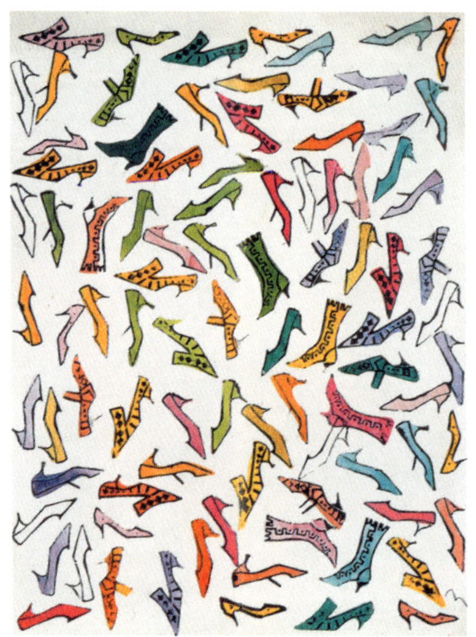

Probably the item that Warhol became most synonymous with in the 1950s was the shoe. His inventive advertising campaigns for I. Miller Shoes, which explored the high-heeled stiletto to its maximum, eventually won him an Art Directors Club award in 1956. A year earlier, *Women's Wear Daily* had described him as 'I. Miller's da Vinci of shoes'.

This particular textile explores a wide range of footwear, from the high-legged Victorian boot to the much more regular, low-heeled 'slip-on'. A more flamboyant type of background is provided, in which yellow, red, pink and white stripes are arranged vertically across the cloth, with the footwear positioned across it.

Above left (a) Printed lithographic hand-coloured cover for *À la Recherche du Shoe Perdu*, a portfolio of prints, c.1955.
Above right (b) Stamped shoe design. Ink on paper, c.1959. **Opposite (c)** Textile (detail of blouse by Jayson Classics).

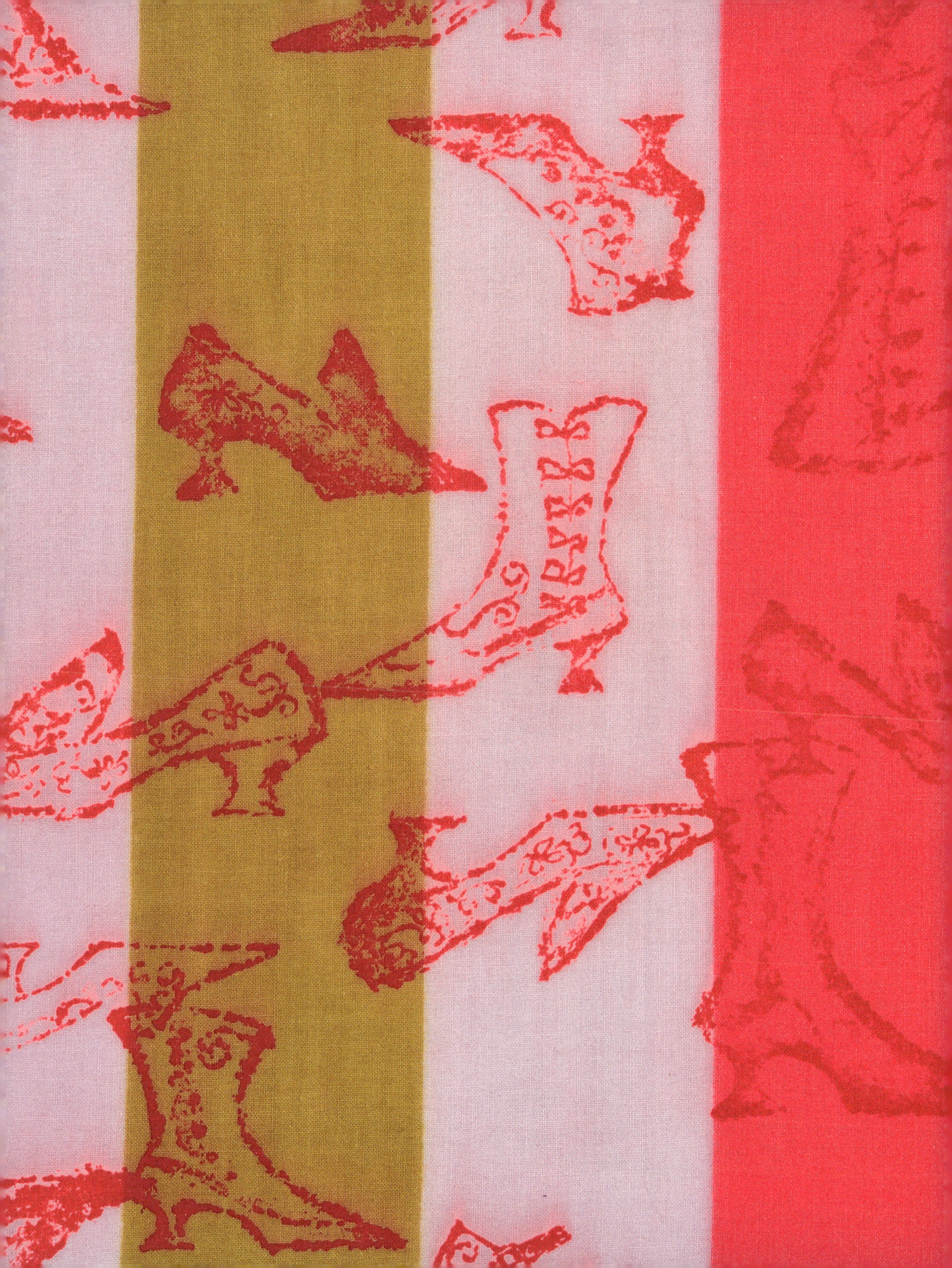

14

TEXTILE WITH
HATS

Printed cotton, *circa* 1957–1958
Compton-Richmond Company, Inc.

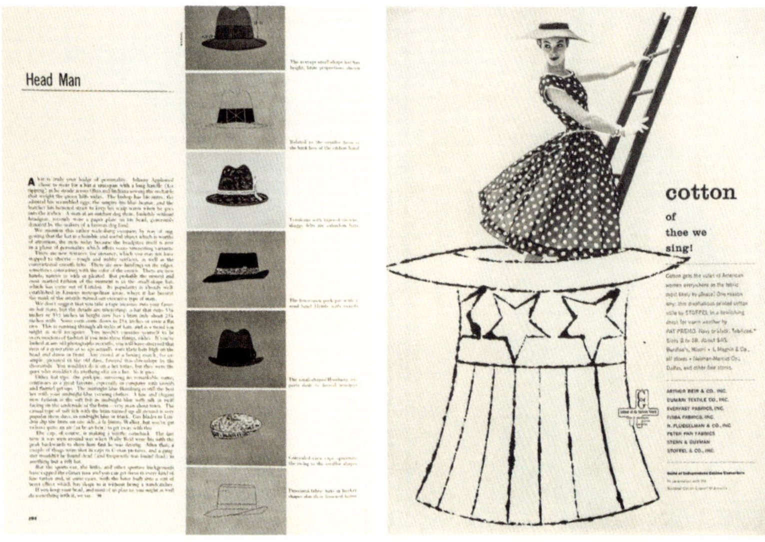

Hats were another of Warhol's repeating patterns, very similar in composition and humour to the socks and shoes textiles he'd created (nos 12 and 13). He employed free reign in his choice of headwear, from high-toned 'horticultural' hats right down to the plebeian tam-o'-shanter. Hats were indeed a perfect subject matter for the novelty or conversational prints that were then so very popular with New York manufacturers.

Above left (a) 'Head Man', *Esquire magazine* (November 1954). **Above right (b)** 'Cotton of Thee We Sing!', *Vogue* (February 1955). Advertisement for the Guild of Independent Cotton Convertors. **Opposite (c)** Textile (detail of dress, maker unknown).

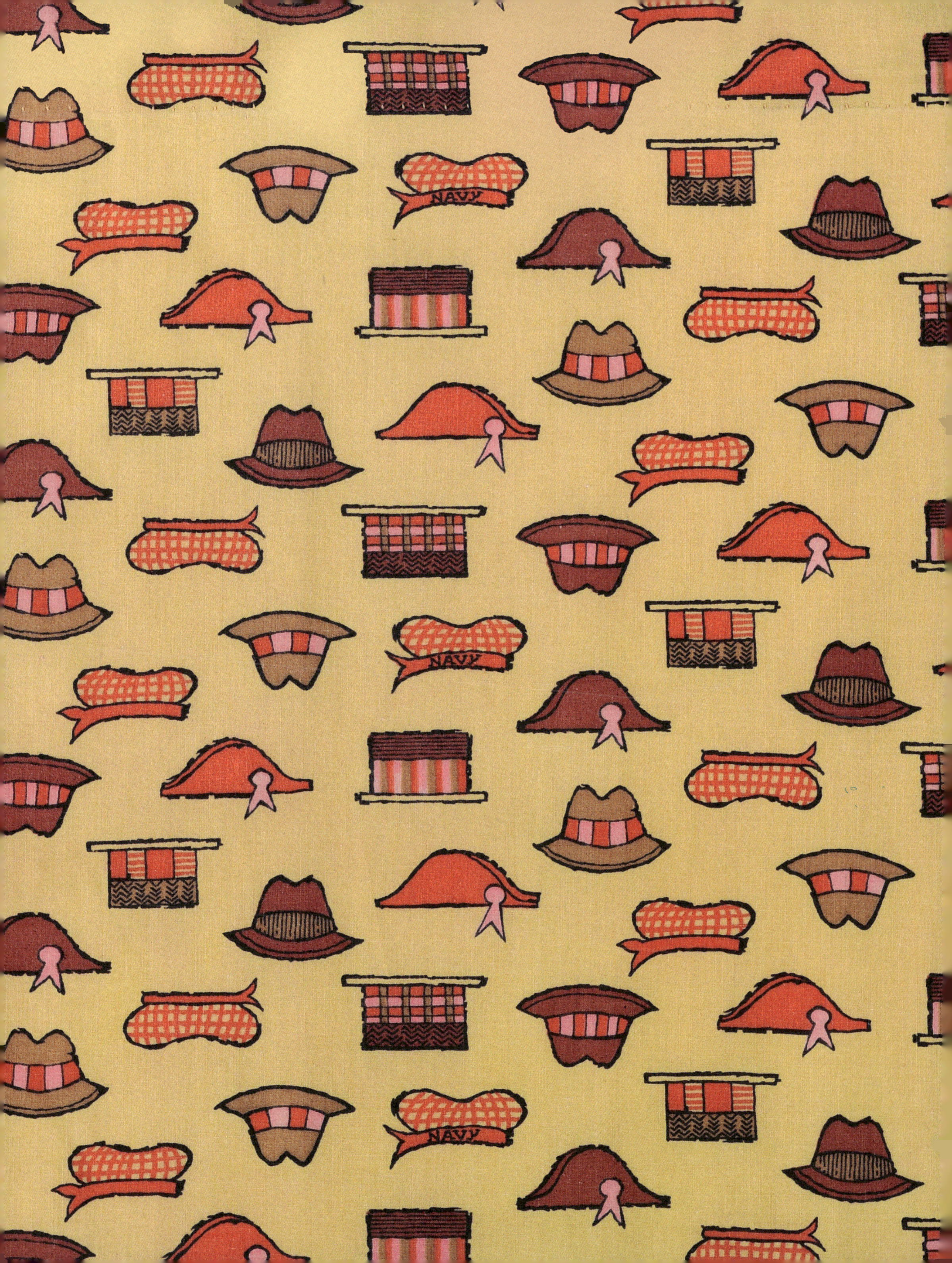
NAVY
NAVY
NAVY

15

TEXTILE WITH
BRUSHES AND BROOMS

Printed cotton, *circa* 1957–1958
Crompton-Richmond Company, Inc.

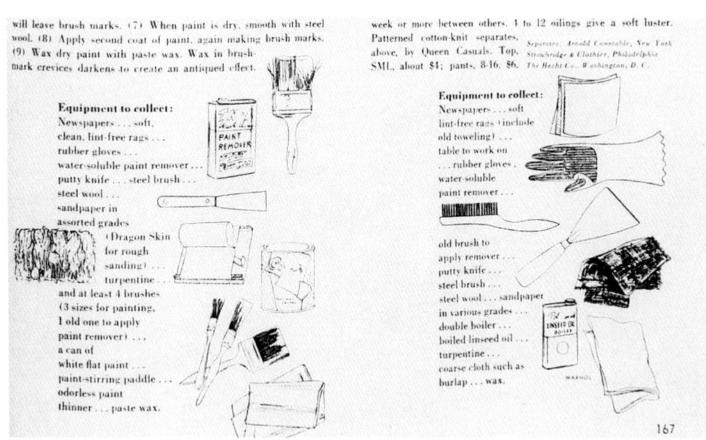

will leave brush marks. (7) When paint is dry, smooth with steel wool. (8) Apply second coat of paint, again making brush marks. (9) Wax dry paint with paste wax. Wax in brush-mark crevices darkens to create an antiqued effect.

Equipment to collect:
Newspapers . . . soft, clean, lint-free rags . . . rubber gloves . . . water-soluble paint remover . . . putty knife . . . steel brush . . . steel wool . . . sandpaper in assorted grades (Dragon Skin for rough sanding) . . . turpentine . . . and at least 4 brushes (3 sizes for painting, 1 old one to apply paint remover) . . . a can of white flat paint . . . paint-stirring paddle . . . odorless paint thinner . . . paste wax.

week or more between others. 4 to 12 oilings give a soft luster. Patterned cotton-knit separates, above, by Queen Casuals. Top, SML, about $4; pants, 8-16, $6.

Separates: Arnold Constable, New York; Strawbridge & Clothier, Philadelphia; The Hecht Co., Washington, D. C.

Equipment to collect:
Newspapers . . . soft lint-free rags (include old toweling) . . . table to work on . . . rubber gloves . . . water-soluble paint remover . . . old brush to apply remover . . . putty knife . . . steel brush . . . steel wool . . . sandpaper in various grades . . . double boiler . . . boiled linseed oil . . . turpentine . . . coarse cloth such as burlap . . . wax.

A long-established textile manufacturer from West Warwick, dating back to 1807, in 1916 the Providence Manufacturing Company had changed their name to Crompton-Richmond, Incorporated. Originally the company had specialised in producing everyday work fabrics such as corduroy. However, in 1936 they moved their selling department to New York City, from where they were able to focus much more on fashion-led textiles.

Two colourways are known, one of which was used for dresses by preppy fashion retailer The Villager.

Warhol's elevation of the everyday, taking ordinary household objects such as brushes and brooms and presenting them in his own unique way, very much informed the Pop art he produced in the early 1960s.

Above (a) Illustrations of brushes, *Glamour* magazine (September 1958). **Opposite (b)** Textile.

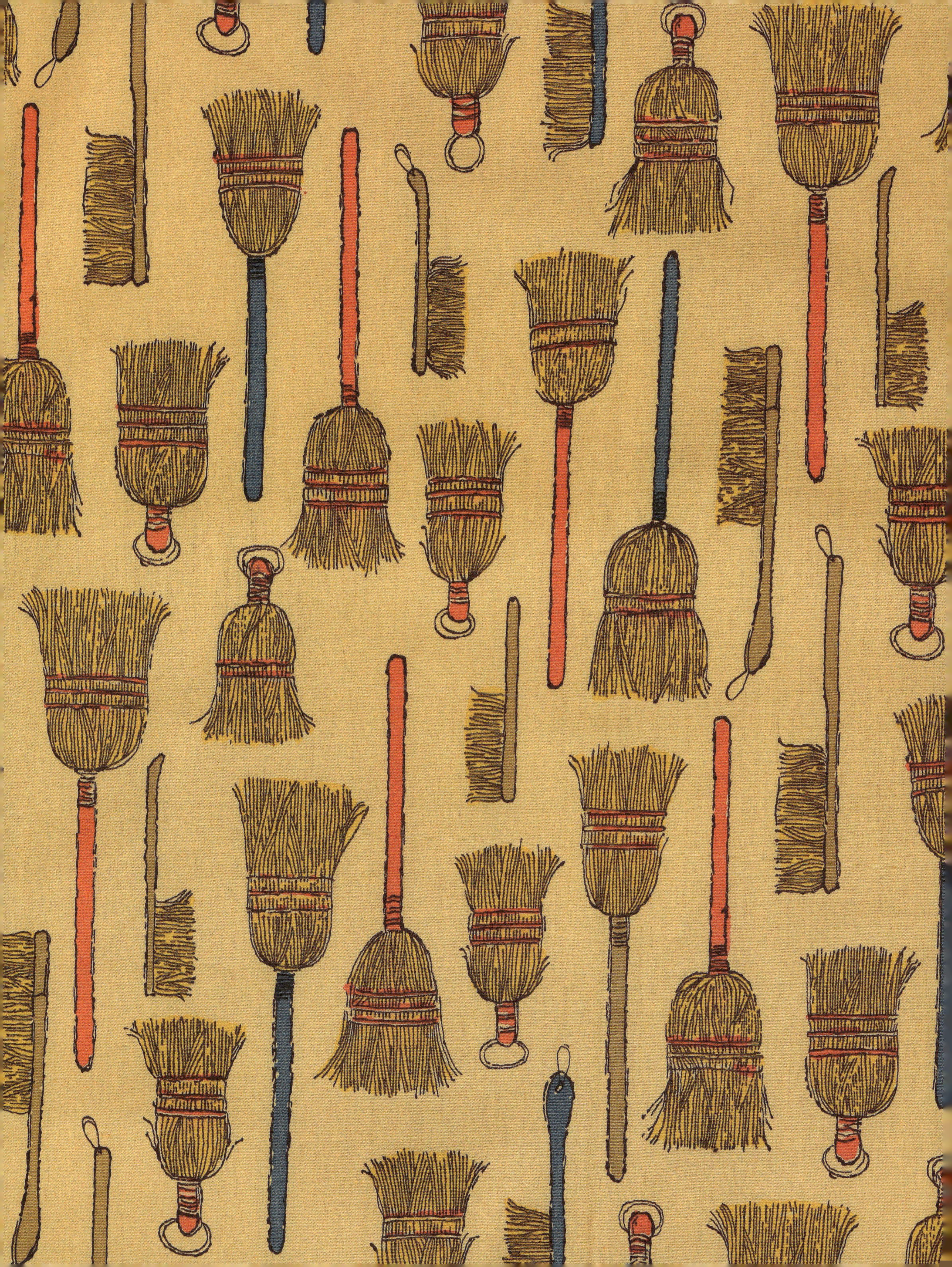

16

TEXTILE ON
THE THEME OF GARDENING

Printed cotton, *circa* 1957–1958
Attributed to M. Lowenstein & Sons, Inc.

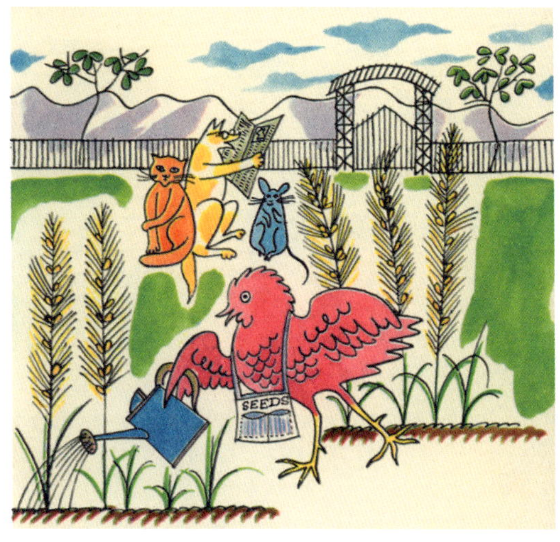

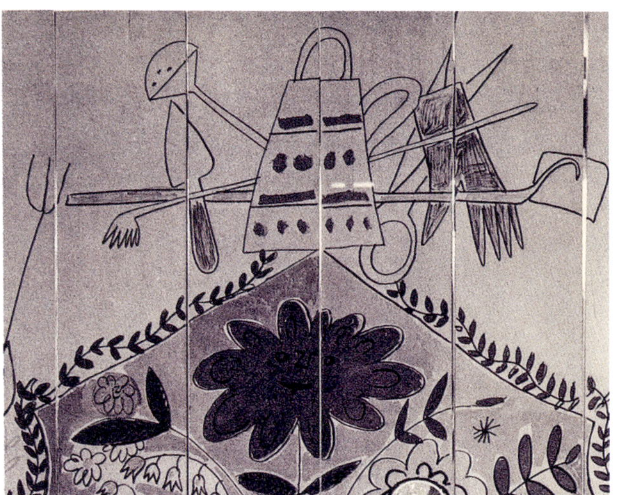

Warhol often took up the subject of gardens and gardening. In illustrations for the children's story of the Little Red Hen, executed at roughly the same time for the Best in Children's Books series, his colourway is identical to that of this textile. The particularly fresh and bright palette used for this fabric is very much a development of the Warholian way of caring for a garden. Warhol's particular style of drawing and colouring in this instance is frankly joyous and depicts the wonder he felt in horticultural pursuits.

Above left (a) Illustration by Andy Warhol from *The Little Red Hen* (New York: Nelson Doubleday, 1958).
Above right (b) Bonwit Teller garden-themed window display designed by Warhol (detail), 1957. Photographer: Virginia Roehl for Gene Moore, Artistic Director, Bonwit Teller. **Opposite (c)** Textile.

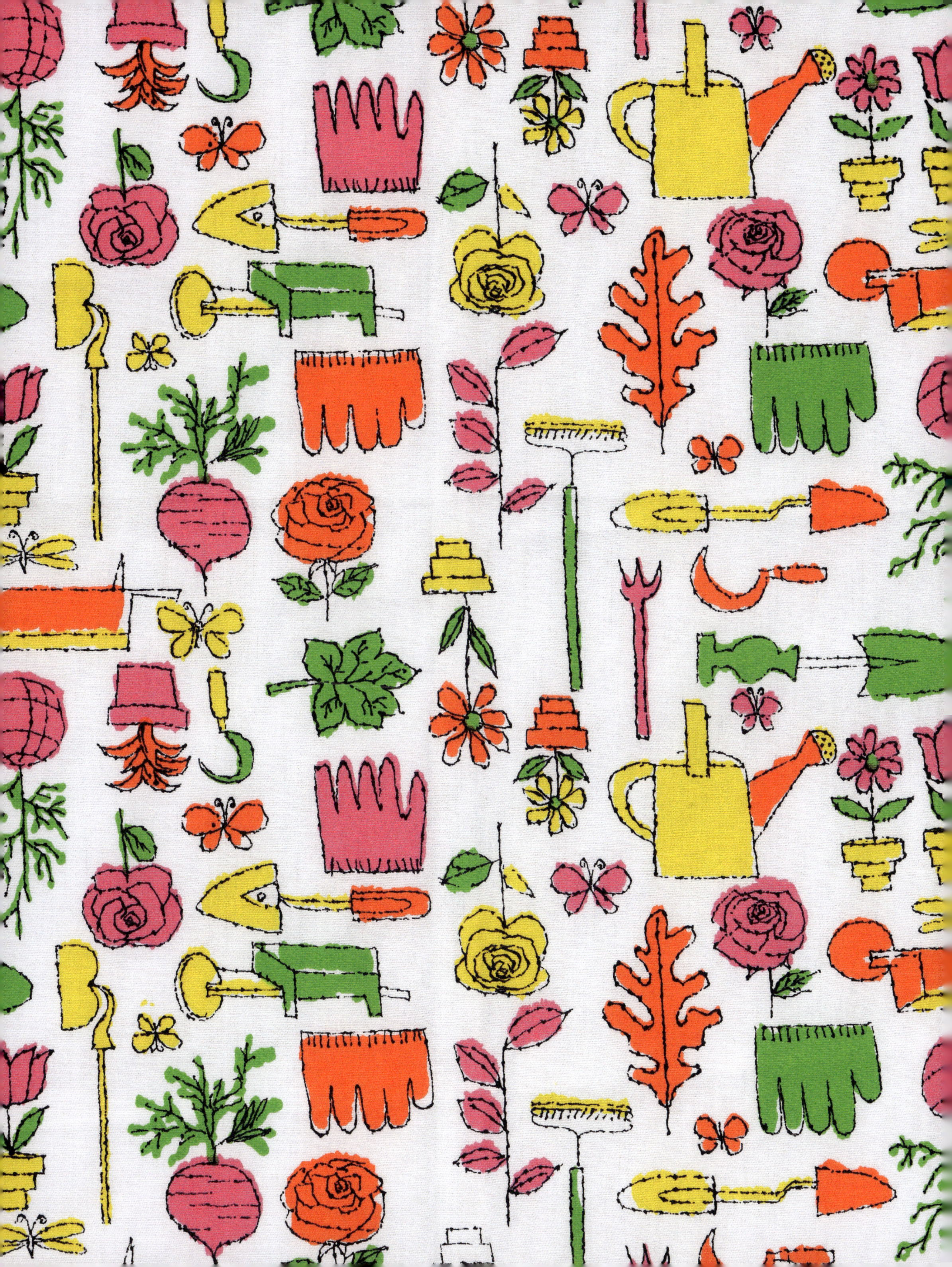

17

POTTED PLANTS

Printed cotton, *circa* 1957–1958
Attributed to D. B. Fuller & Co., Inc.

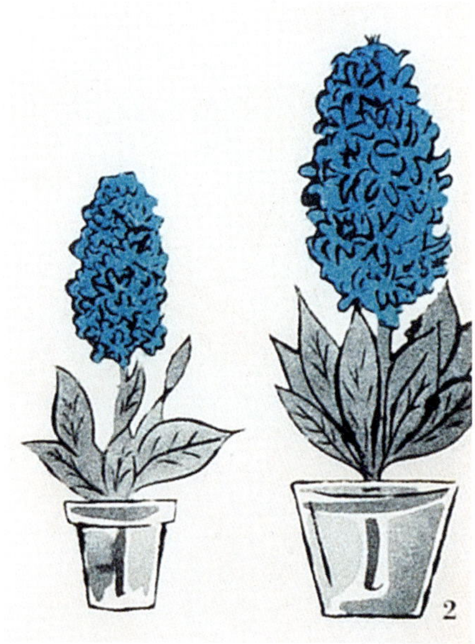

Potted plants such as flowering perennials and succulents appear frequently in Warhol's repeating patterns and magazine work, for example for I. Miller Shoes and greetings cards and illustrations for *Harper's Bazaar*. John Rombola still remembers Warhol making textile designs with floral decoration for Dan Fuller of Fuller Fabrics.

Above (a) Illustration of potted plants, *Harper's Bazaar* (July 1958). **Opposite (b)** Textile (detail of skirt overleaf).

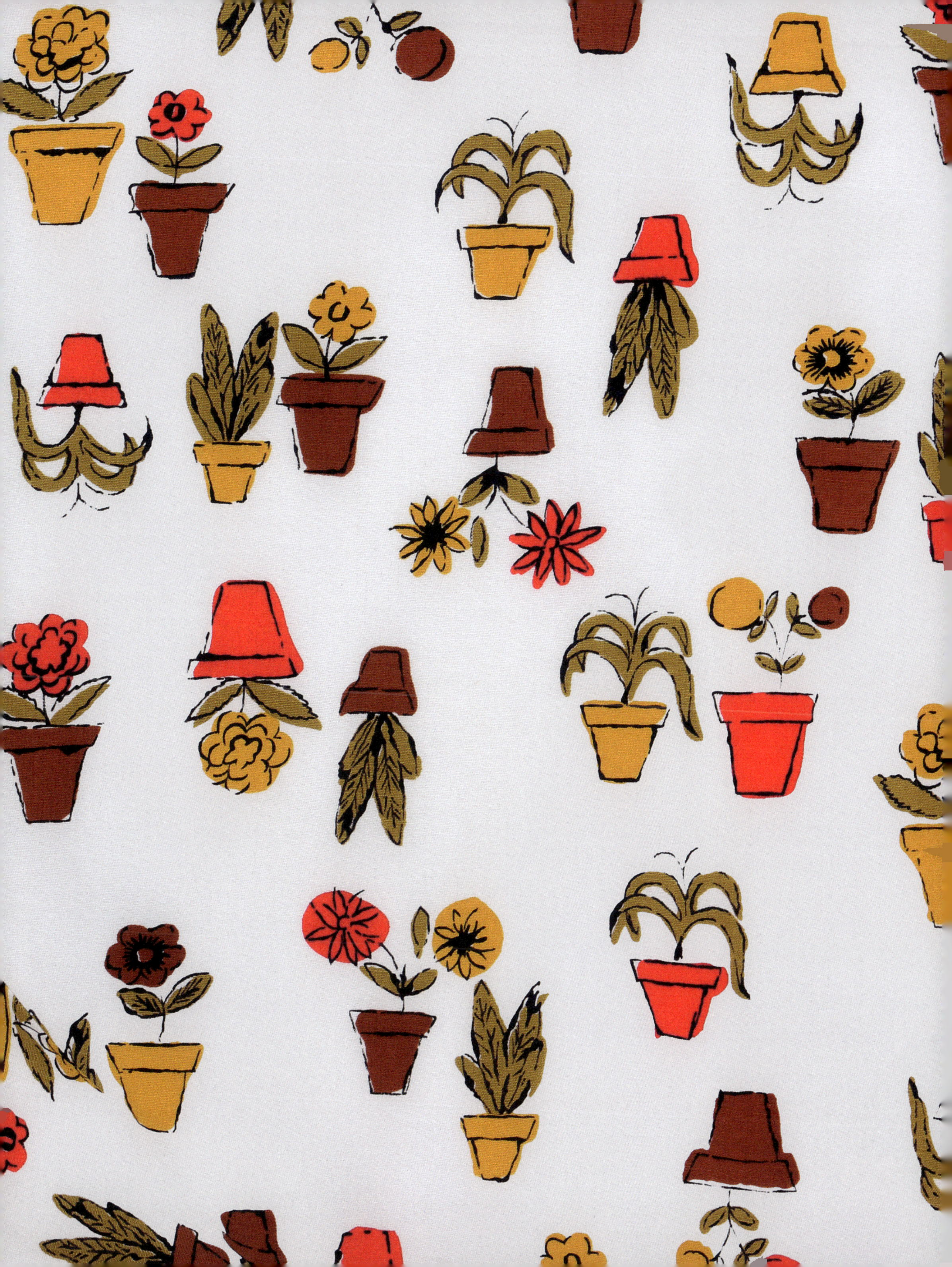

(b) Skirt, maker unknown.

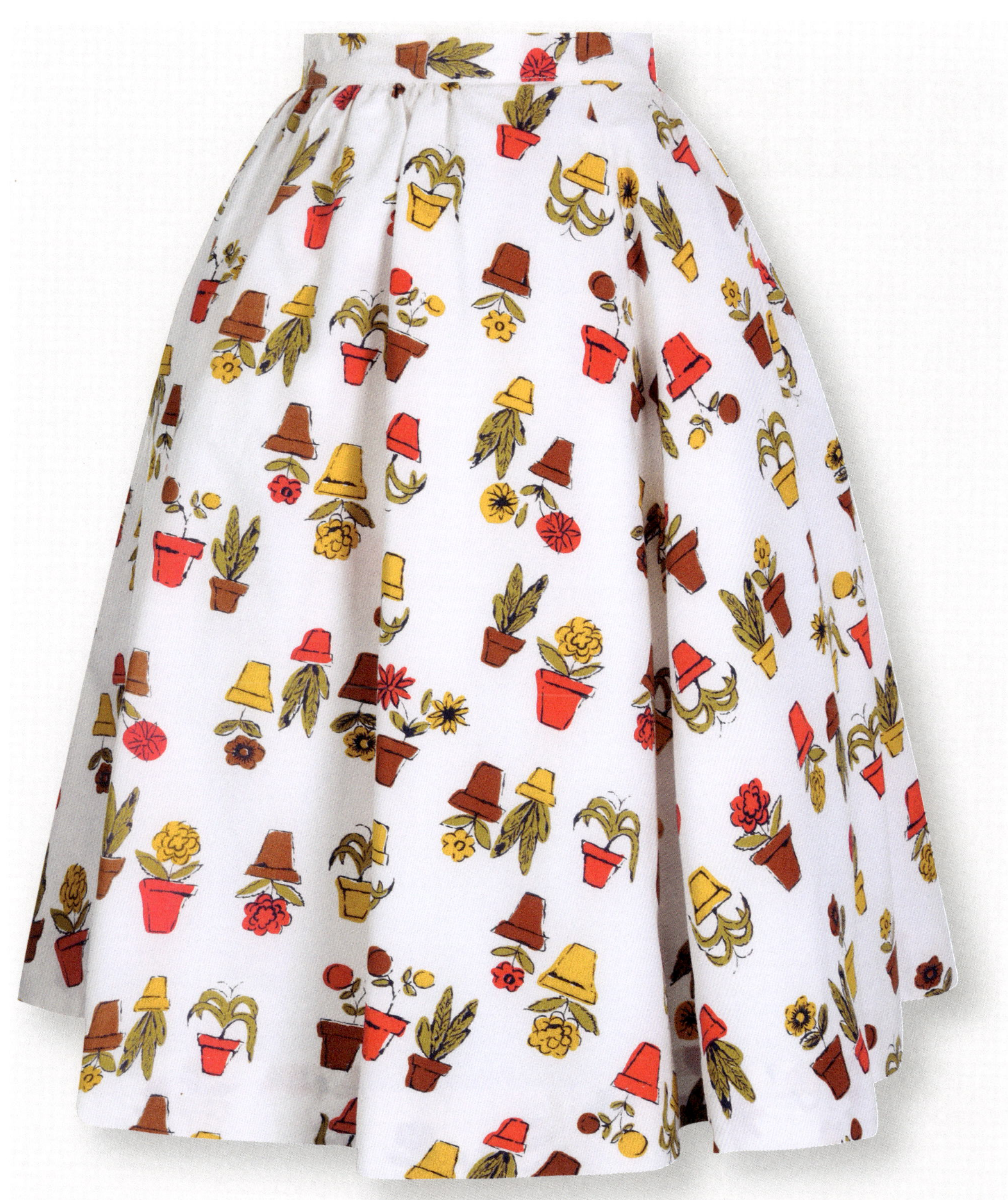

18

THE BALMORAL LOOMS DESIGNS

Printed silk, 1957–1959
Balmoral Looms, Inc.

The textile designer and entrepreneur Jack Schondorf was an acquaintance of Warhol's in the 1950s. At the end of the decade Warhol created a number of textiles which he gave to Schondorf, who was then able to sell them on the commercial textile market. Schondorf sold seven of Warhol's drawings to Joseph Slifka, the owner of Balmoral Looms. Slifka, together with his wife Sylvia, owned at least eight individual textile companies in New York City in the 1950s, Balmoral Looms being one of them.

(a) Advertisement from *Women's Wear Daily* featuring Jack Schondorf, c.1964.

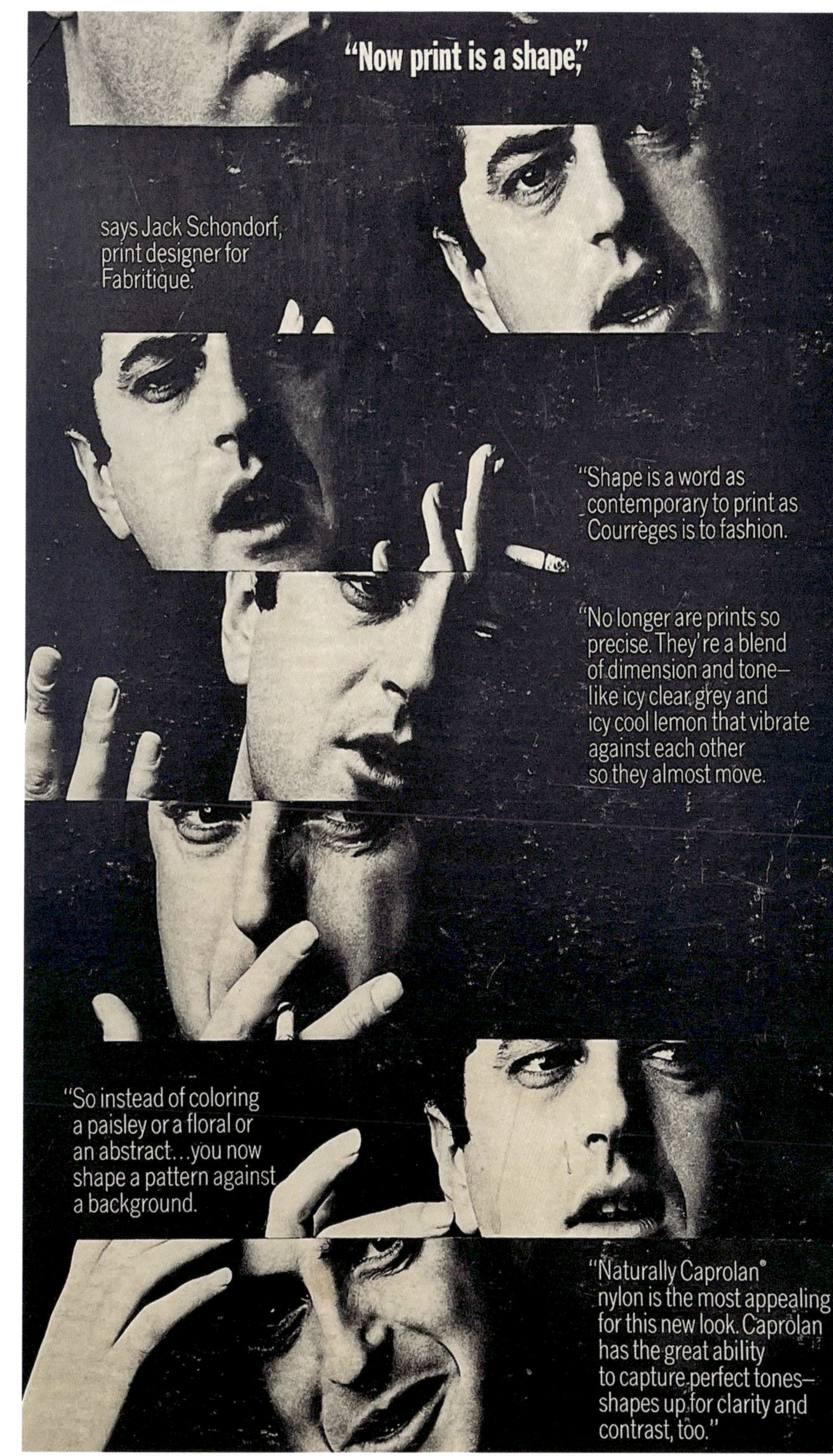
"Now print is a shape,"
says Jack Schondorf, print designer for Fabritique.
"Shape is a word as contemporary to print as Courrèges is to fashion.
"No longer are prints so precise. They're a blend of dimension and tone—like icy clear grey and icy cool lemon that vibrate against each other so they almost move.
"So instead of coloring a paisley or a floral or an abstract…you now shape a pattern against a background.
"Naturally Caprolan® nylon is the most appealing for this new look. Caprolan has the great ability to capture perfect tones—shapes up for clarity and contrast, too."

TEXTILE WITH
NASTURTIUMS

Printed silk, 1959

This textile has a selvedge intact with details that identify the manufacturer as Balmoral Looms. It is one of six silk fabrics now in the collection of the Warhol Museum in Pittsburgh.

(b) Textile.

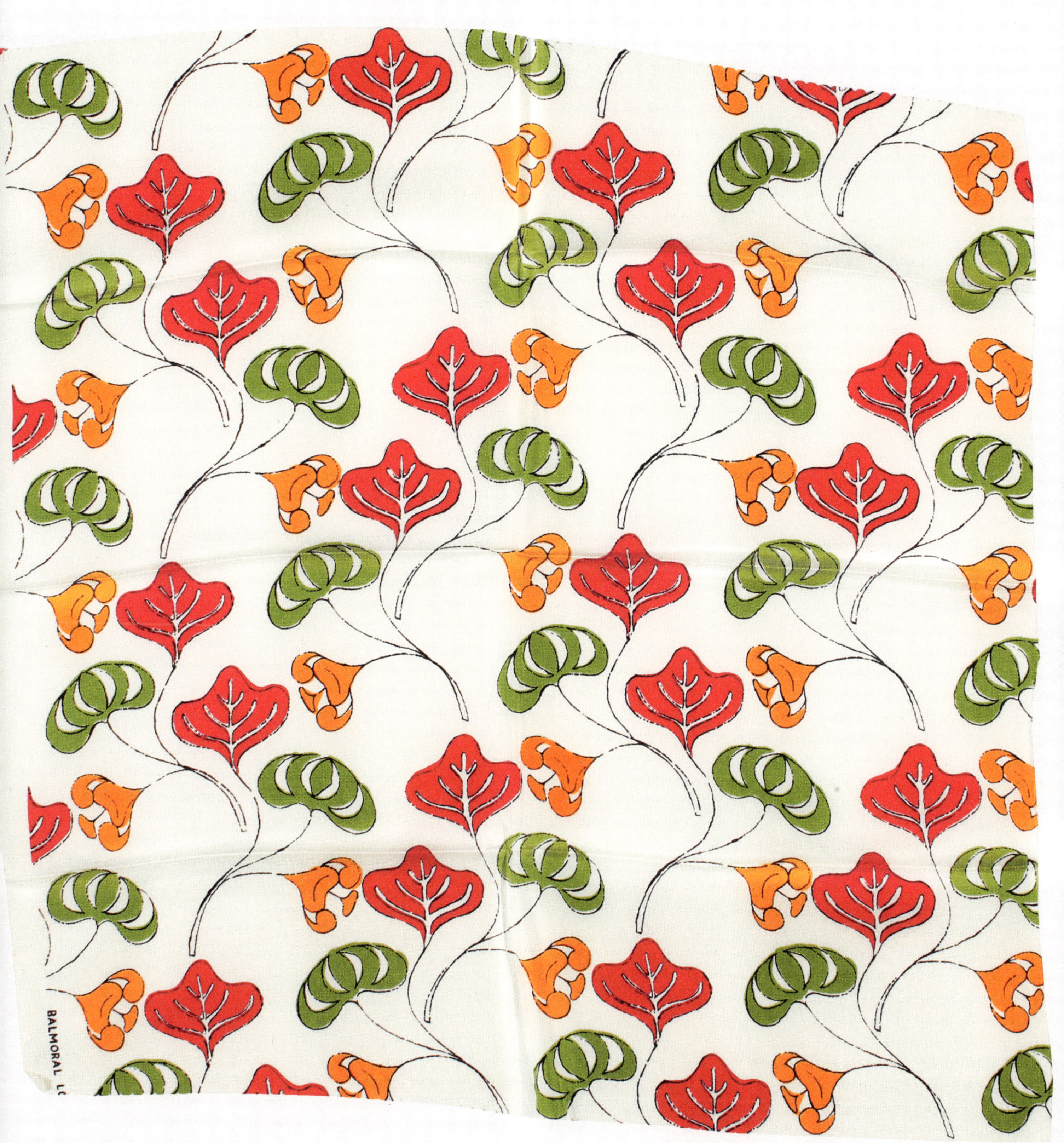
BALMORAL

FLORAL DESIGN NO. 1

Printed silk, 1959

Here Warhol is already playing with the exaggerated shapes and patterns of flowers, a number of years before his Pop art floral carpet designs of the 1960s first emerged.

(c) Textile.

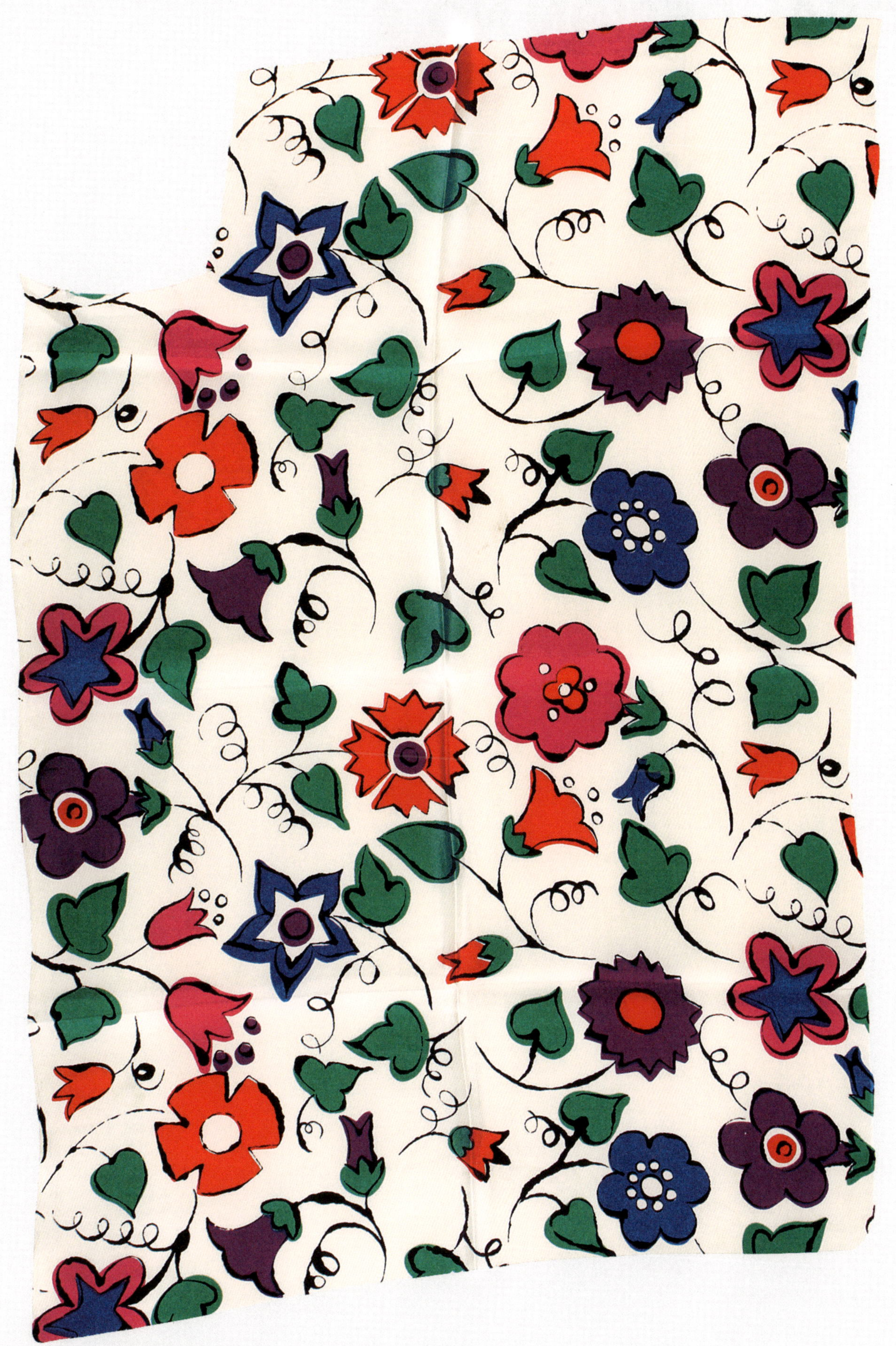

FLORAL DESIGN NO. 2

Printed silk, 1959

Somewhat larger in scale than Floral Design No. 1, this textile yet again uses the shapes and colours of flowers in a Pop art fashion.

(d) Textile.

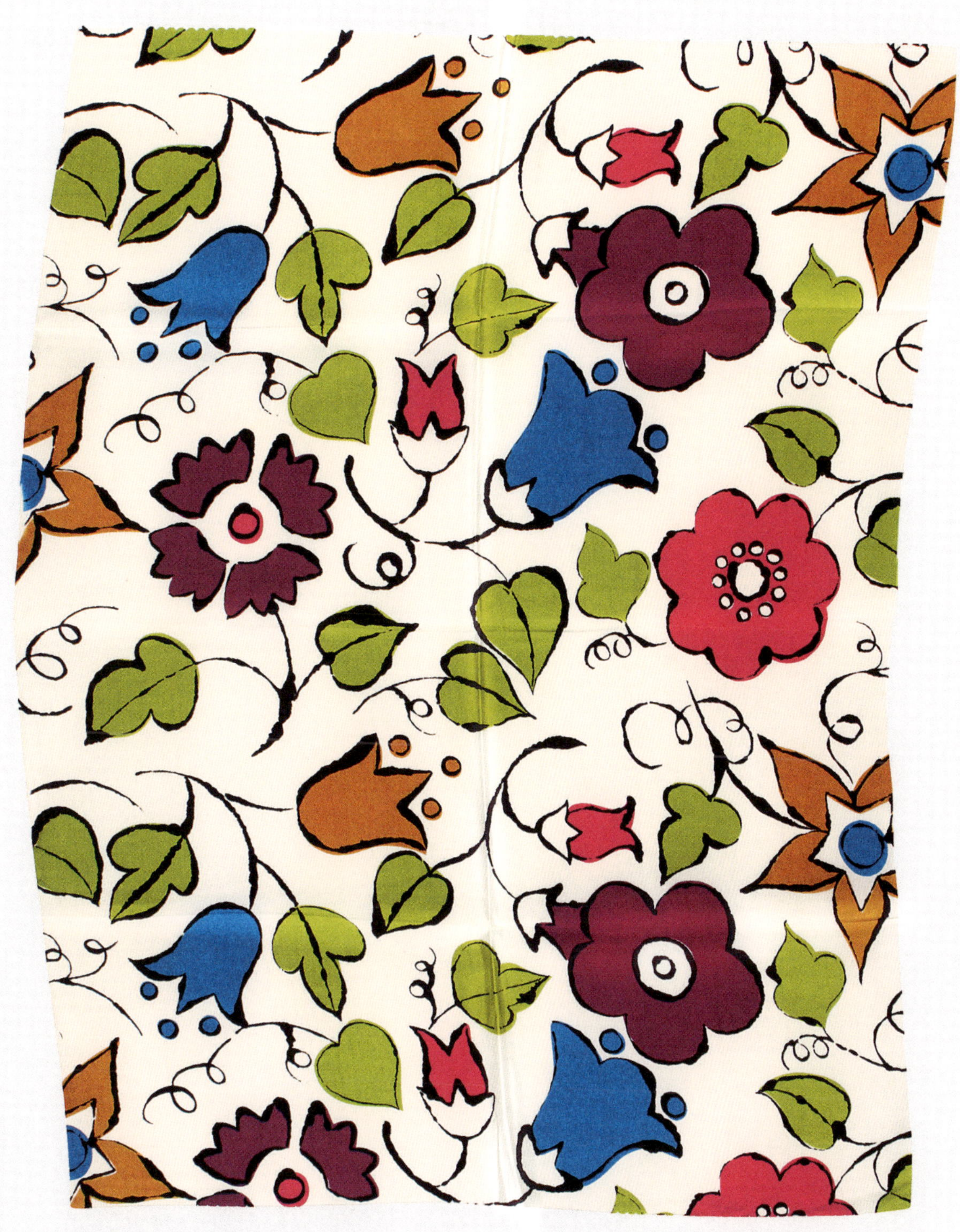

LILIES

Printed silk, 1958–1959

Warhol uses a lily flower here to create a pattern of floral shapes. Taken together with the plant's wayward stems and leaves, this is a motif that at the same time can be viewed within the broader art historical framework of Art Nouveau.

(e) Textile.

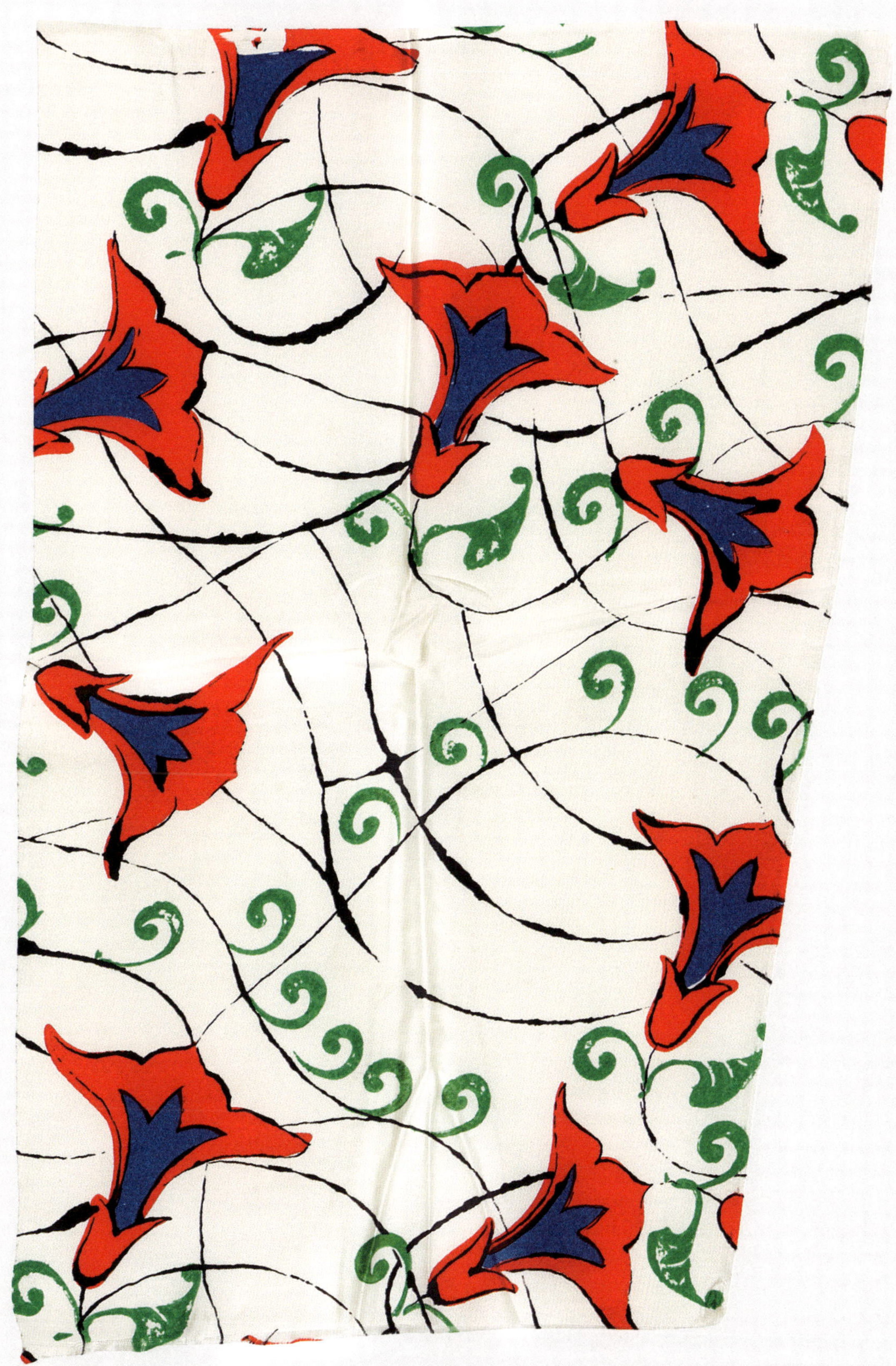

WATER LILIES

Printed silk, 1958–1959

The pattern of water lilies used here is a more structured image, which as such offers a stronger rhythmic definition of the plant. This, however, is relieved by a much more spontaneous use of stems and leaves.

The early reappraisal of Art Nouveau in Europe and America was only then beginning to burgeon, with great interest being shown in Tiffany lamps, Aubrey Beardsley illustrations and bentwood furniture. This was especially important for Warhol, referencing as it did his strong connection to the New York café Serendipity 3, then a Mecca for the Art Nouveau revival in the United States.

(f) Textile.

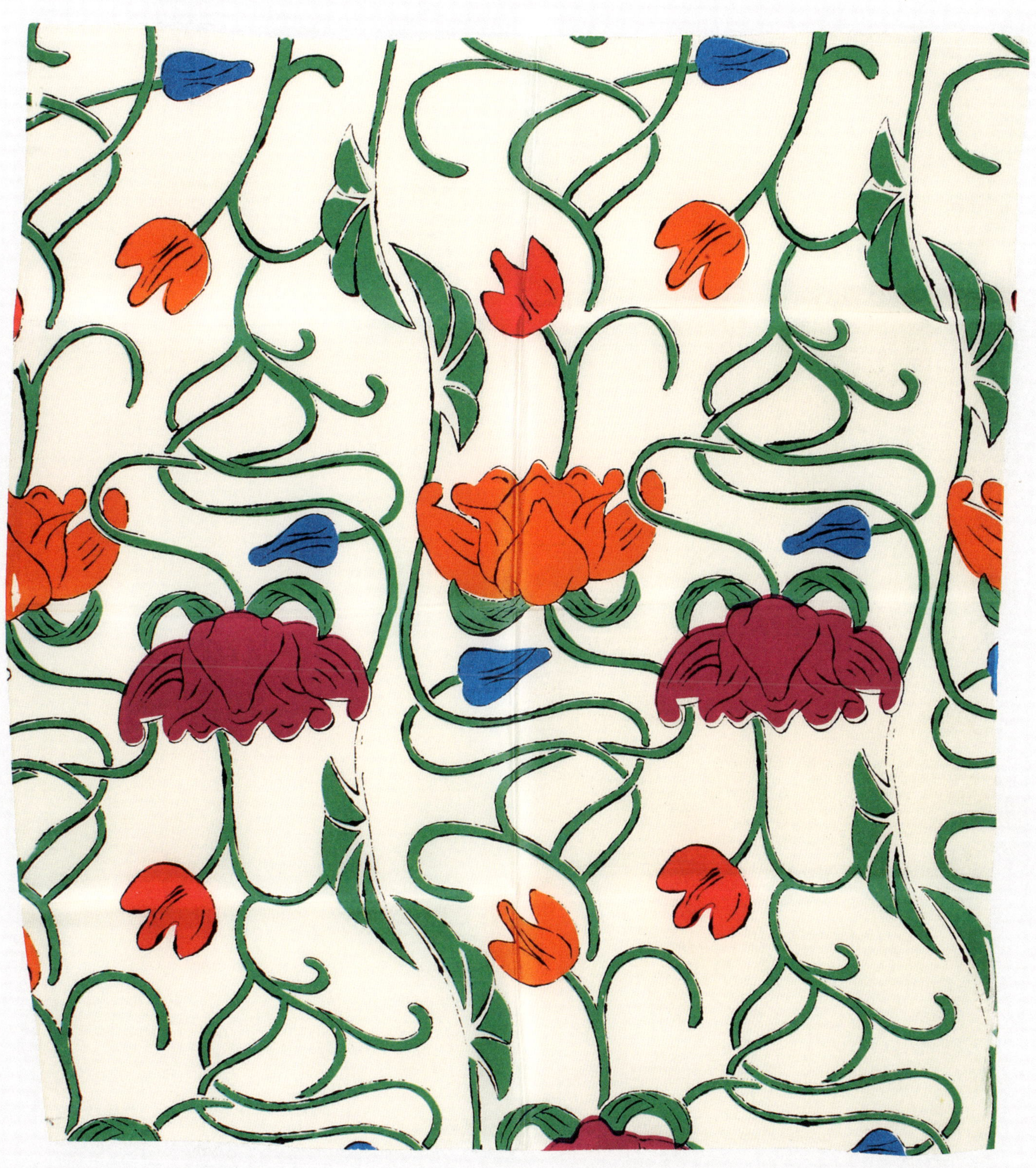

PAISLEY TEXTILE DESIGN

Ink on paper, 1959

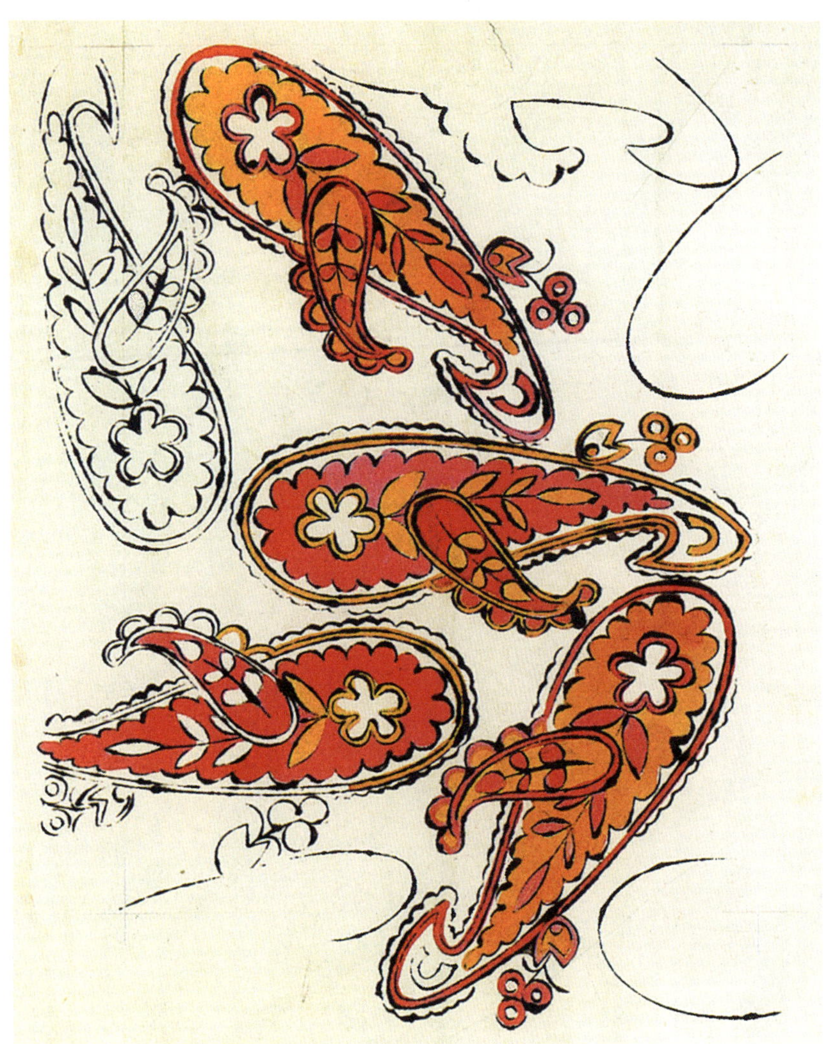

In this design given to Balmoral Looms, although he is using a traditional Paisley pattern, Warhol has added a fin or wing to each individual form, which gives a zoomorphic quality to the overall effect.

(g) Textile design. Ink on paper.

HOLIDAY PRINT

Textile design, 1959

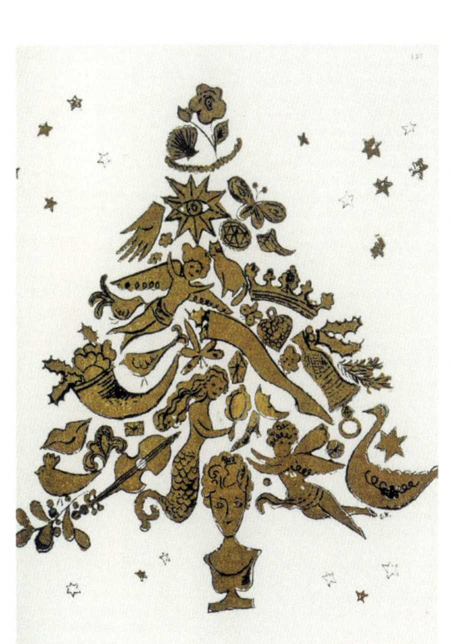

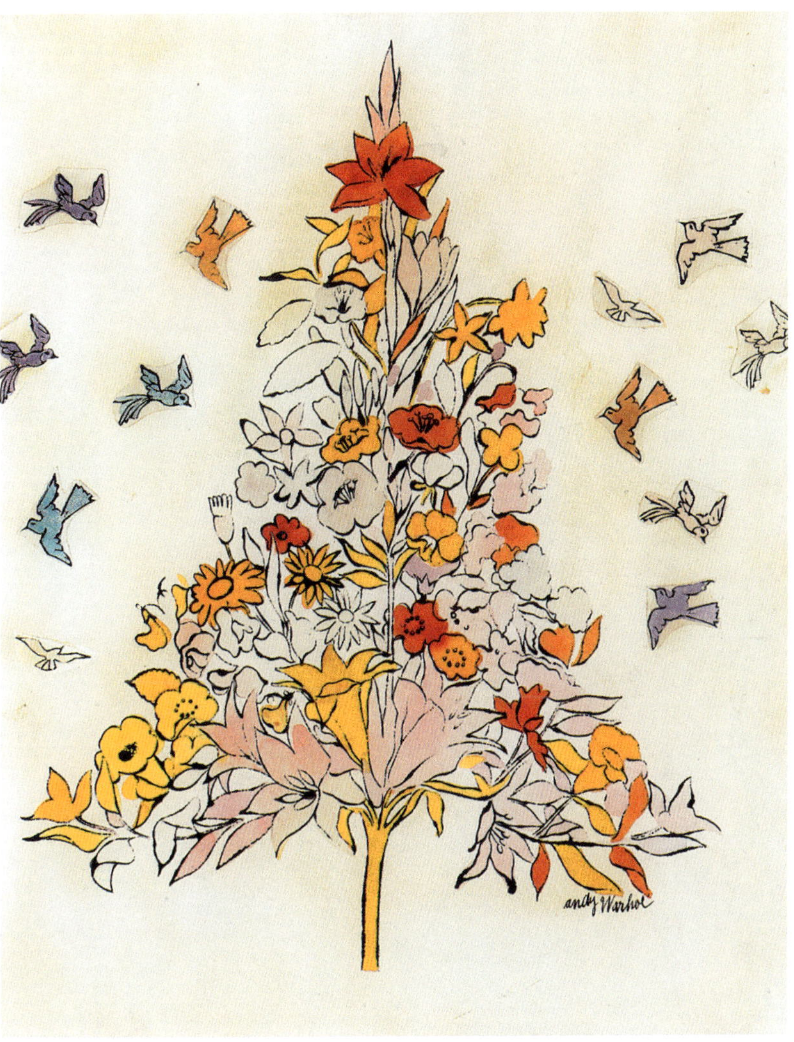

'Holiday Print', drawn by Warhol and supplied to Balmoral Looms by Jack Schondorf, takes the form of a Christmas tree but is composed of flowers and leaves rather than the usual sprigs of fir normally connected with the season. Also, the tree is surrounded by upsurging flights of birds, instead of the customary Christmas motifs. The design is not only unusual for Christmas but also allows for use on textiles and cards for other types of holiday.

Above left (h) A similar design in *Harper's Bazaar* (December 1957), with stars instead of birds. **Above right (i)** Textile design.

TEXTILE OF

FLORAL DESIGN

Printed nylon, *circa* 1957–1958

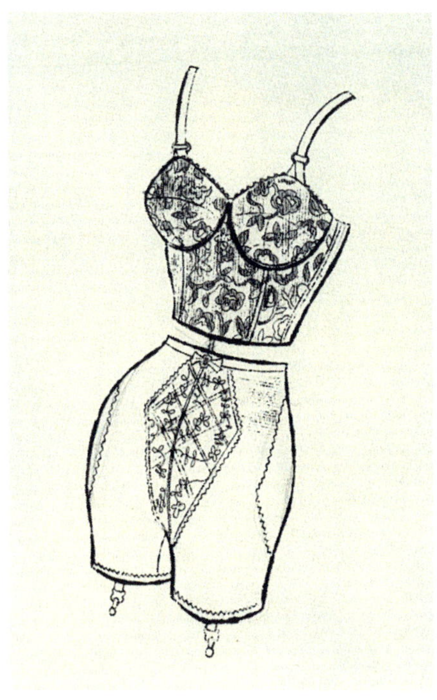

This design, primarily meant for women's underwear, was produced by Balmoral Looms on nylon in the late 1950s. The delicately rendered textile of floral design is used here, for example, as an underslip. Warhol produced many illustrations of underwear for advertisements at the time, often incorporating light, airy patterns such as this.

Above (j) Illustration of underwear, *Harper's Bazaar* (March 1958). **Opposite (k)** Textile (detail of underslip, maker unknown).

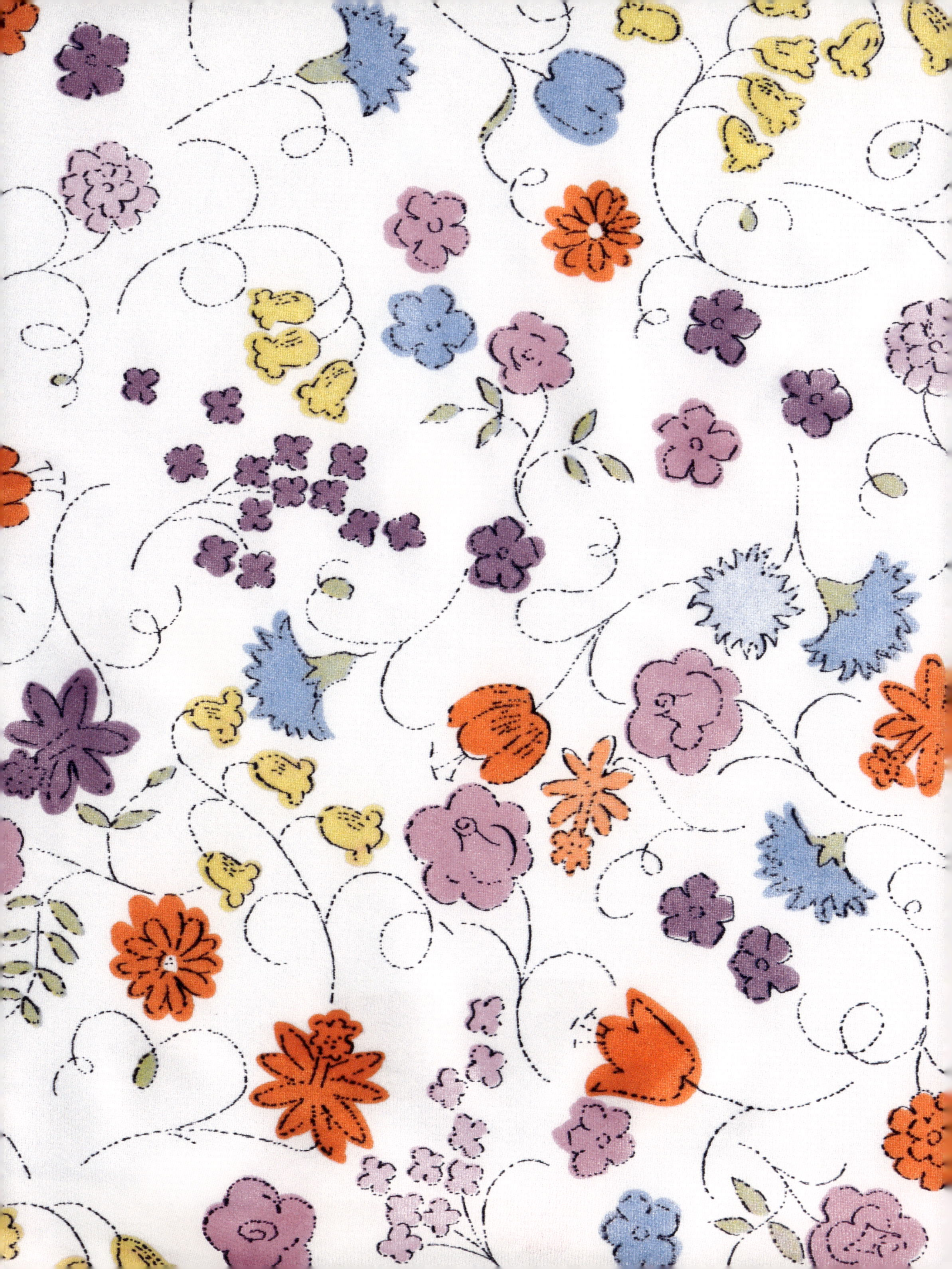

19

TEXTILE WITH
PHILODENDRONS

Printed arnel triacetate, *circa* 1958–1959
Attributed to Balmoral Looms, Inc.

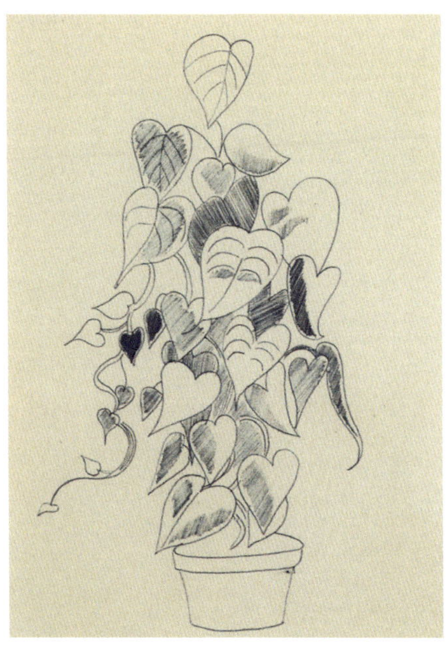

The cultivar philadendron was introduced to the US in the 1950s and became a top-selling houseplant alongside the Swiss cheese plant. This pattern once again draws on the sinuous and meandering properties of Art Nouveau, a style that was only then beginning to return to fashion following its heyday in the nineteenth century. Warhol would have found the distinctive heart-shaped leaf an irresistible subject matter.

Palm Fashions of Deland, Florida, made dresses from this textile, using it to great effect.

Above (a) Drawing of a philodendron. Ballpoint pen on paper, c.1957. **Opposite (b)** Textile in yellow colourway (detail of dress by Palm Fashions, Deland, Florida, c.1959).

(c) Dress in pink colourway by Palm Fashions, Deland, Florida, *c.*1959.

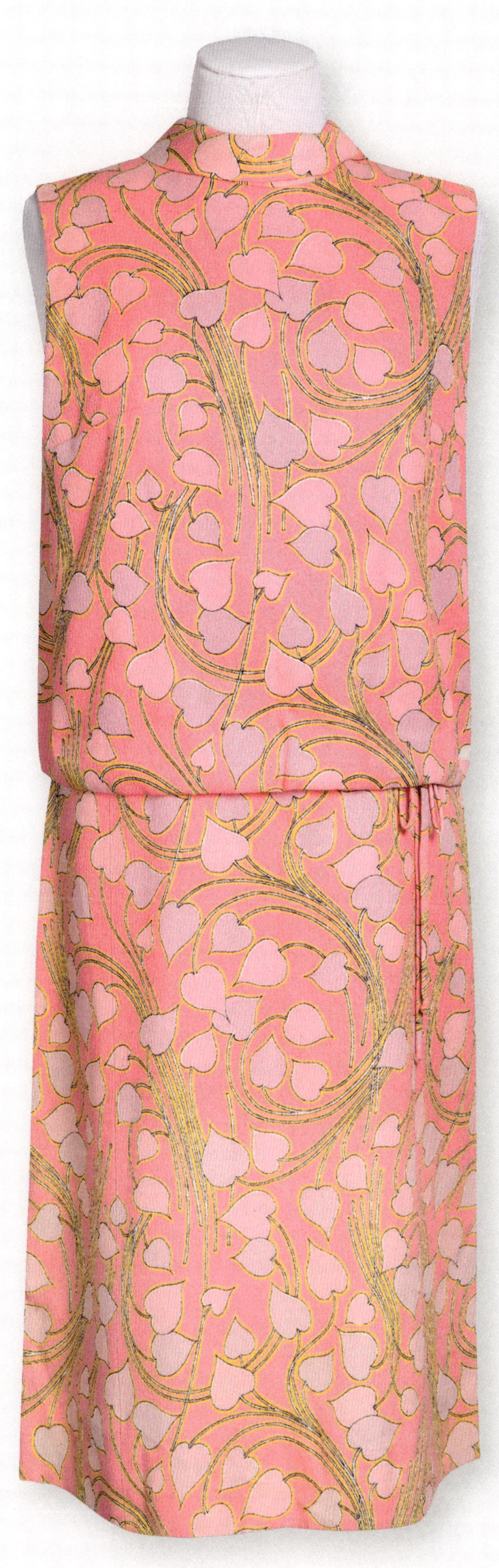

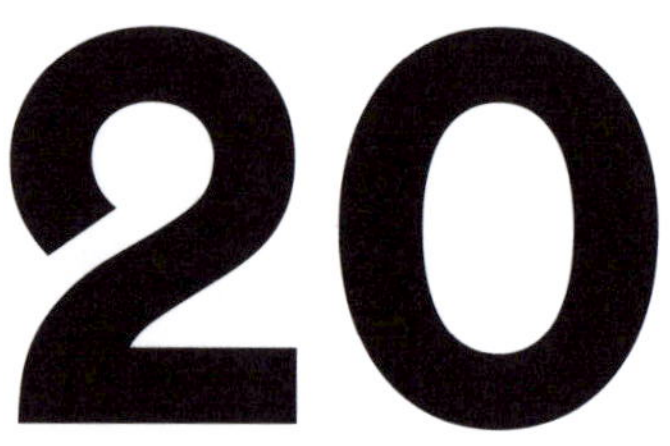

TEXTILE WITH
STARS, ANGELS AND BUGS

Printed rayon, *circa* 1958
Manufacturer unknown

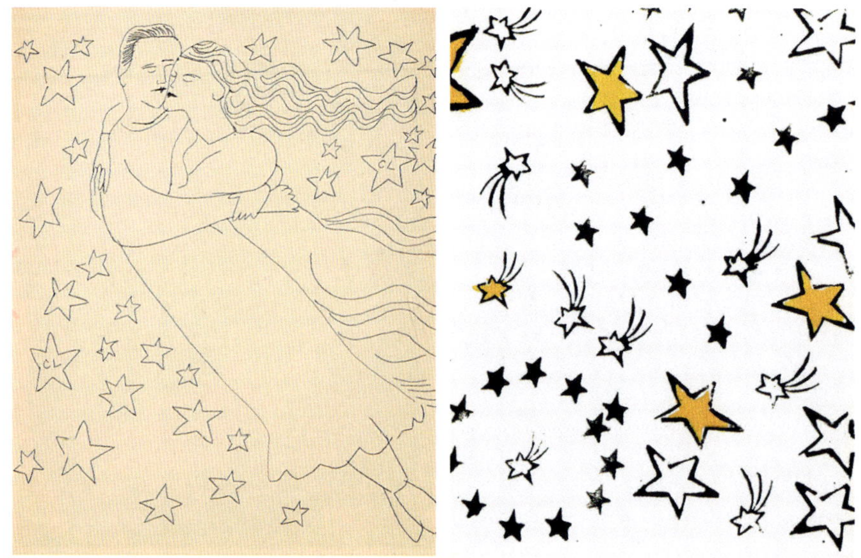

This textile displays dancers floating against a background of stars. The figures float in a void lit with starlight and filled with a myriad of moths and other flying creatures.

Unusually, the background to this textile is reversed. The black shows the figures outlined in white, a design which conveys the depths of space. Warhol rarely used backgrounds such as this, although his frequent work in the early 1950s for the journal *Dance Magazine* was another such exception.

Above left (a) Drawing of Charles Lisanby flying with a woman, surrounded by stars. Ink on paper, c.1956. **Above right (b)** 'So Starry' (detail), a stamped and coloured design. Ink on paper, c.1958. **Opposite (c)** Textile (detail).

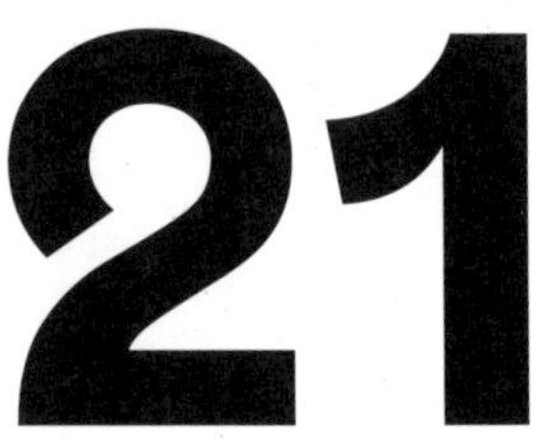

TEXTILE WITH
LARGE NAUTICAL FLAGS

Printed cotton, *circa* 1958–1959
Manufacturer unknown

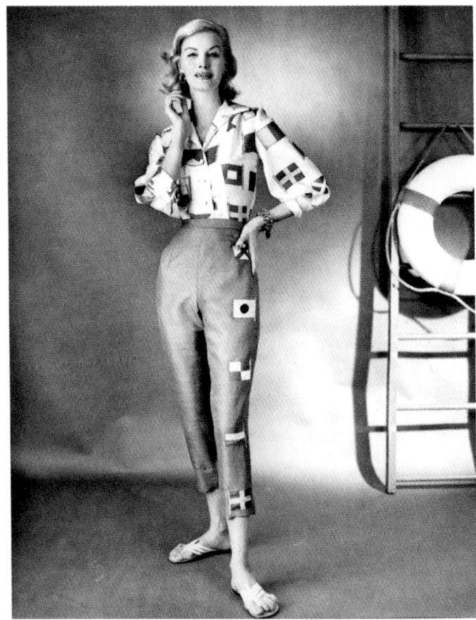

The variety of different designs offered by nautical flags, with their brightly coloured geometric elements, provided Warhol with the perfect theme for conversational prints, intended for use on high days and summer vacations.

The print in this case is enlarged on an impressive scale to provide for border-printed skirts.

Above (a) Press photograph of 8 January 1960 featuring a silk textile of nautical flags, the design attributed to Warhol. Printed by Nat Wager Associates, blouse manufactured by Arbe. **Opposite (b)** Skirt by Marden Classics, late 1950s.

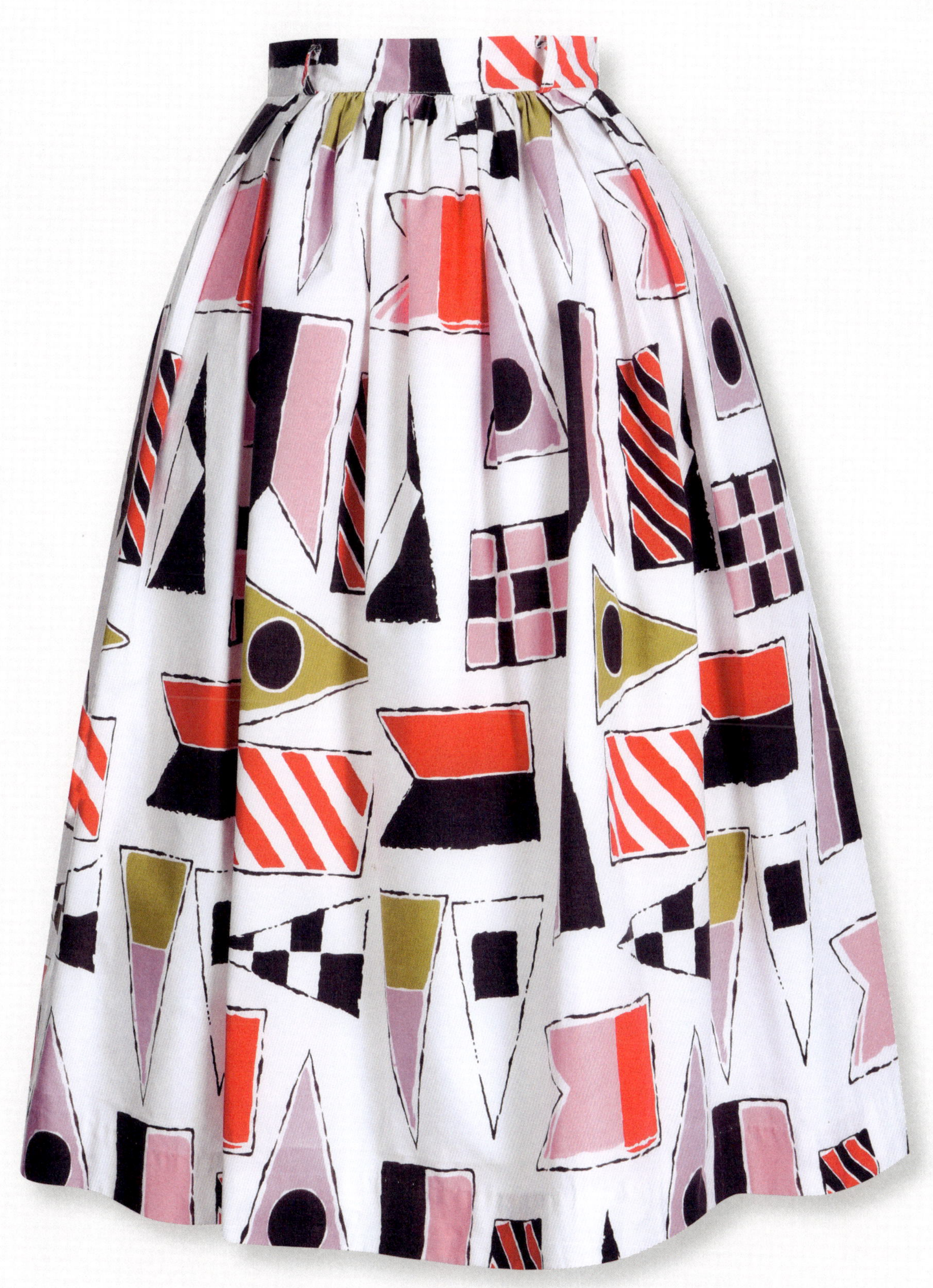

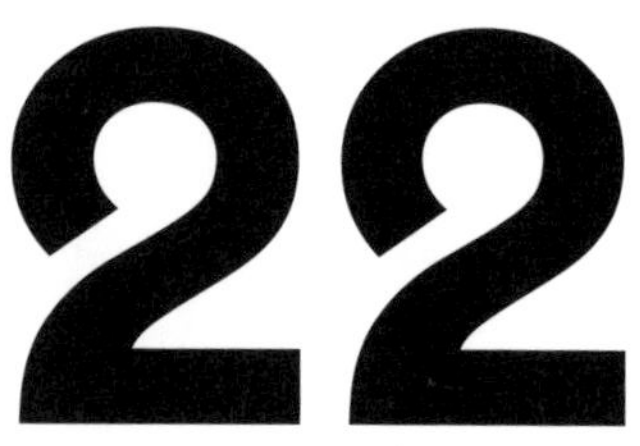

TEXTILE WITH
SMALL NAUTICAL FLAGS

Printed cotton, late 1950s
Manufacturer unknown

Warhol's delicately rendered design of small nautical flags was produced in at least two different colourways. It was used almost exclusively on various types of beach and resort wear.

Opposite left (a) Pedal pushers in green and red colourway, maker unknown. **Opposite right (b)** Beach costume in orange and blue colourway, maker unknown.

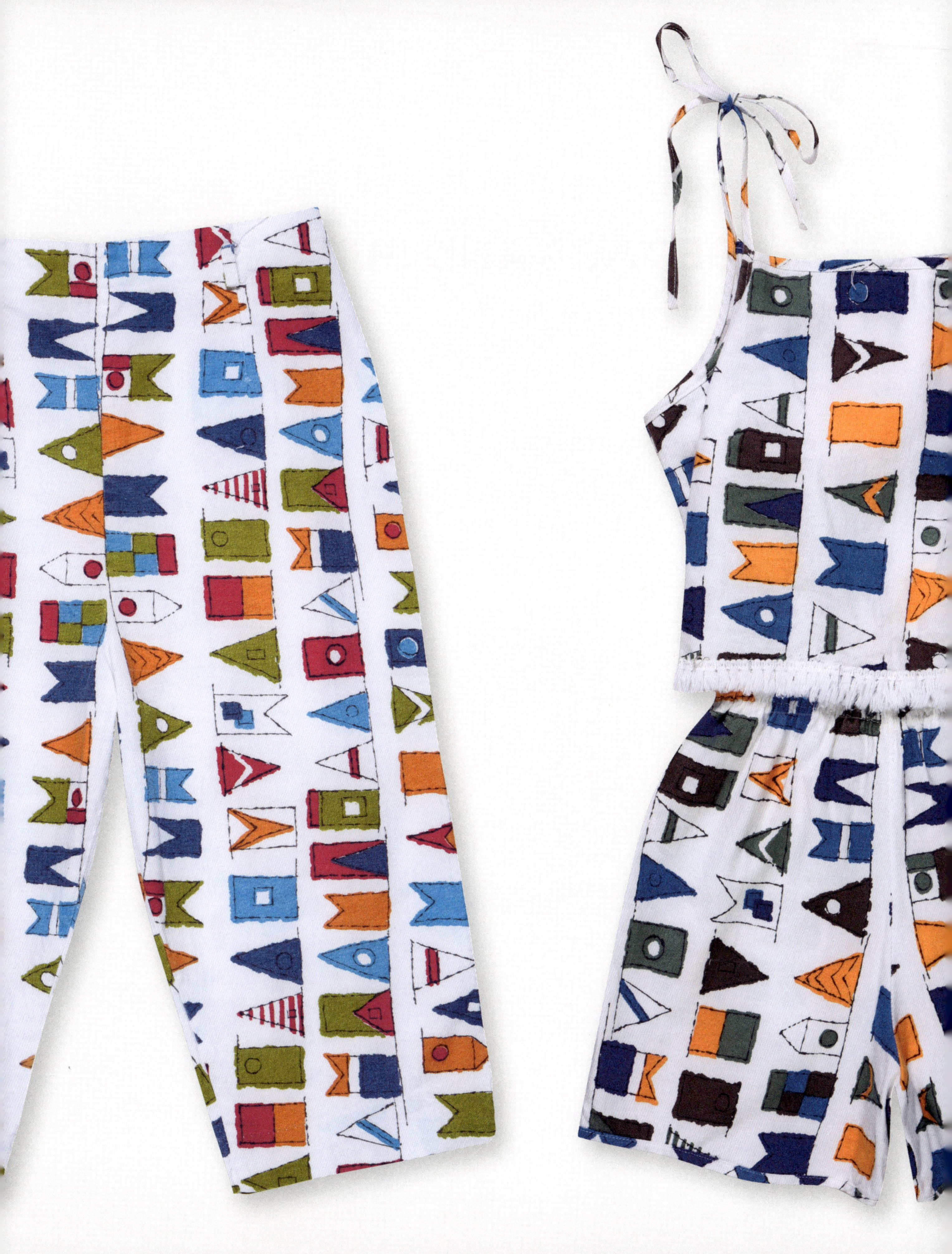

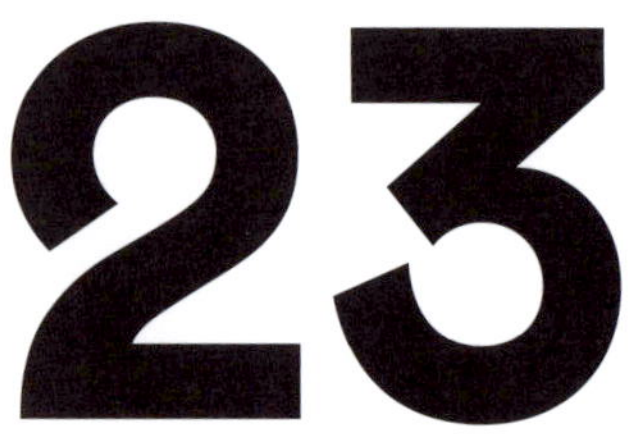

TEXTILE WITH
LUGGAGE TAGS AND SUITCASES

Printed lycron, *circa* 1958–1959
Cohama

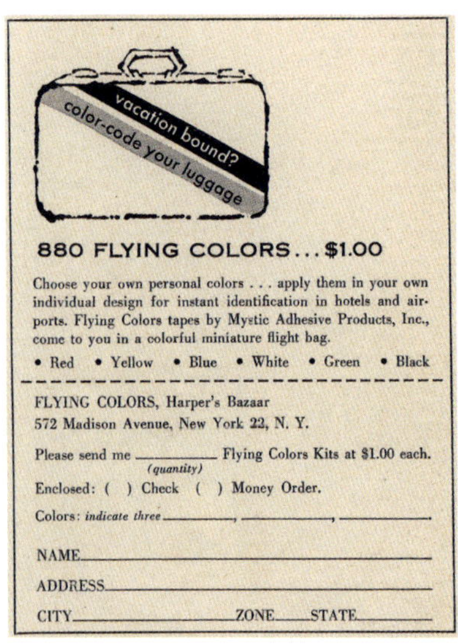

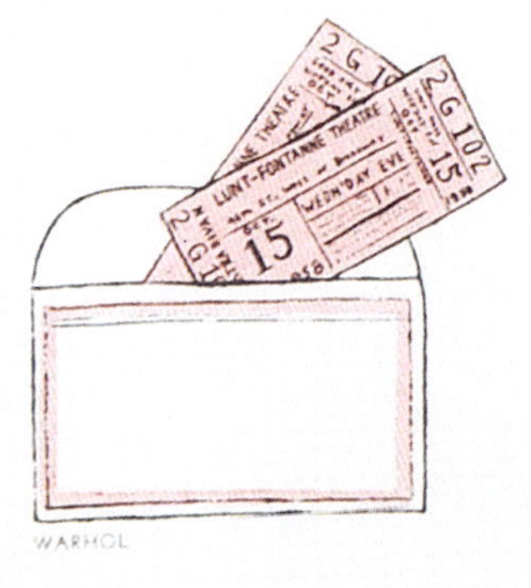

So-called resort or cruise wear had originally been intended for a wealthy international elite, who travelled widely in the 1920s and 1930s. However, designs of this type from the 1950s also helped bring to life for the American public at large the idea of increased leisure-time pursuits as well as the concept of foreign travel.

This design was printed on lycron, a man-made, crease-resistant fabric, by the textile company Cohama, the brand name of Cohn-Hall-Marx, New York. Originally established in 1912, Cohama had by the 1940s grown into a sizeable and profitable concern. By then the company had a reputation for commissioning young talented artist-designers, such as Angelo Testa, a recent graduate from the Institute of Design in Chicago.

Above left (a) Advertisement, *Harper's Bazaar* (July 1960). **Above right (b)** Illustration of theatre tickets in an envelope, *Harper's Bazaar* (July 1958). **Opposite (c)** Textile (detail of blouse by Majestic).

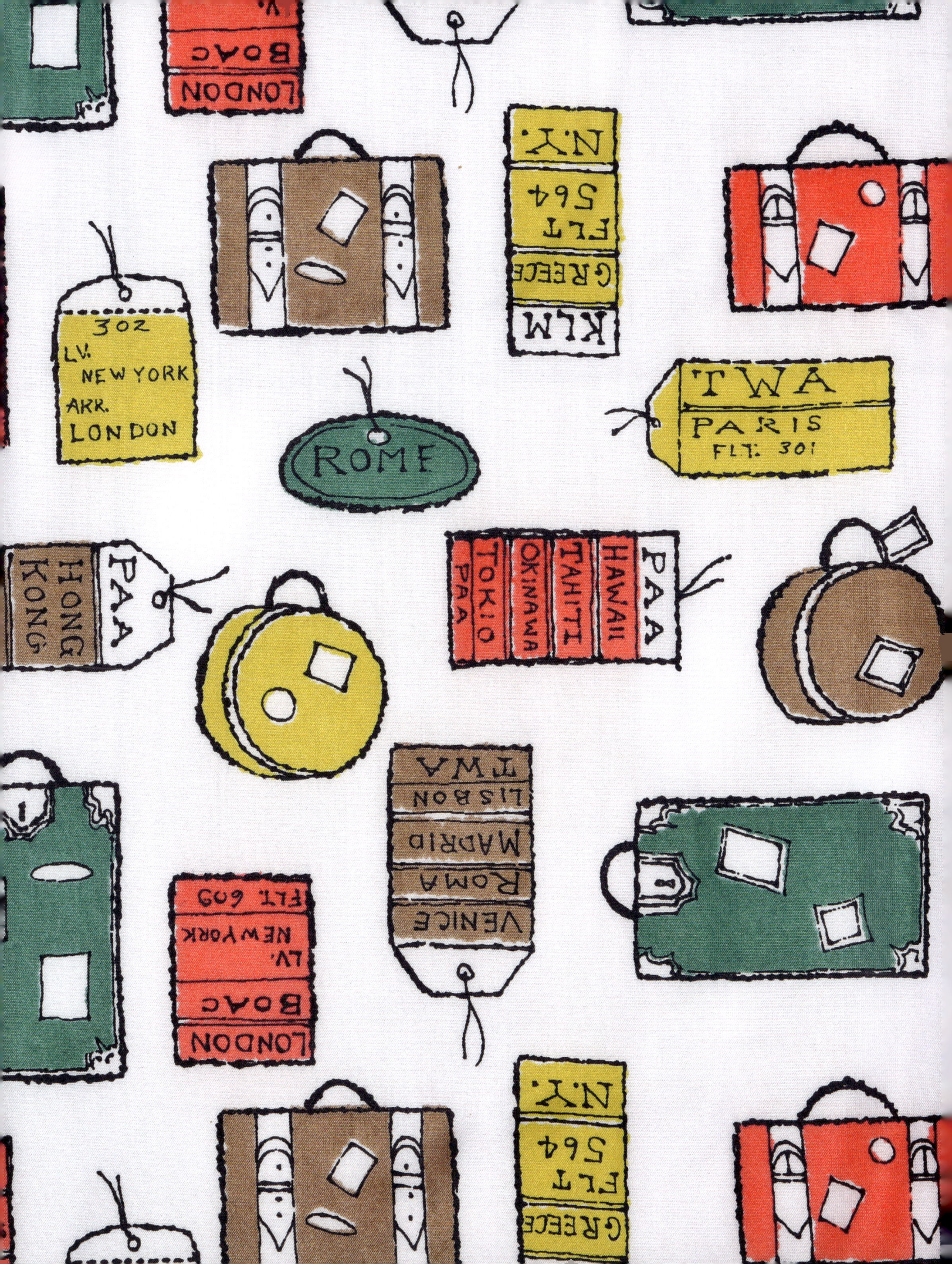
LONDON
BOAC
N.Y.
FLT 564
GREECE
KLM
3OZ
LV. NEW YORK
ARR. LONDON
ROME
TWA
PARIS
FLT. 301
PAA
HONG KONG
PAA
HAWAII
TAHITI
OKINAWA
TOKIO
PAA
TWA
LISBON
MADRID
ROMA
VENICE
FLT. 609
LV. NEW YORK
BOAC
LONDON

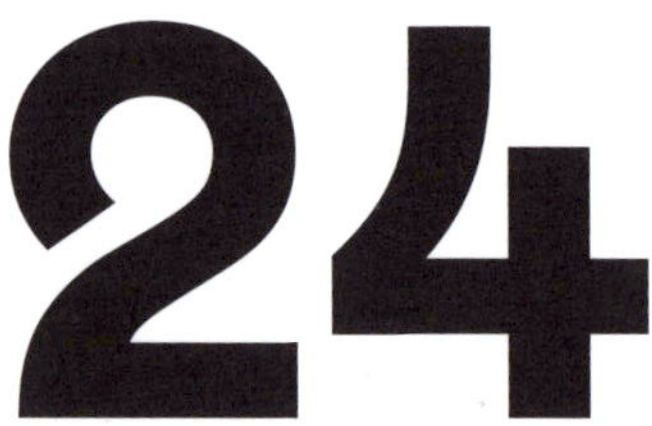

TEXTILE WITH
PERFUME AND SCENT BOTTLES

Printed cotton, *circa* 1958–1959
Attributed to D. B. Fuller & Co., Inc.

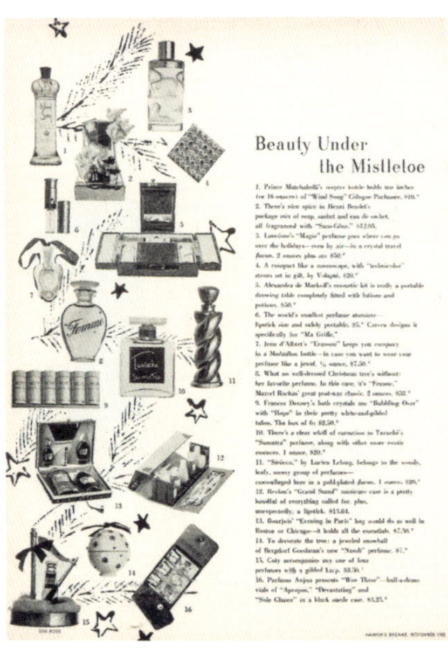

Warhol drew many bottles of perfume throughout the 1950s, and it is hardly a surprise that he designed a textile inspired by them. The bottles grouped together here make an icon out of the subject, but not without some irony since bottles marked 'Fanel No. 6' are clearly a send-up of Chanel No. 5.

Some of Warhol's more important commissions for perfumes and cosmetics came from *Harper's Bazaar*, who were offering limited-edition, specially curated Beauty Boxes, which Warhol frequently illustrated.

Above left (a) 'Beauty Under the Mistletoe', photo-collage illustration of perfume bottles and cosmetics by Warhol and the photographer Ben Rose for *Harper's Bazaar* (November 1955). **Above right (b)** Perfume bottles, *Harper's Bazaar* (April 1956). **Opposite (c)** Textile (detail of skirt, maker unknown).

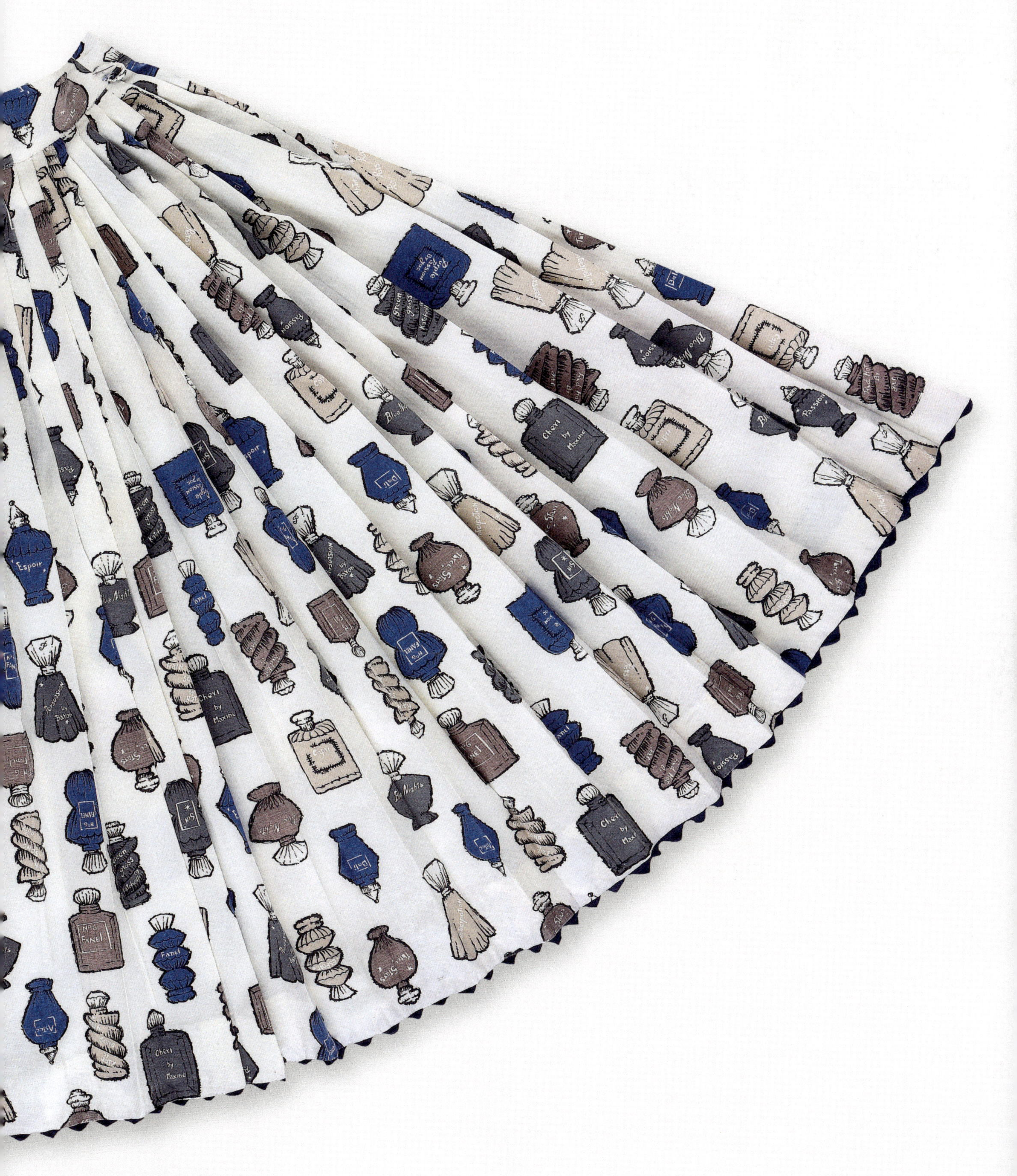
Espoir
Blue Nights
Cheri by Maxine
Passion
Dali

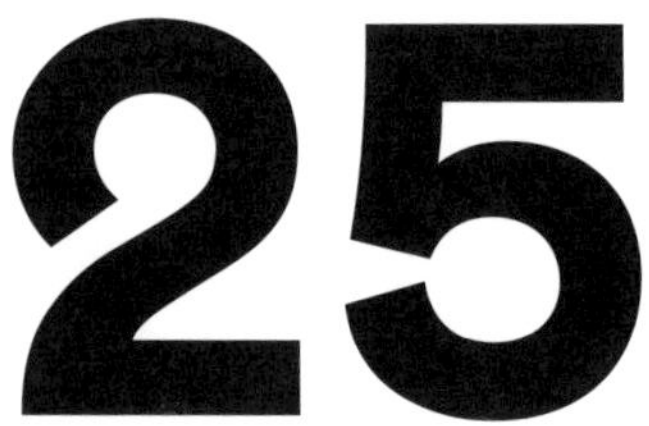

TEXTILE WITH
POCKET WATCHES

Printed silk, acetate twill or cotton, *circa* 1958–1959
Attributed to Leon B. Rosenblatt

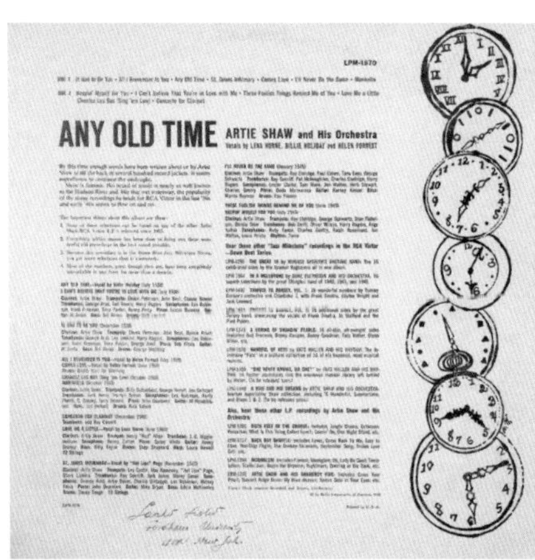

Pocket watches and timepieces of all types were a recurrent theme of Warhol's. For instance, he drew them as a group illustration for the reverse side of the dust cover for Artie Shaw's long-playing record *Any Old Time*, which was released in 1958.

Jerry Gilden, one of the top five manufacturers of women's fashions in the United States at the time, used the silk version of this textile to make dresses.

Above (a) *Any Old Time* by Artie Shaw and His Orchestra (1958). LP record sleeve, reverse side. **Opposite (b)** Yellow and green colourway.

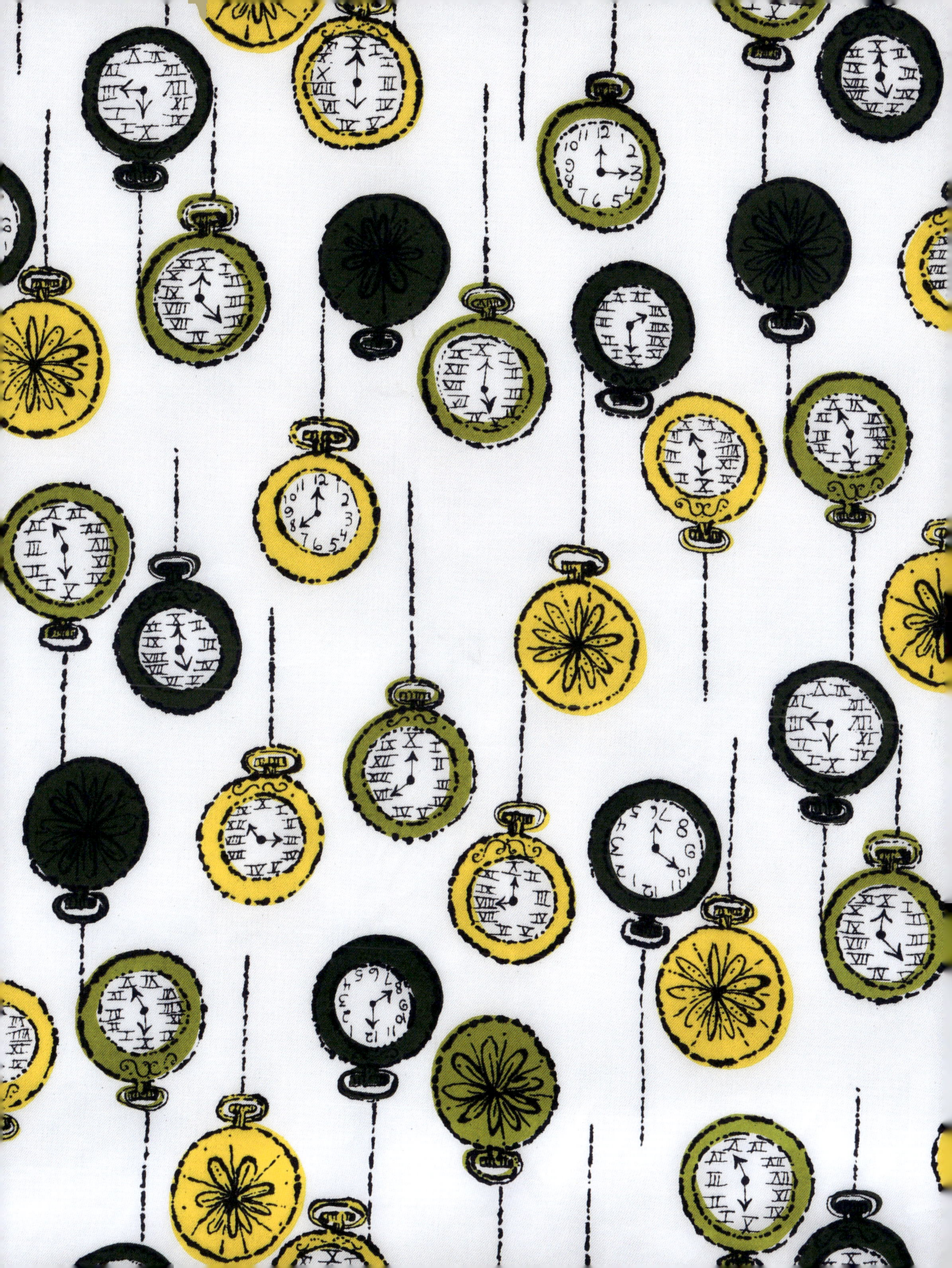

(c) Brown and grey colourway.

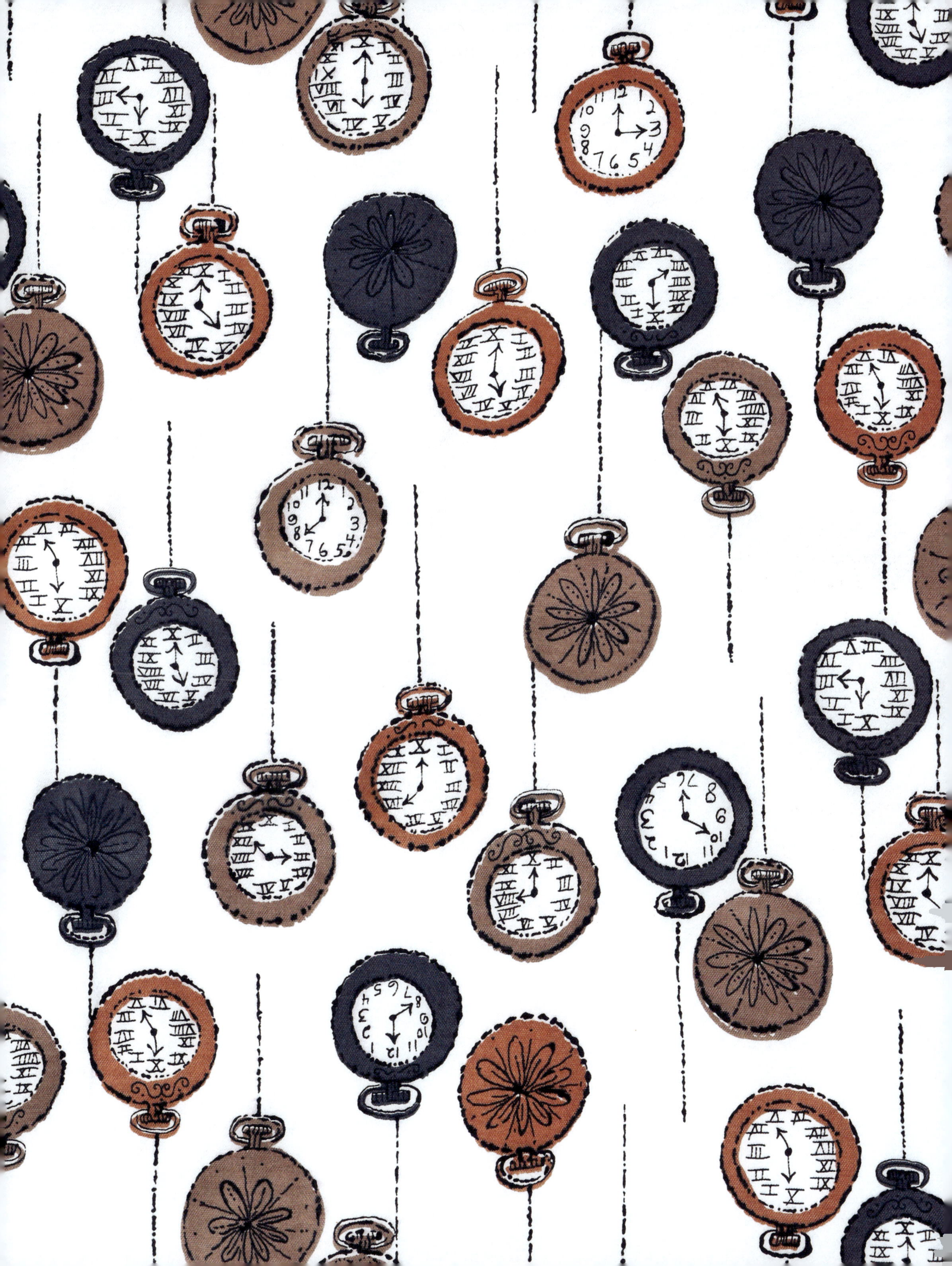

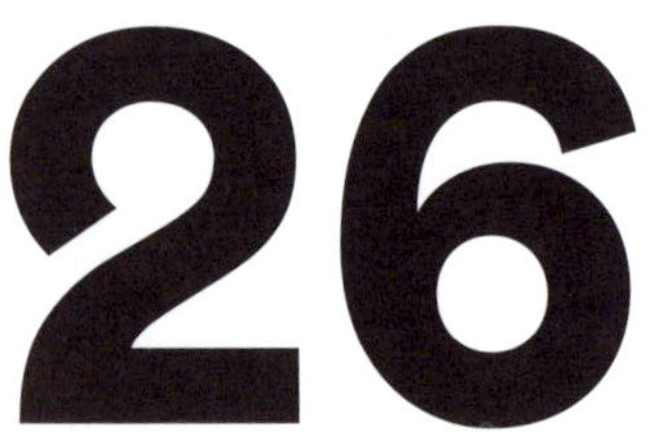

TEXTILE WITH
OBJECTS PRINTED USING RUBBER STAMPS

Printed silk, *circa* 1959–1960
Attributed to Stehli Silks Corporation, Inc.

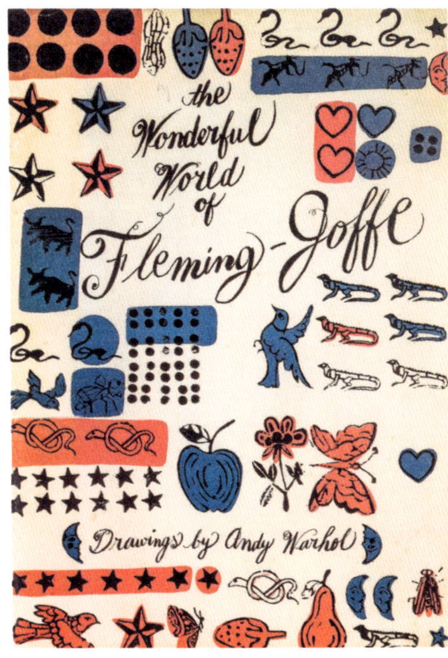

The artwork for this printed silk textile was mainly created by Warhol using inked rubber stamps laid down on paper and then hand-coloured.

Warhol created a large number of rubber stamps, which he used in numerous permutations in combination with a wide variety of media, from large three-dimensional folding screens to hand-coloured wrapping paper. Even promotional material for Fleming-Joffe, an exclusive leather goods company based in New York, was given a certain amount of Warhol's rubber stamp decoration. Some stamps were also used to create two-dimensional pattern designs, an example of which, *Bow Ties* (1960), is in the collection of the Whitney Museum of Art, New York.

Above (a) 'The Wonderful World of Fleming-Joffe', promotional colouring portfolio, front cover, 1960. **Opposite (b)** Scarf, maker unknown.

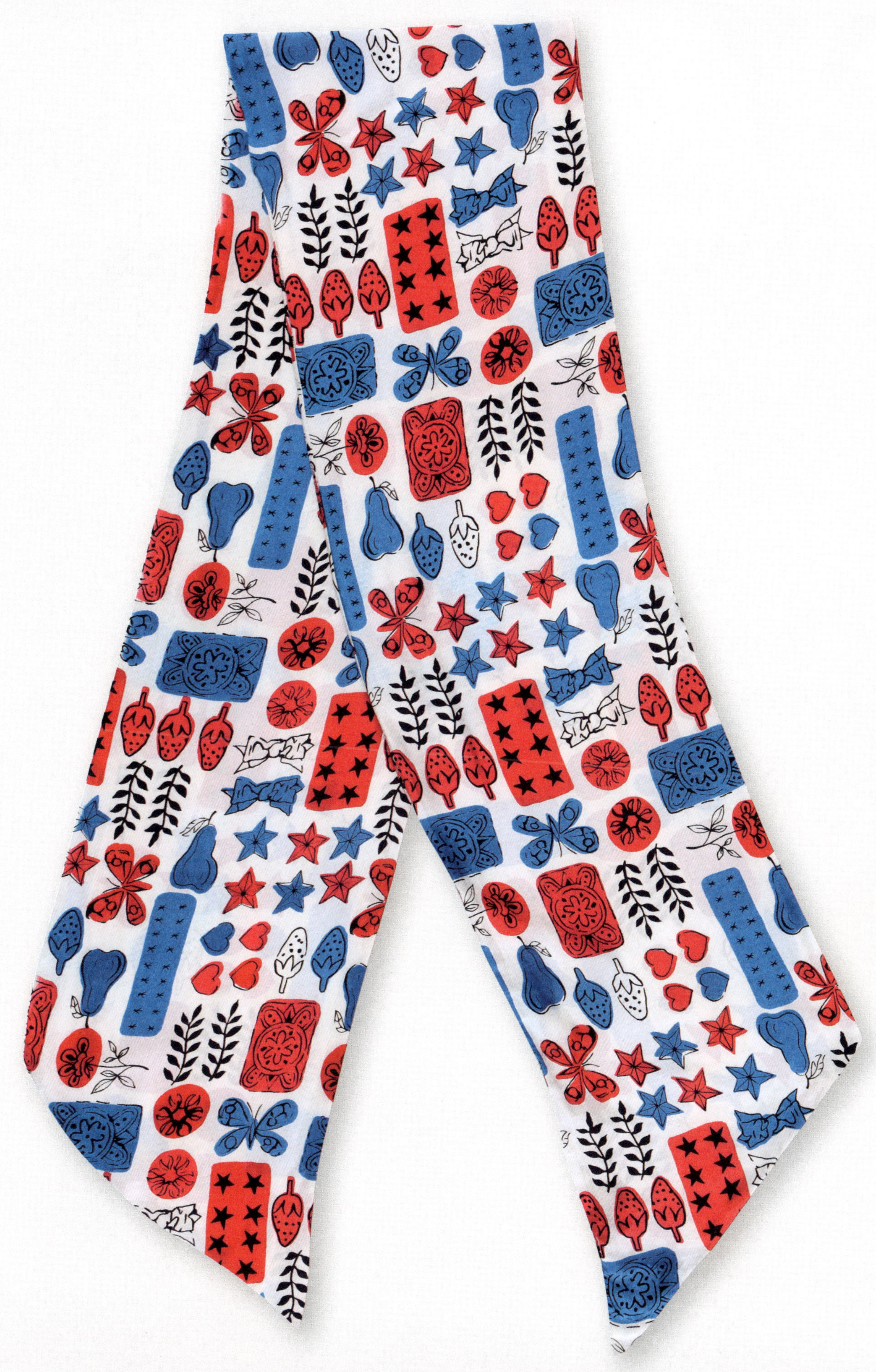

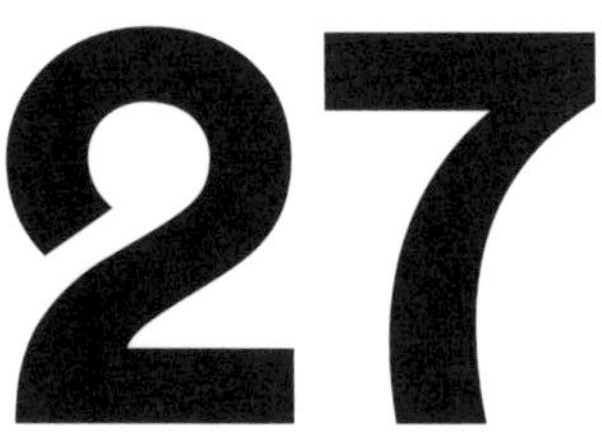

TEXTILE WITH

BUTTONS AND COTTON REELS

Printed cotton, *circa* 1959–1960
Manufacturer unknown

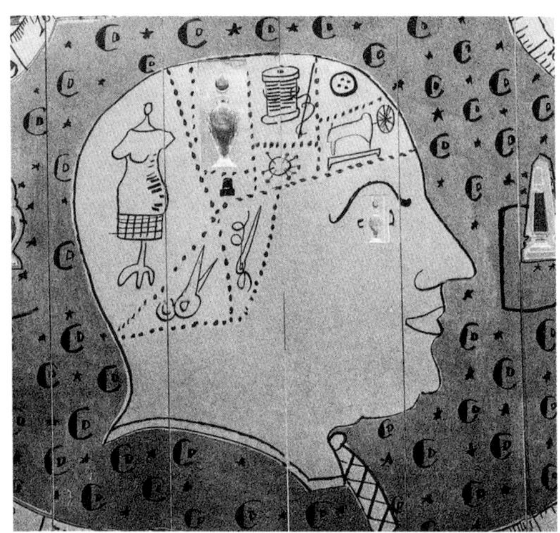

In this textile design, which is very closely allied to textile no. 26, the buttons are augmented with reels of cotton that are depicted unravelling or stacked on end. The motif is somewhat akin to magazine illustrations Warhol had created for merchandising such items as sewing materials. It is also very close in style to a 'snake' shop window awning he executed for Fleming-Joffe's St Louis store in 1960.

Above (a) Window display for Miss Dior (detail), designed by Warhol for the Bonwit Teller Store, New York, 1957. Photographer: Virginia Roehl for Gene Moore. **Opposite (b)** Collar, maker unknown.

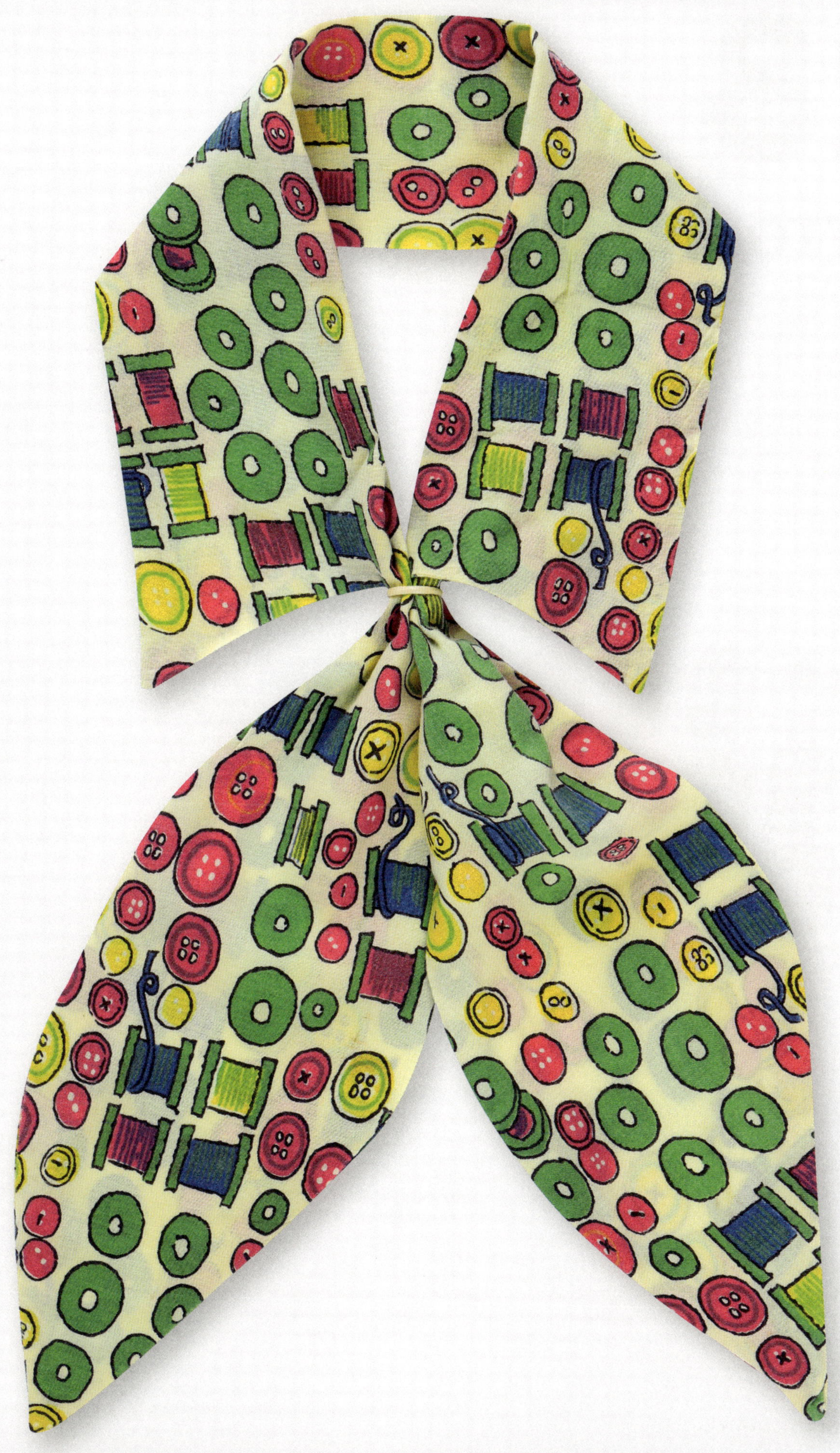

28

BUTTONS

Printed cotton or silk, *circa* 1959–1960
Leon B. Rosenblatt

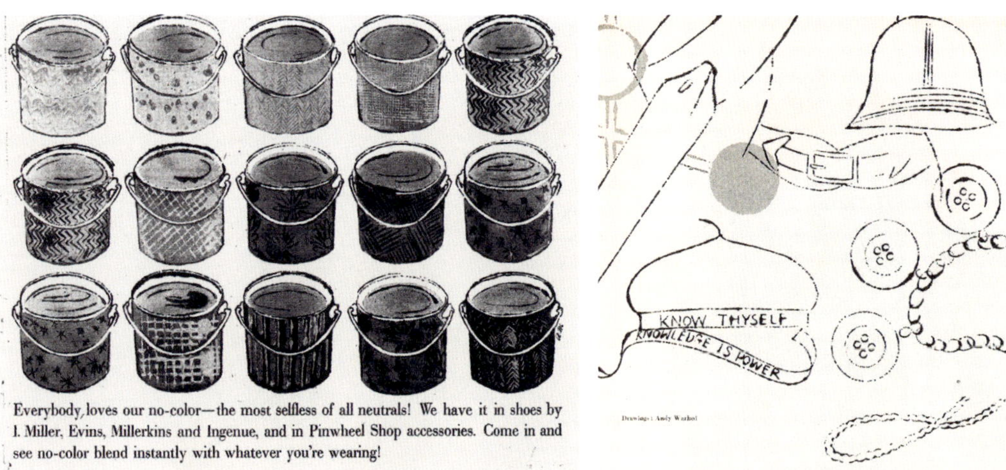

The selvedge of this textile is printed with the name of Leon B. Rosenblatt, a New York-based textile company, established in 1954 by Leon Beryl Rosenblatt and responsible for several famous Pop art textiles dating from about 1970. These include 'Love Comic', commissioned by the company from the comic book artist Nicky Zann.

Particularly prescient of Warhol's first Pop art paintings from the early 1960s, 'Buttons' uses a repetitious subject, though with some slight variation. An early example of Warhol's work in the fine arts employing this concept are his Coca-Cola bottle paintings from 1962.

An important and very early exploration of working with a repeating theme, this textile was printed in eight different colourways in total and produced on both cotton and silk mixes. A variation is also known with a blue background. The number of surviving examples attests to the textile's commercial success in 1959–60.

Above left (a) Advertisement to promote I. Miller's 'no colour' range of neutral-toned footwear, *New York Sunday Times*, 21 October 1956. An early example of Warhol's use of a repetitious theme depicted with slight variations. This concept was to come to its ultimate fruition in his iconic soup can paintings of 1962. **Above right (b)** Illustration for *American Girl* (August 1961). **Opposite (c)** Multicoloured colourway.

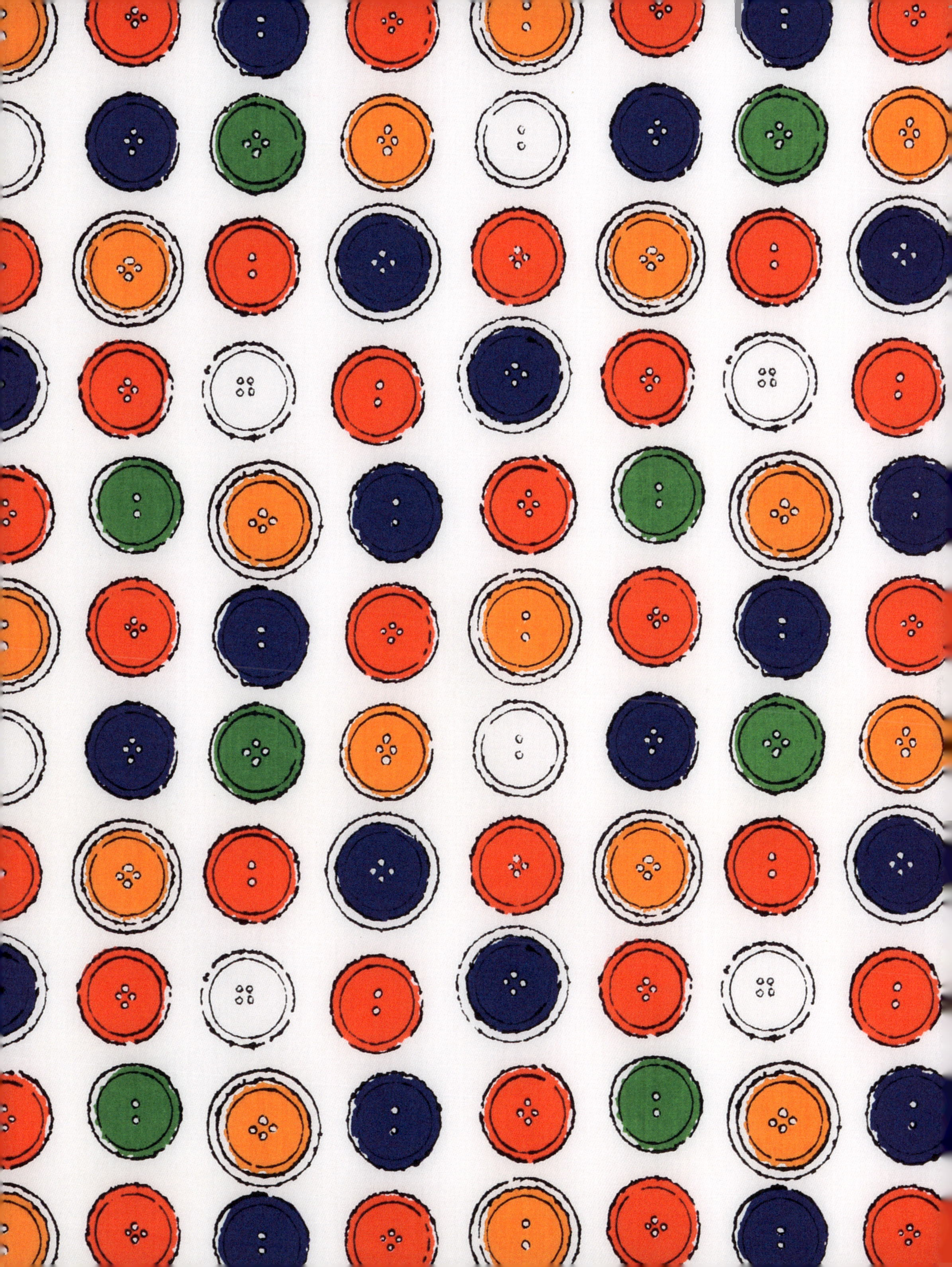

(d) Brown, red and orange colourway.

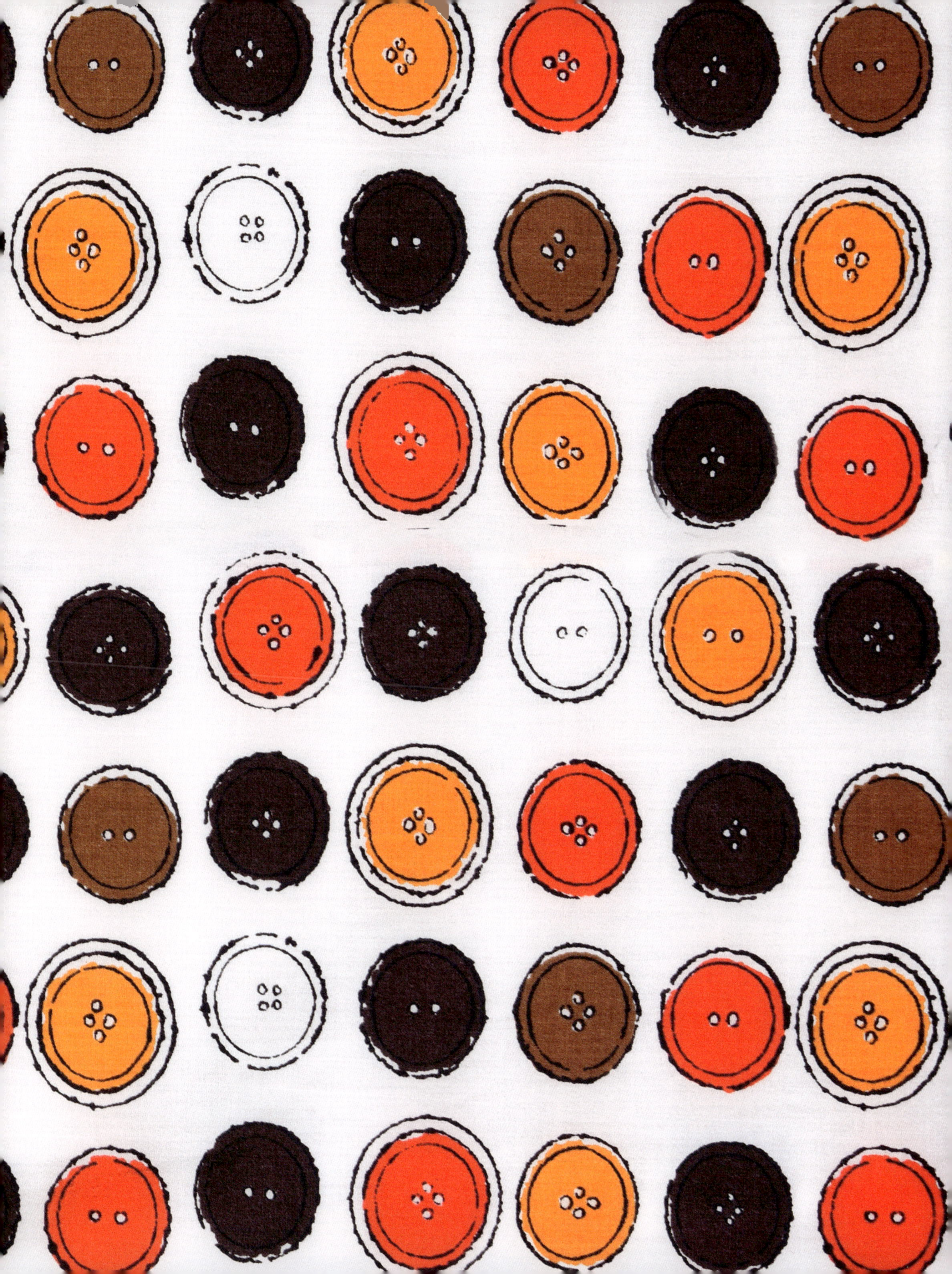

(e) Orange, blue and yellow colourway.

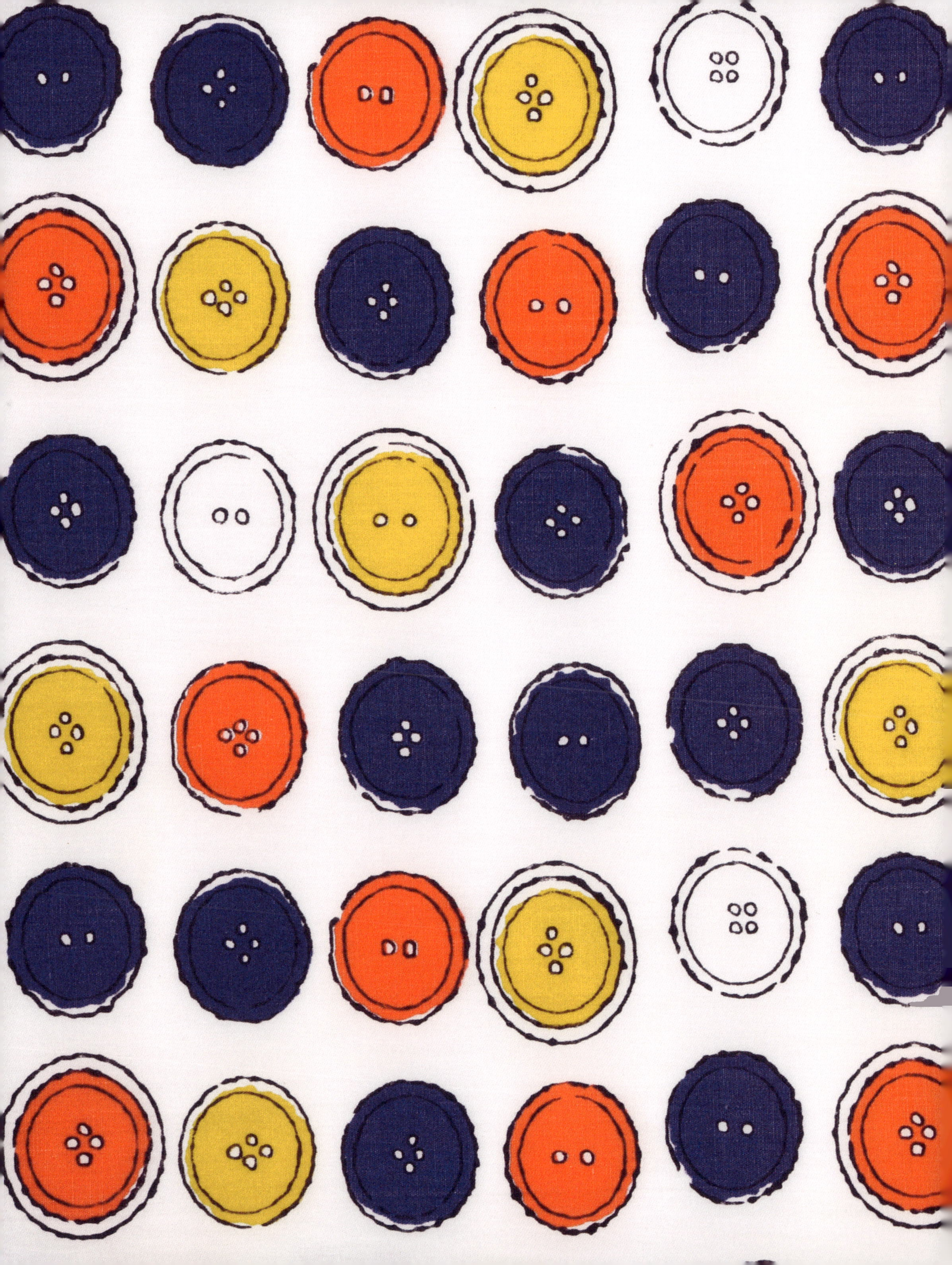

(f) Red, orange and green colourway.

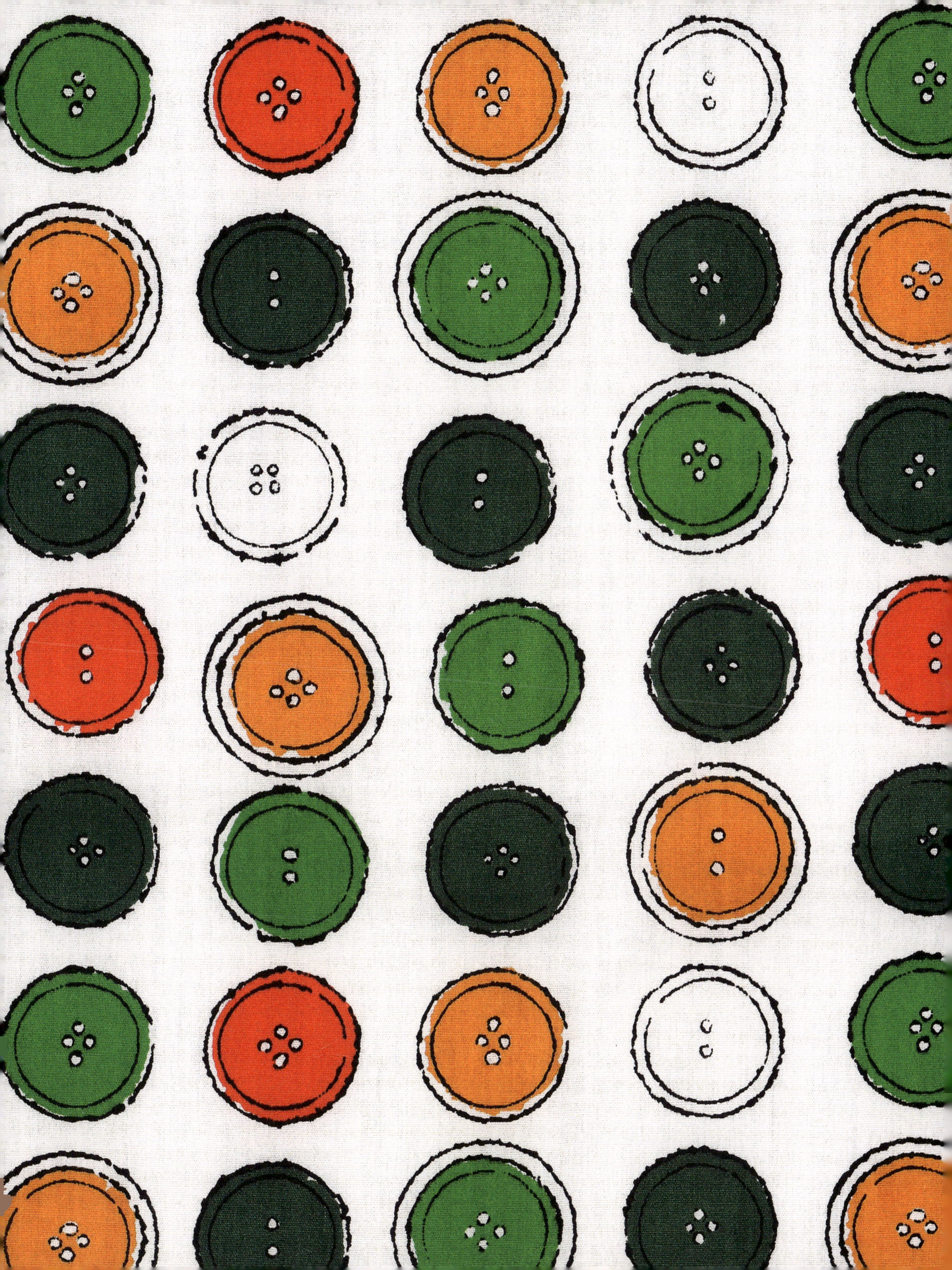

(g) Blue, yellow and green colourway.

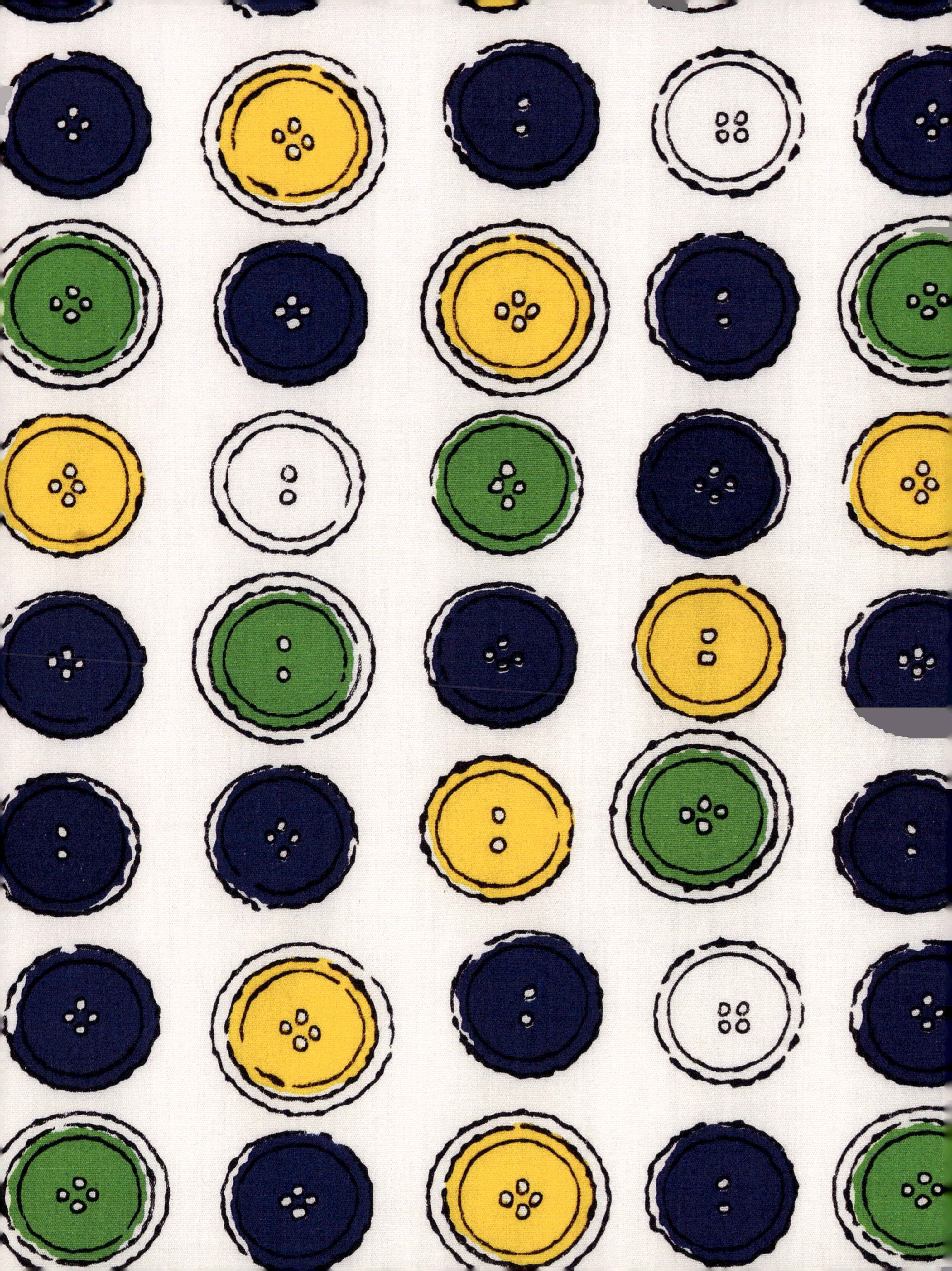

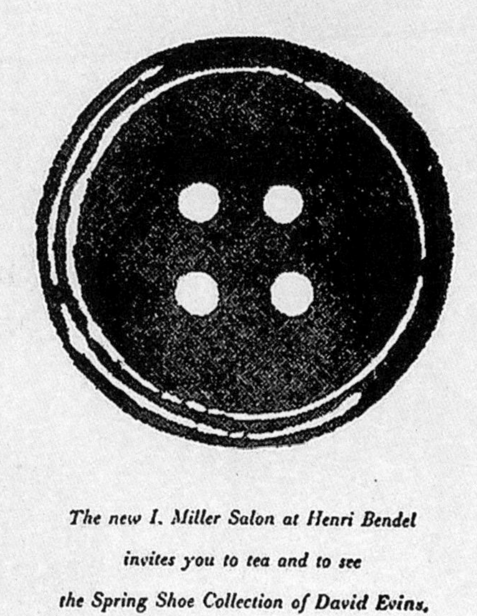

Above (h) Advertisement for the I. Miller salon at Henri Bendel department store, New York, originally printed in the *New York Sunday Times* and featured in the *37th Annual of Advertising, Editorial Art and Design* (New York: Directors' Club, 1958). **Opposite (i)** Silk cocktail dress in grey and brown colourway by Carnivale, New York.

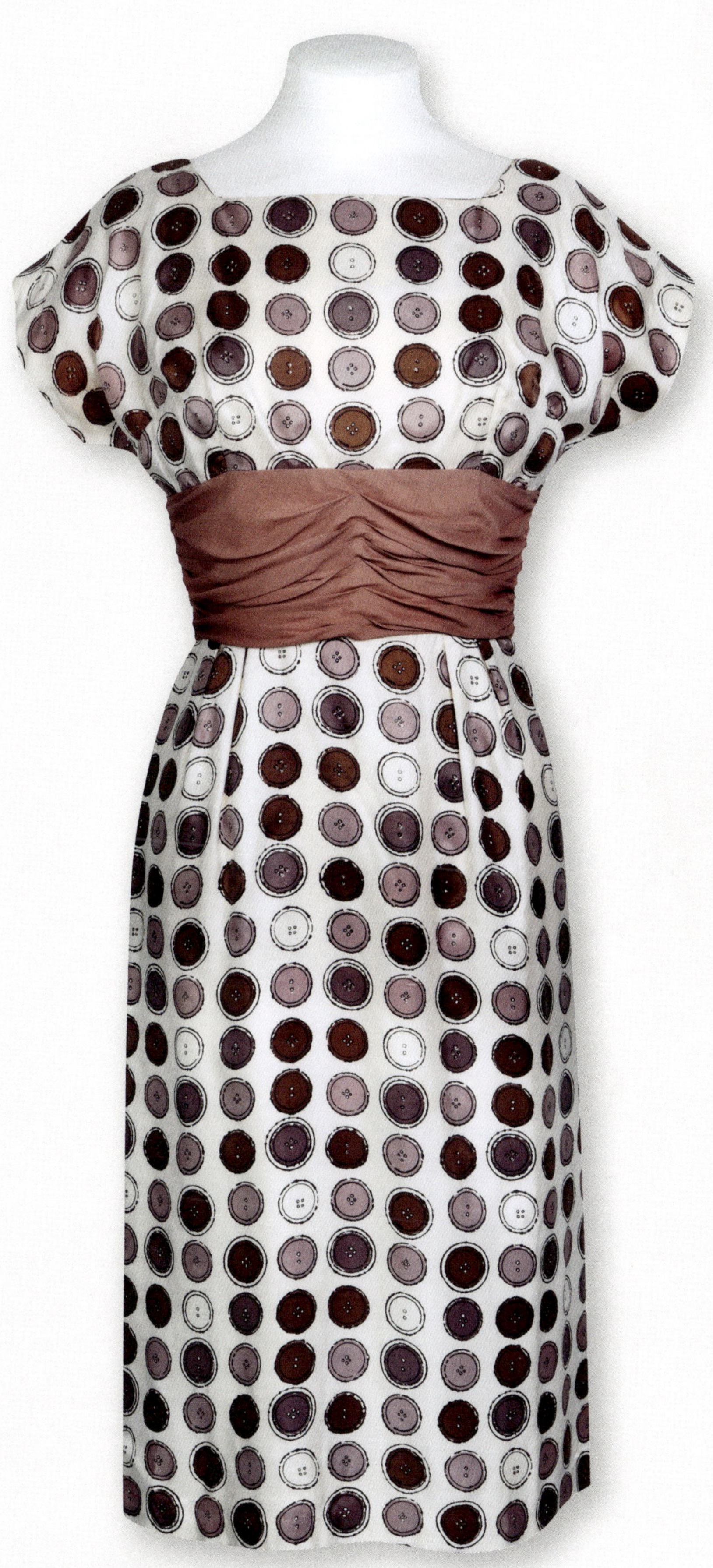

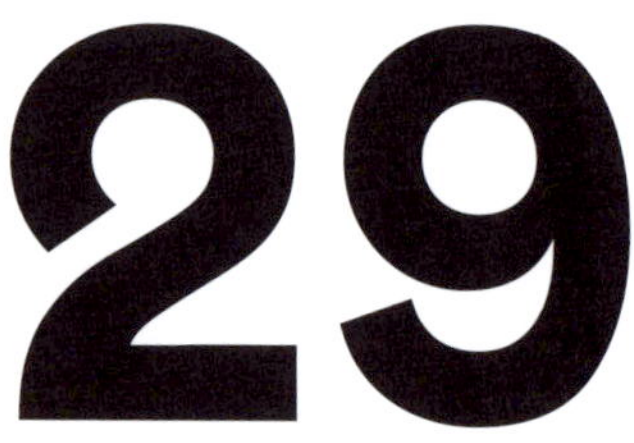

BRIGHT BUTTERFLIES

Printed silk surah or 'silky linen-like' rayon, 1960
Nat Wager Associates, Inc.

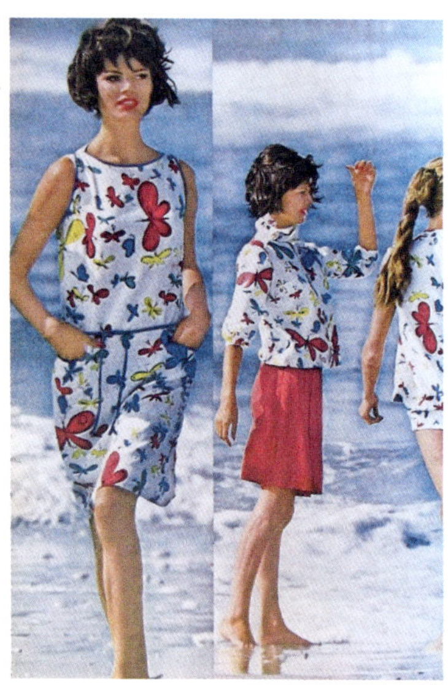

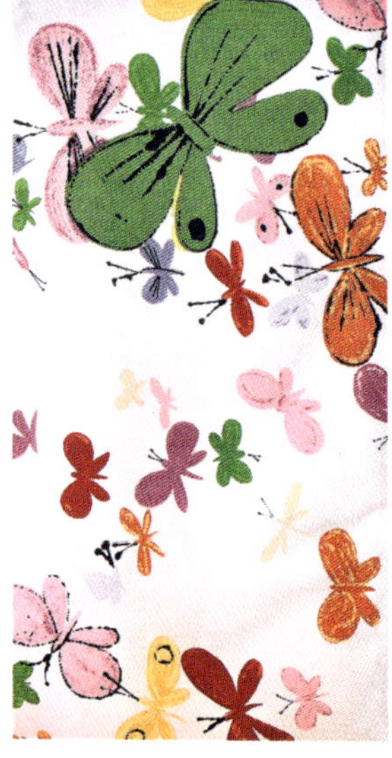

Produced on silk surah by Nat Wager, this textile was given a four-page feature by the magazine *Glamour* in December 1960.

The dress shown here was designed by Sylvia De Gay for Robert Sloan and retailed by Saks of New York, Halle Bros of Clevedon, Ohio, and D. H. Holmes of New Orleans. De Gay, who had studied at the Pratt Institute of Design and had been a model before turning to design, became known for her elegant sportswear. She became head designer for Robert Sloan, expanding the firm's ranges to dresses and swimwear, including some radical designs in clear plastic in the mid 1960s.

Glamour magazine referred to the textile as 'Bright Butterflies designed by Andy Warhol and printed by Nat Wager'. The article also mentioned that the garments featured were made in both silk surah and 'a silky linen-like rayon'. The Warhol Museum, Pittsburgh, holds an example of this textile in the red, blue and yellow colourway.

Above left (a) Part of a feature on the textile, *Glamour* (December 1960). **Above right (b)** Textile design. Ink and collage on paper, *c.*1958. **Opposite (c)** Textile (detail of dress overleaf).

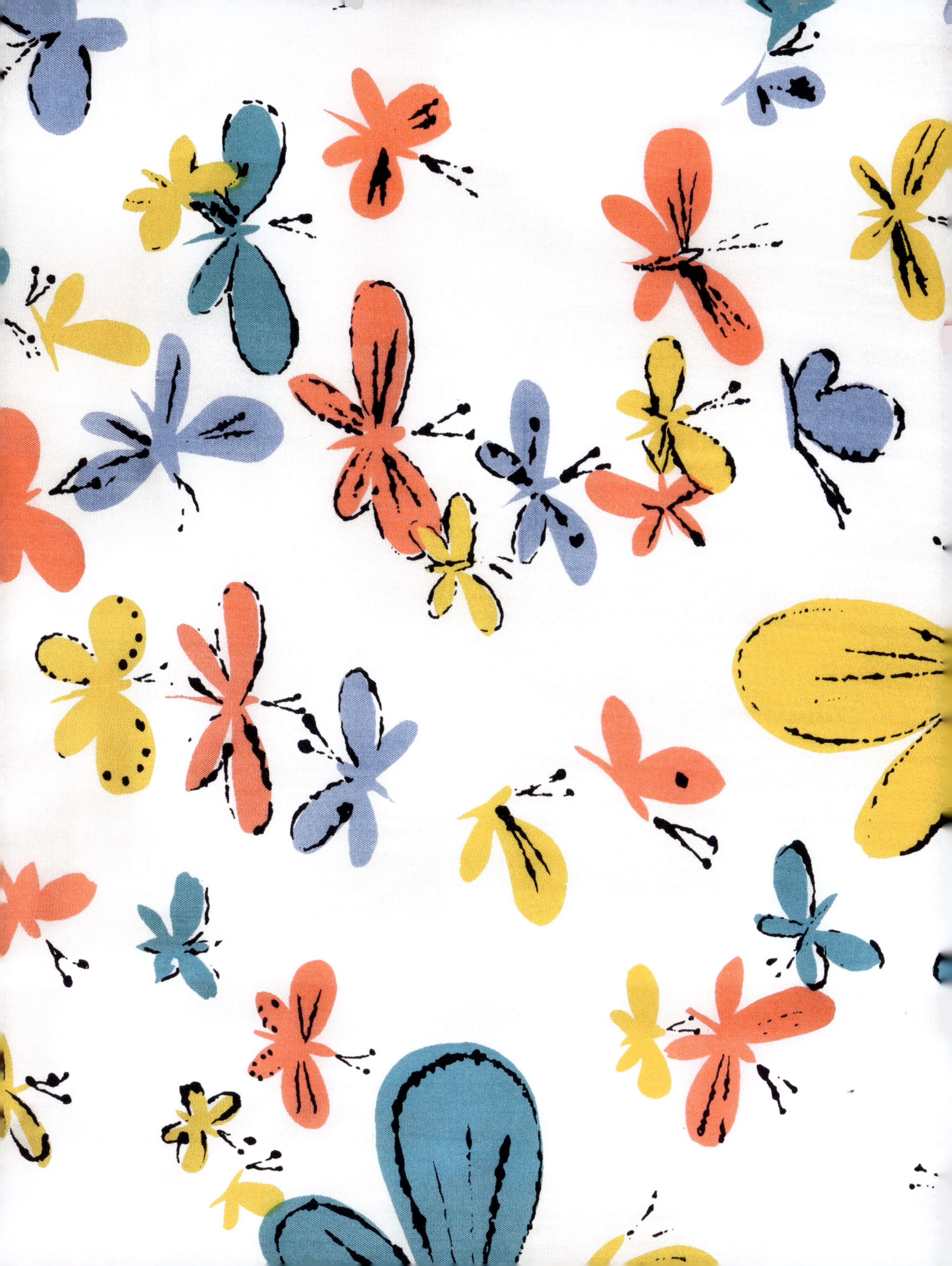

(d) Dress in yellow and sky blue colourway by Sylvia De Gay for Robert Sloan.

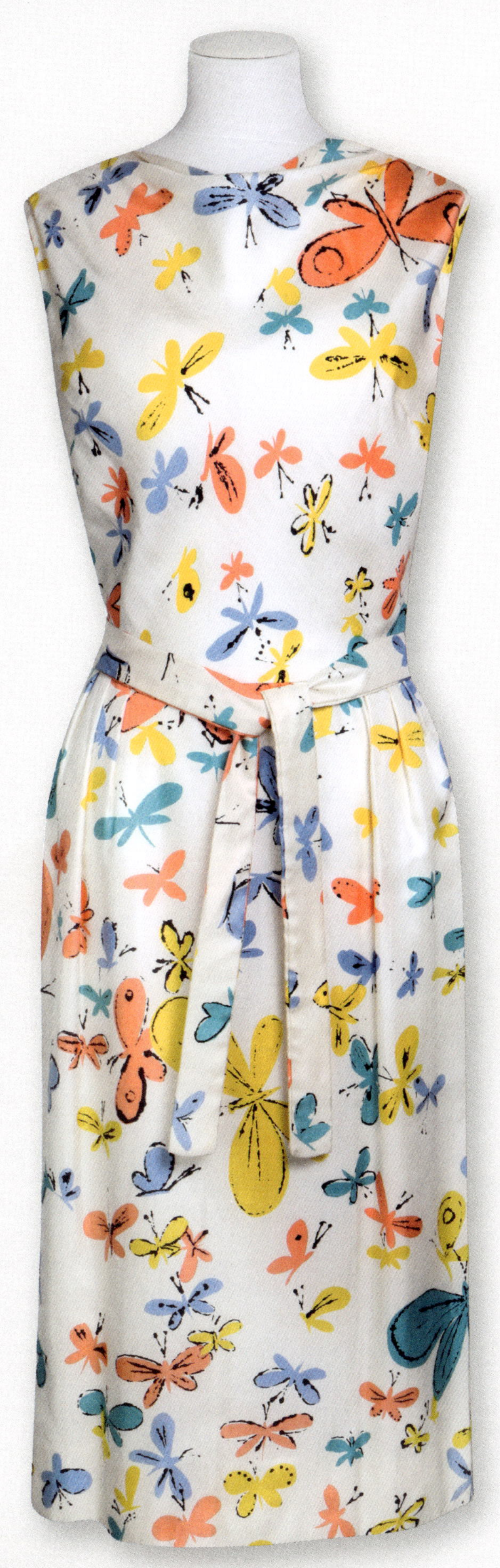

30

TEXTILE WITH
ICE CREAM DESSERTS

Printed cotton, *circa* 1960
M. Lowenstein & Sons, Inc.

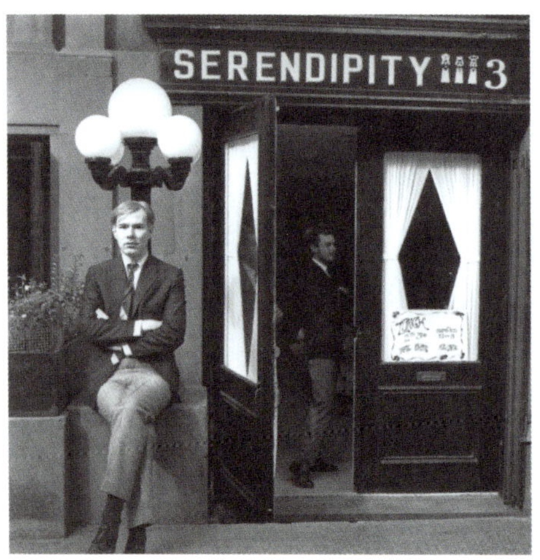

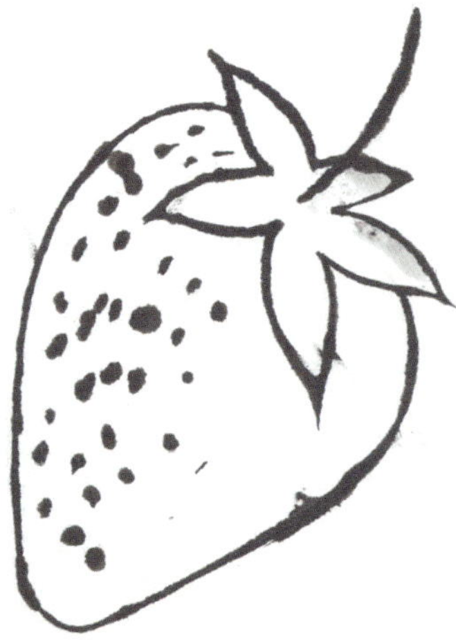

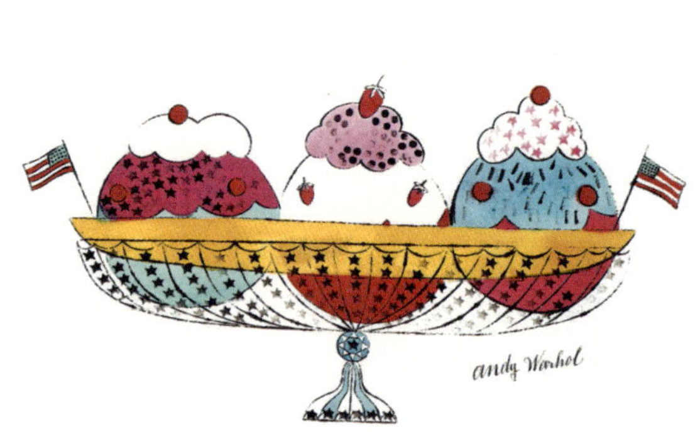

It is widely known that Warhol had an incredibly sweet tooth. His favourite foods throughout his life were desserts of various types, including Frozen Hot Chocolate, a speciality of Serendipity 3. Warhol, a regular habitué of the New York café-bistro, was able to keep a large tab there, even bartering drawings in exchange for his regular orders. In his biography *Warhol: A Life as Art* (2020), Blake Gopnik records that the last meal Warhol purchased, just before his untimely death in 1987, was at Serendipity 3: it consisted only of desserts.

It comes as no surprise, therefore, that Warhol created, in about 1960, a textile which pays homage to the ice cream desserts he was so fond of. Delicately rendered in his finest broken, dotted line style, he lovingly created drawings for this textile of the various types of pudding that gave him so much pleasure, from banana splits to ice cream floats. The colourway shown here is pink, blue and orange. A second is also known in green, blue and yellow.

Above left to right (a) Andy Warhol and Stephen Bruce at Serendipity 3, 1961. Photographer: John Ardoin. Courtesy of Stephen Bruce; **(b)** Drawing of a strawberry, c.1959. Ink on paper; **(c)** *Ice Cream Dessert*, c.1959. Ink on paper. **Opposite (d)** Textile in pink, blue and orange colourway.

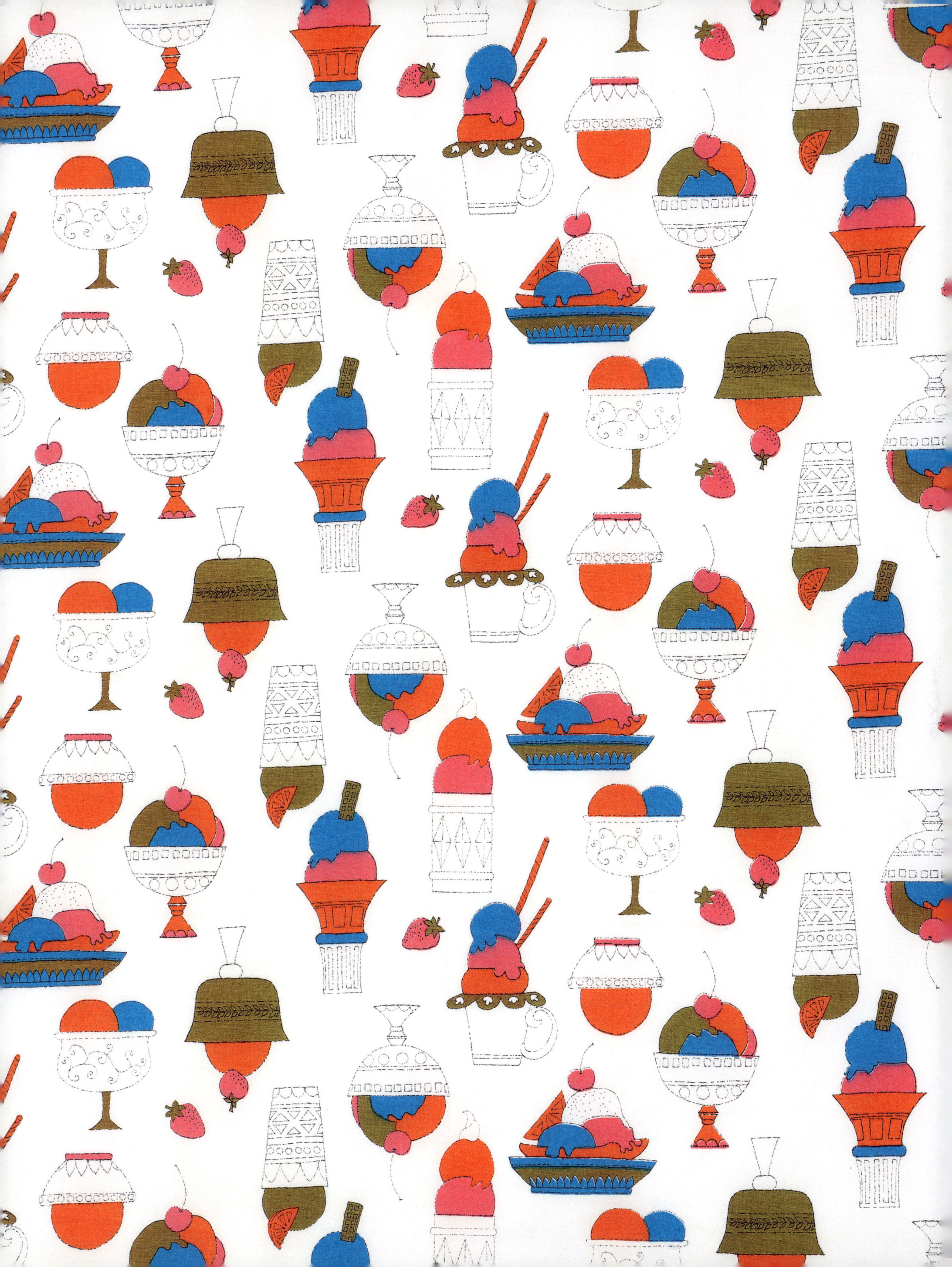

31

TEXTILE WITH
ICE CREAM CONES

Printed silk, 1962–1963; polyester, mid 1960s
Stehli Silks Corporation, Inc.

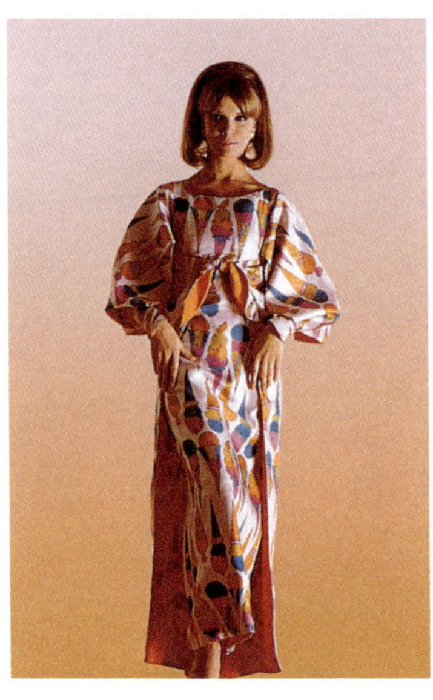

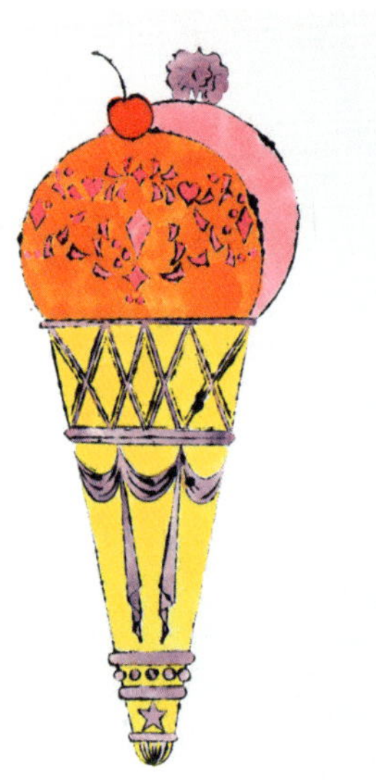

Between 1962 and 1963 Warhol sold, as far as is understood, his last three known commercial textiles to the Stehli Silks Corporation. Visually, this textile of large-scale ice cream cones is the most dramatic of them, with the play of the various brightly coloured cones arresting one's attention.

There are five colourways at least that are known of. Two are printed on silk, the first in pink and blue and the second in purple and green, each with a white ground. The other three, printed on polyester, have red, lilac and black backgrounds. The two silk versions are on a much larger scale than the ones on polyester.

Above left (a) Girl in a silk ice cream cone dress designed by Stephen Bruce and Leila Larmon for the Serendipity 3 fashion collection, 1964. Photograph courtesy of Stephen Bruce. **Above right (b)** *(Untitled) Ice Cream Dessert*, c.1959. Ink on paper. **Opposite (c)** Silk textile in purple and green colourway (detail of dress overleaf). **Following spread (d)** Silk dress in pink and blue colourway, maker unknown; **(e)** Silk dress in purple and green colourway by Castelli.

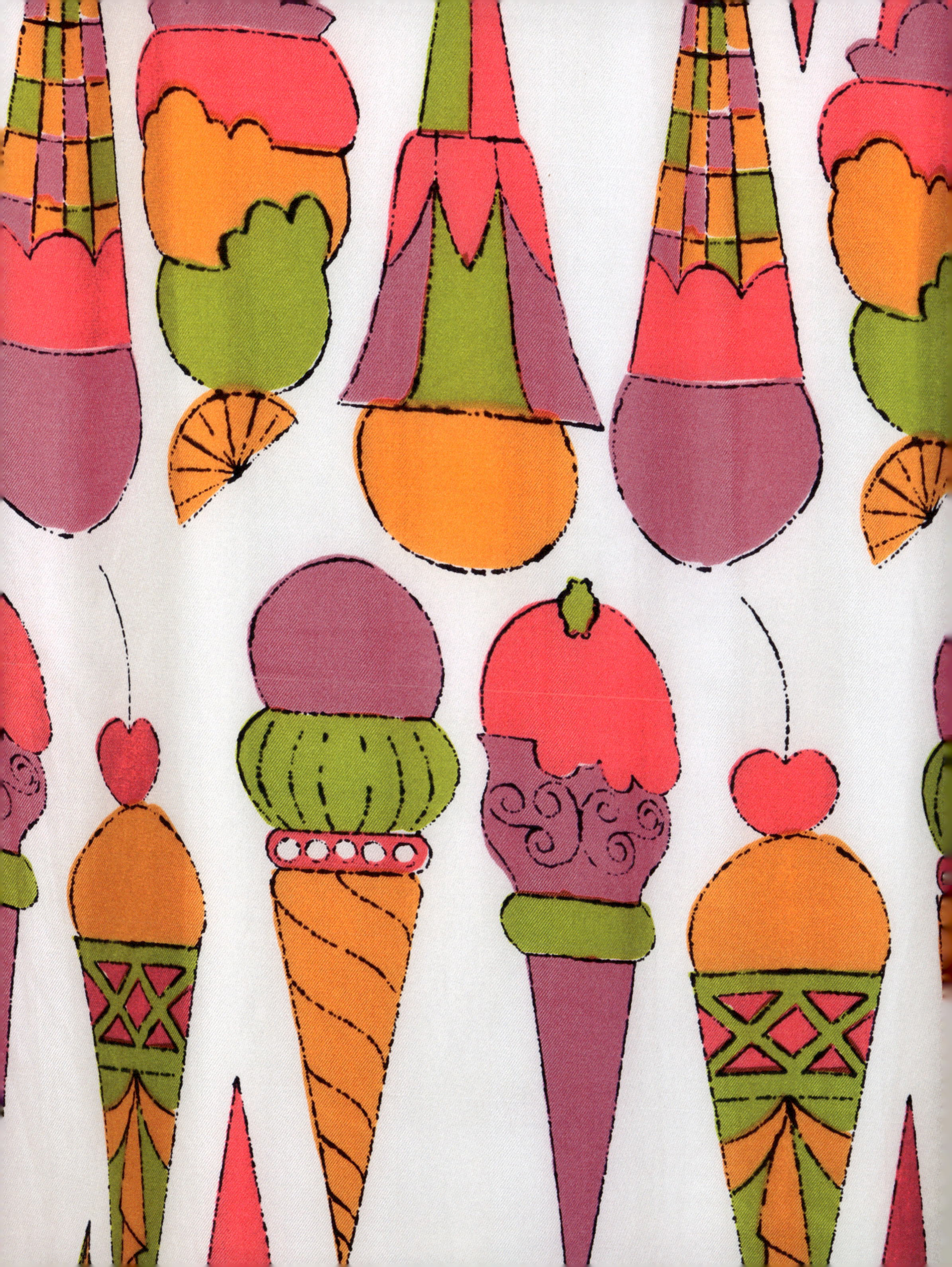

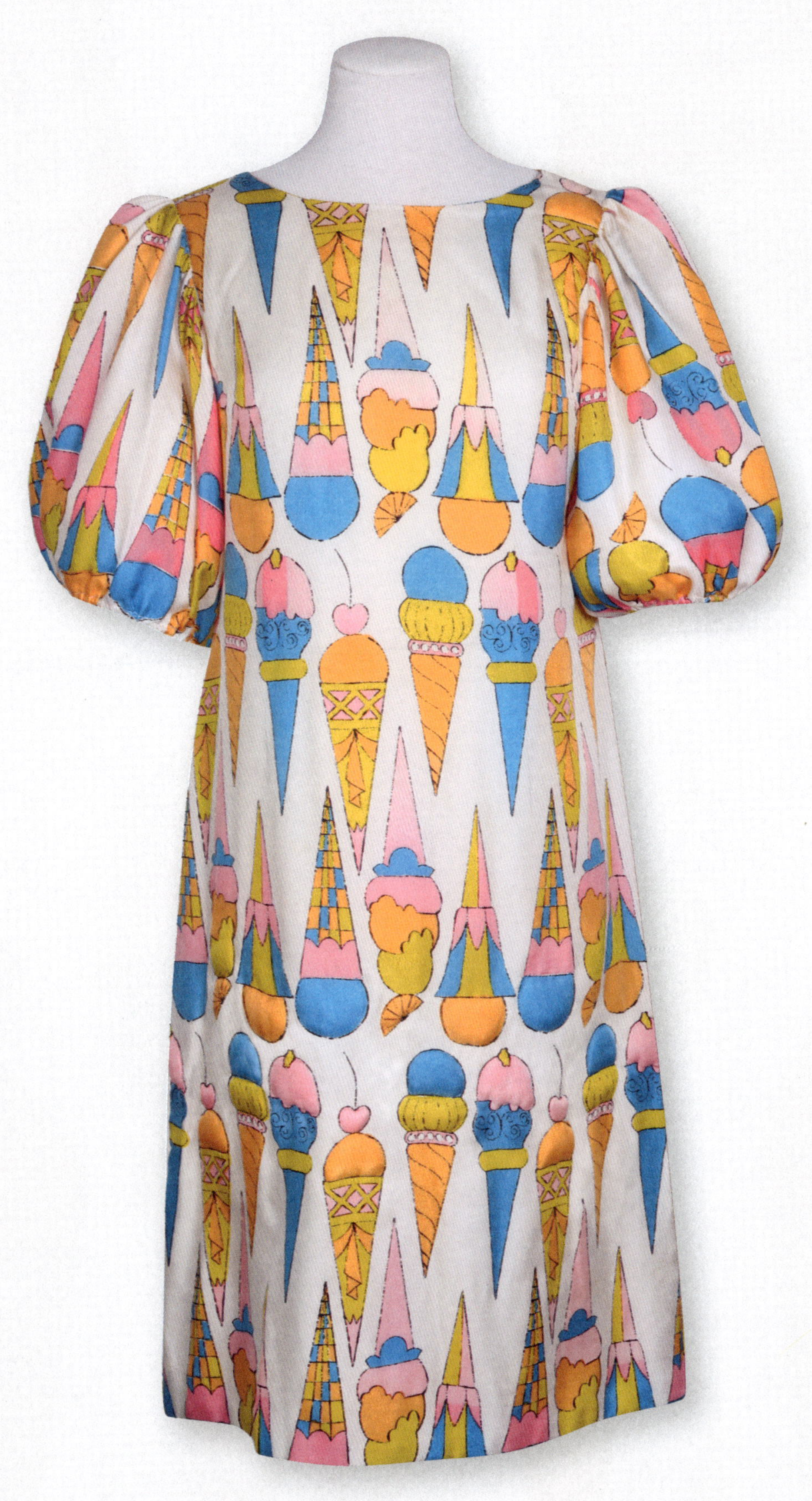

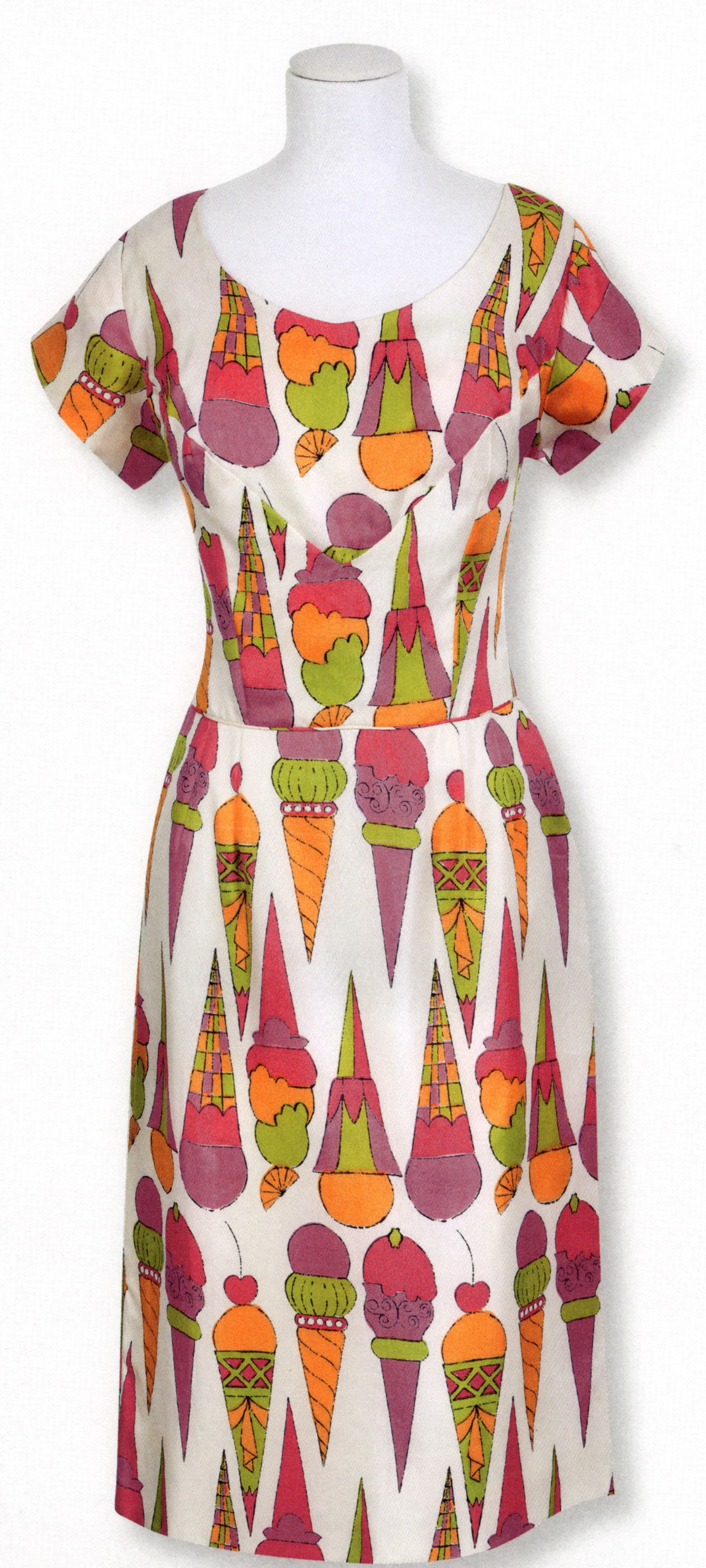

Opposite left (f) Lilac evening dress in polyester, maker unknown. **Opposite right (g)** Red evening dress in polyester, maker unknown.

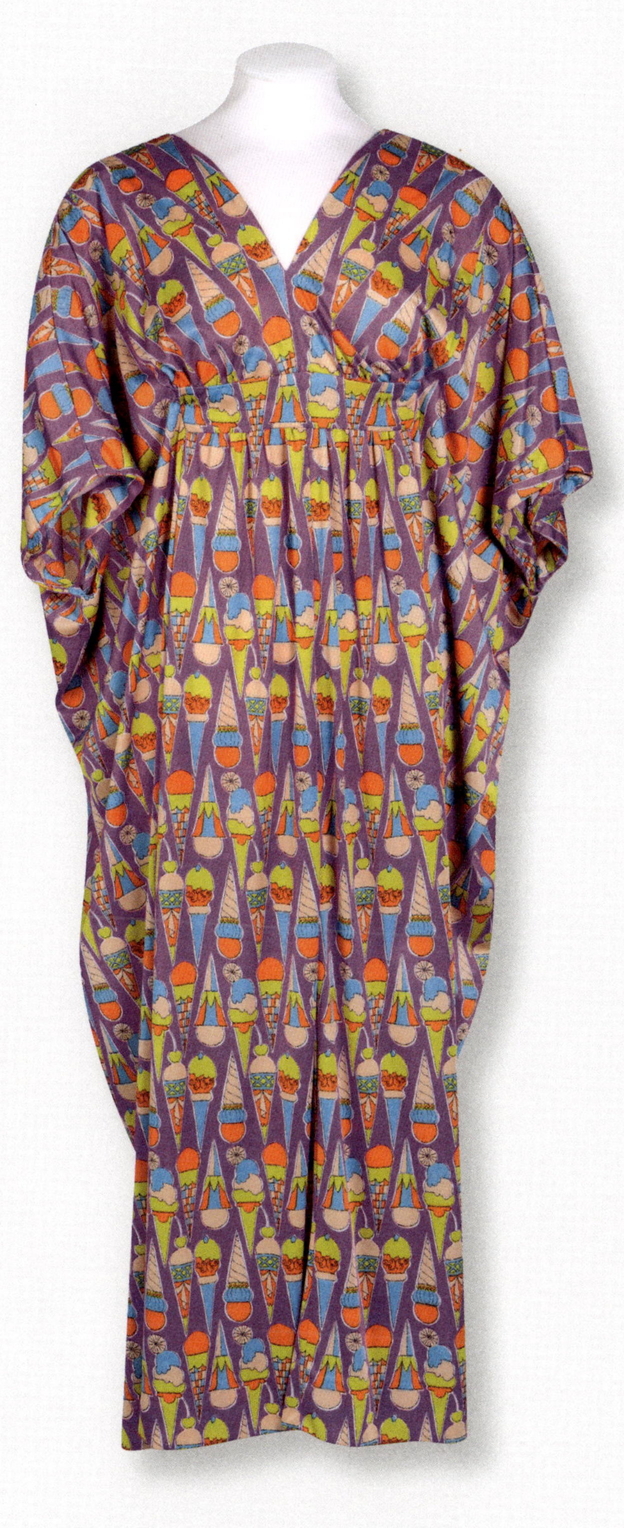

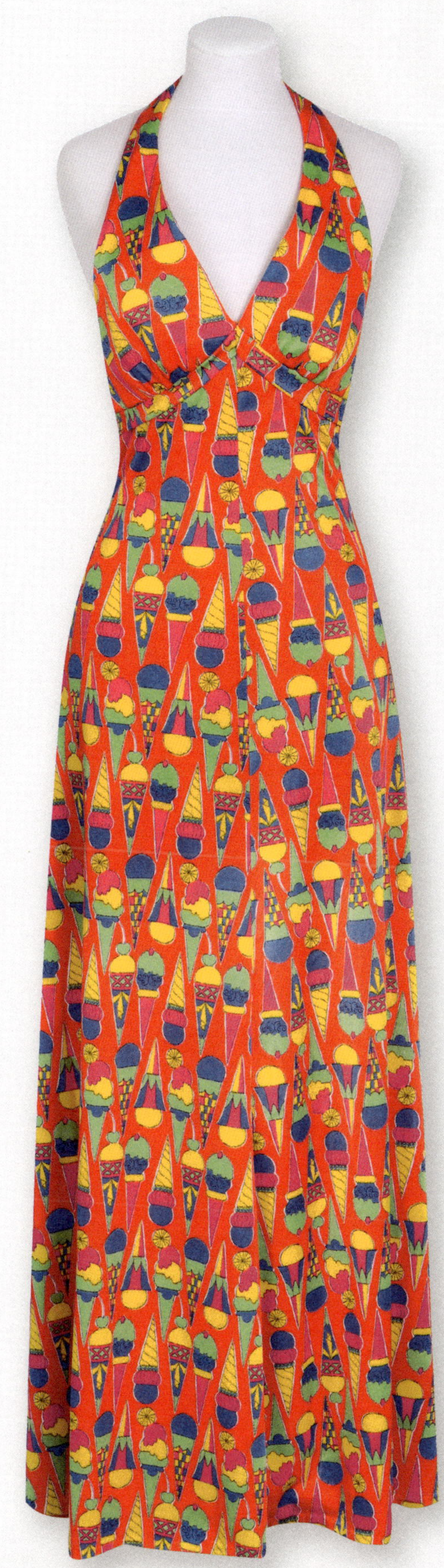

TEXTILE WITH
PRETZELS

Printed silk, 1962–1963; polyester, mid 1960s
Stehli Silks Corporation, Inc.

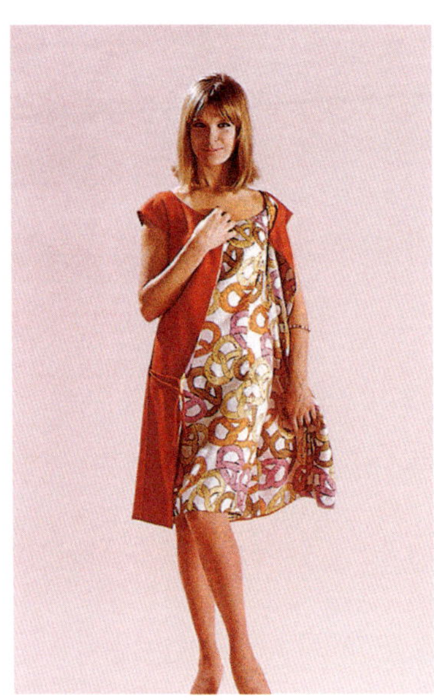

This is the second of Warhol's textiles made by Stehli Silks. The pattern is of giant interlocking pretzels. It was this textile, and the ice cream cones one (no. 31), that Stephen Bruce, the owner of Serendipity 3, eventually received from Warhol, and made into dresses for a fashion collection in 1964. In the mid 1960s a second version of the pretzels design in polyester was also made, with a smaller image of the design.

Above (a) Girl in a silk pretzel dress designed by Stephen Bruce and Leila Larmon for the Serendipity 3 fashion collection, 1964. Photograph courtesy of Stephen Bruce. **Opposite (b)** Silk pretzel dress, Serendipity 3 collection, Spring/Summer 1964. Metropolitan Museum of Art, New York.

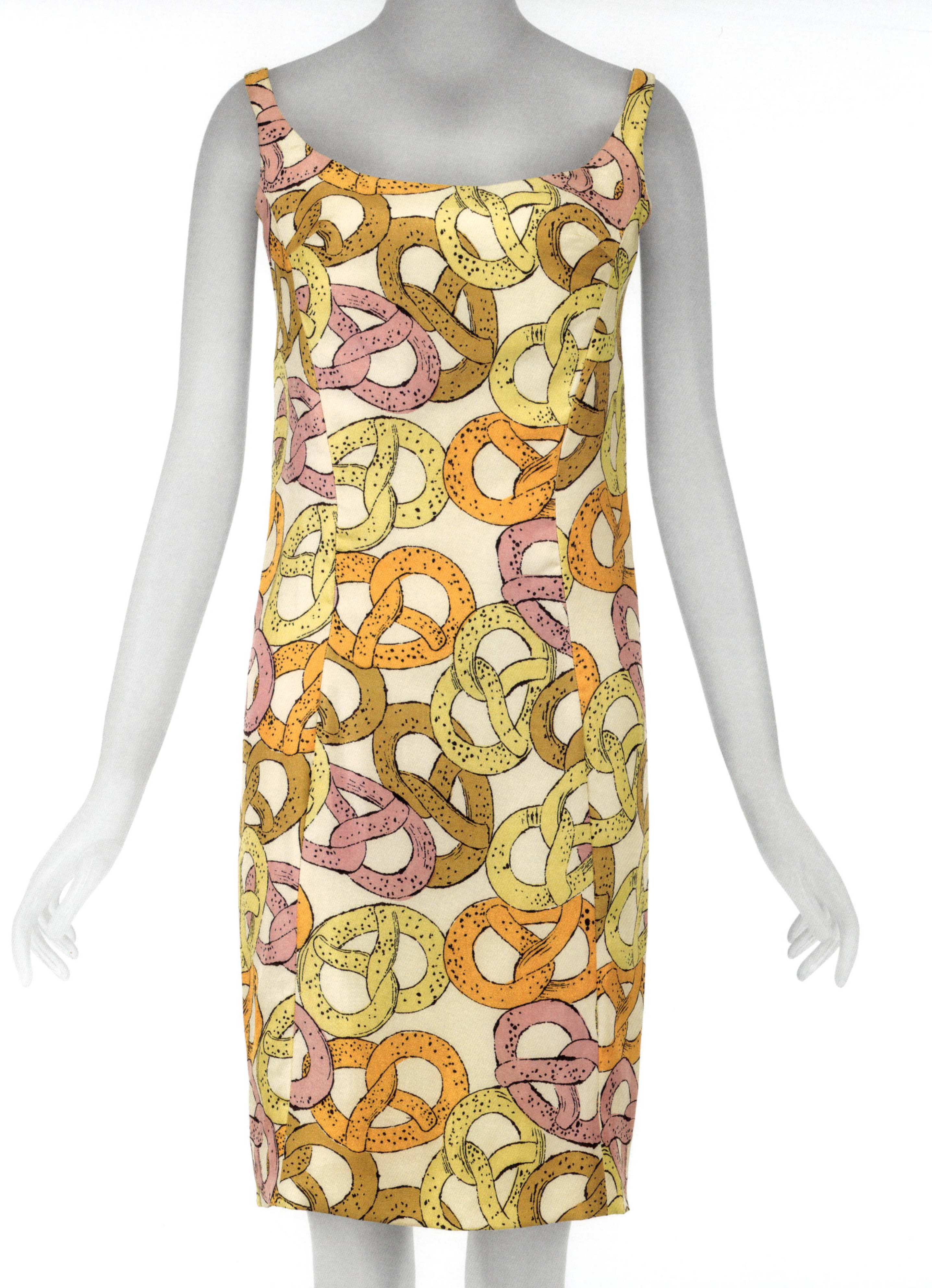

Opposite left (c) Culottes in polyester, lime green colourway, maker unknown. **Opposite right (d)** Evening dress in polyester, lilac and orange colourway, maker unknown.

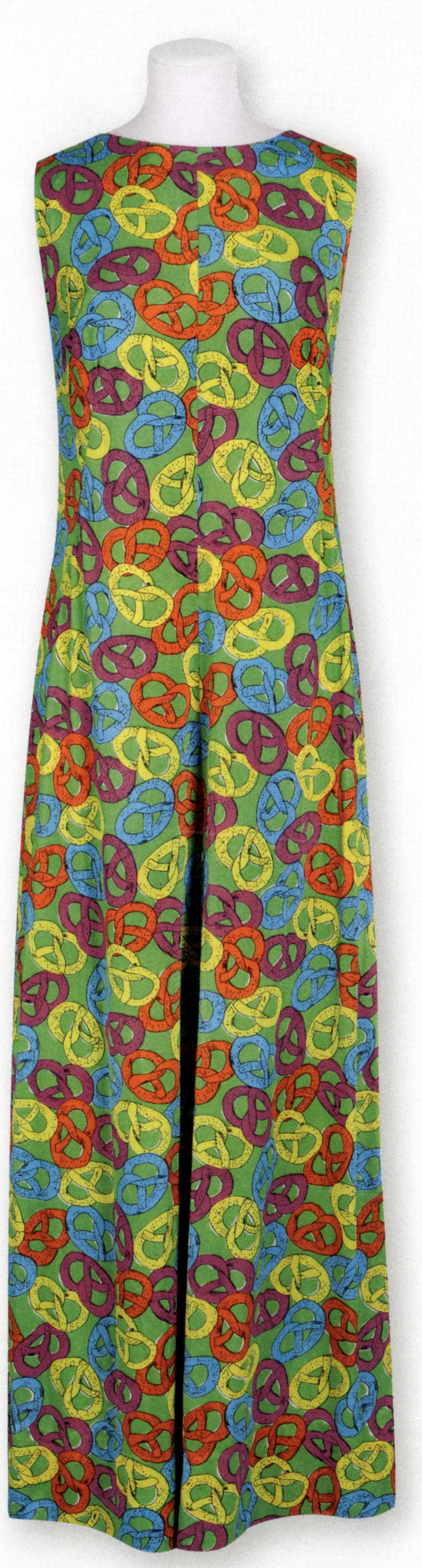

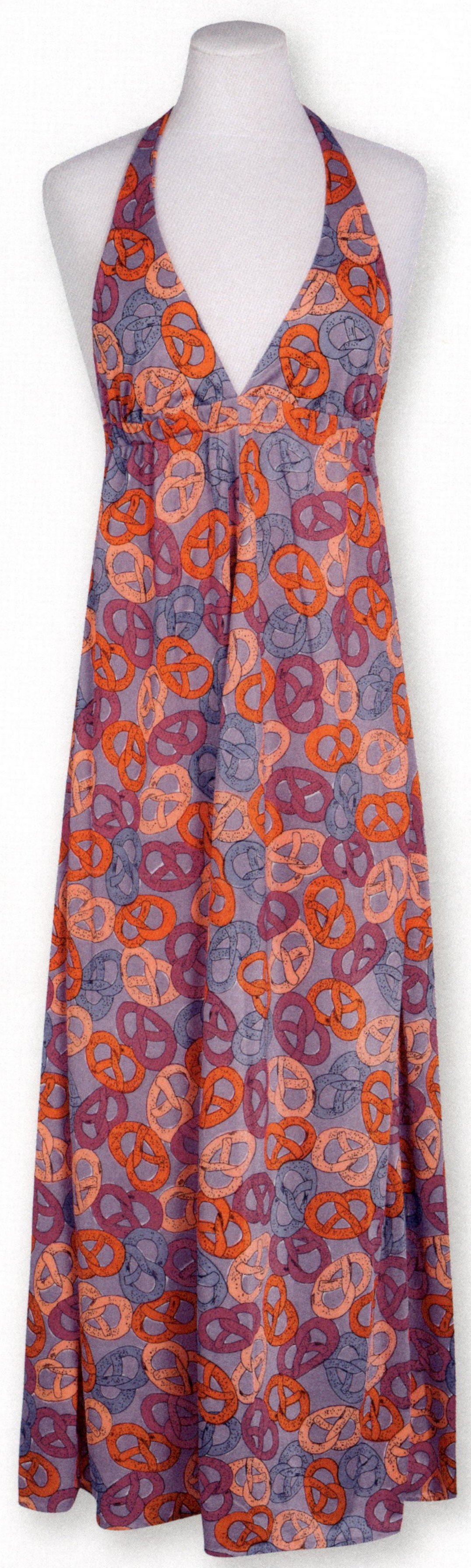

TEXTILE WITH
CANDY APPLES

Printed silk, 1962–1963; polyester, mid 1960s
Stehli Silks Corporation, Inc.

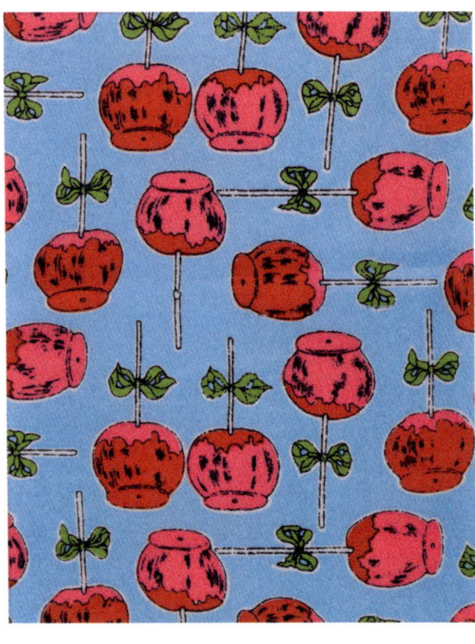

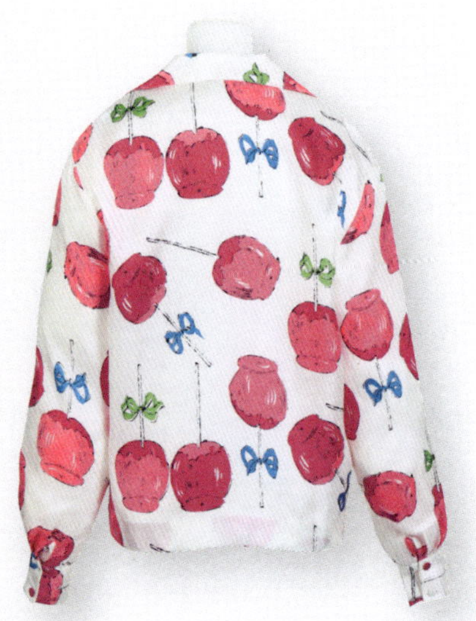

The third of the food-related textiles Warhol designed for the Stehli Silks Corporation is the candy apples textile (see also nos 31 and 32). Two versions are recorded, a silk from 1962–3, with a freely spaced, large-scale pattern, and a second, more tightly grouped pattern printed on polyester from the mid 1960s.

Above left (a) Textile in polyester, light blue and pink colourway. **Above right (b)** Blouse (reverse) in silk by Adelaar, New York. **Opposite (c)** Blouse in silk by Adelaar, New York.

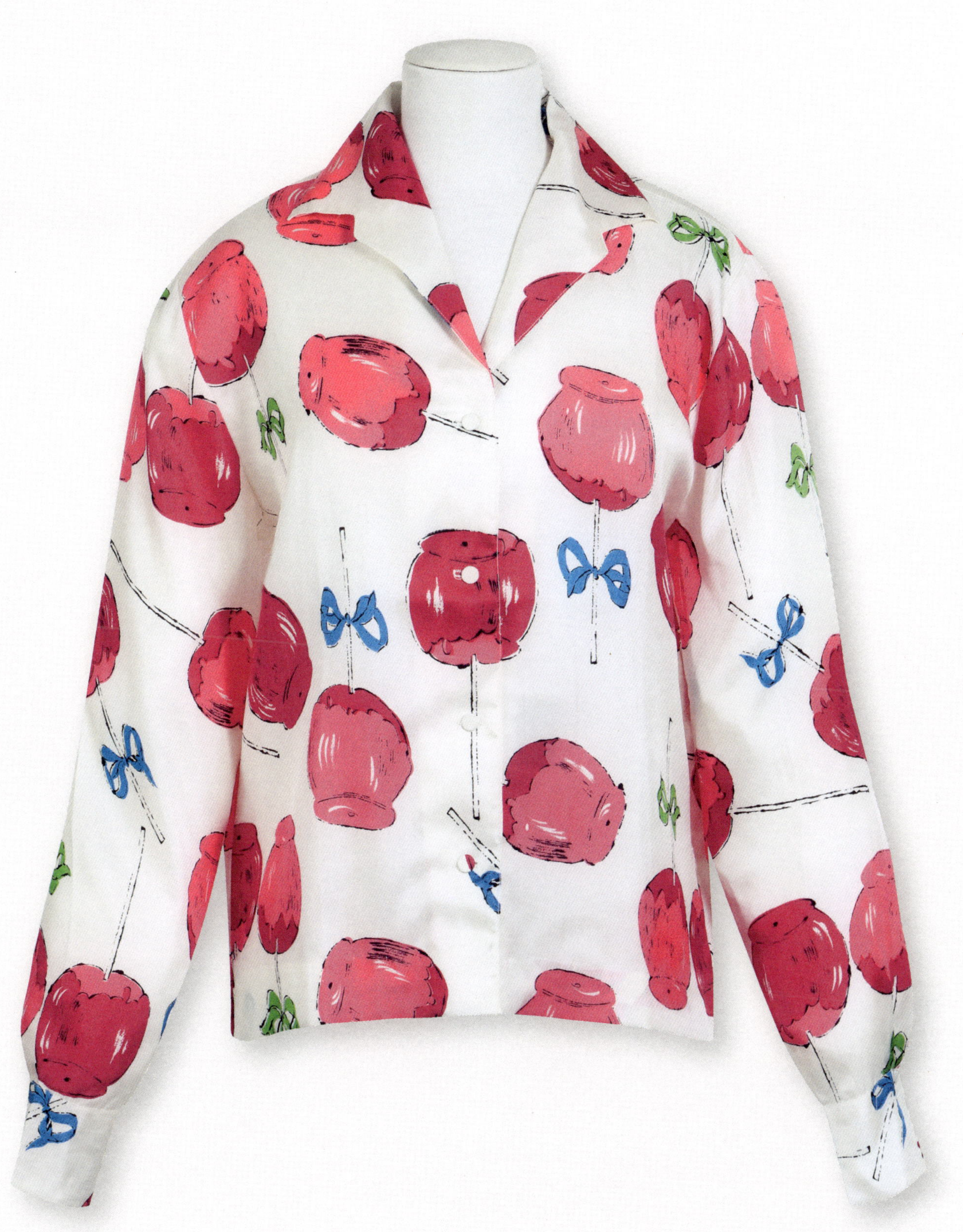

Opposite left (d) Evening dress in polyester, lilac and orange colourway by Alexa, California. **Opposite right (e)** Evening dress in polyester, black, red and pink colourway; maker unknown.

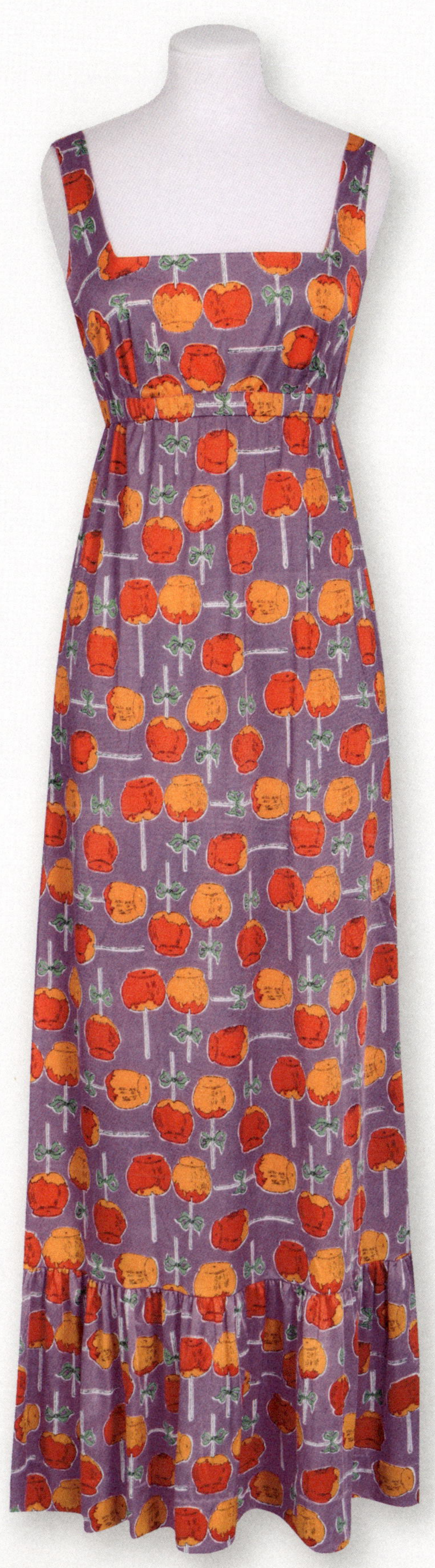

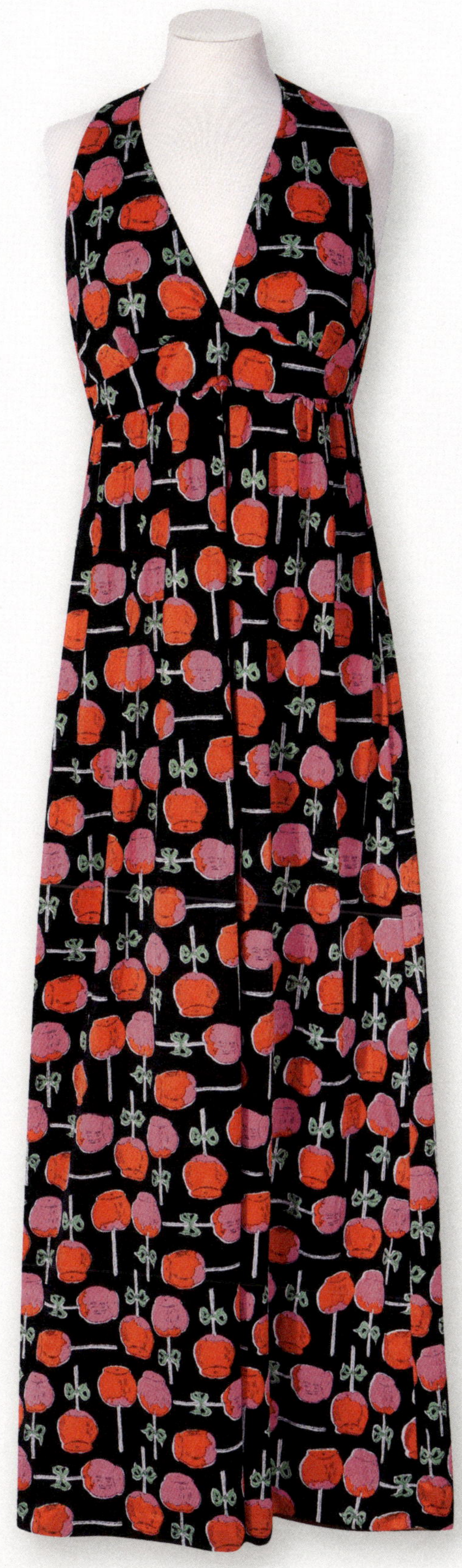

FURTHER READING

Andy Warhol: Drawings and Illustrations of the 1950s. Introduced by Ivan Vartanian. New York: Goliga Books, 2000.

Andy Warhol—From A to B and Back Again. Edited by Donna De Salvo. Exhibition catalogue. Whitney Museum of American Art, New York, 2018.

Andy Warhol: His Early Works 1947–1959. Exhibition catalogue. Gotham Book Mart & Gallery, New York, 1971.

Francis, Mark and King, Margery, et al. *The Warhol Look: Glamour Style Fashion*. New York, Toronto, London: Little, Brown in association with The Andy Warhol Museum, Pittsburgh, 1997.

Gopnik, Blake. *Warhol: A Life as Art*. London: Penguin, 2020.

Kornbluth, Jesse. *Pre-Pop Warhol*. New York: Panache Press at Random House, 1988.

Maréchal, Paul. *Andy Warhol, The Complete Commissioned Magazine Work, 1948–1987*. Catalogue raisonné. Munich, London, New York: Prestel, 2014.

Maréchal, Paul. *Andy Warhol, The Complete Commissioned Record Covers 1949–1987*. Second edition. Munich, London, New York: Prestel, 2015.

Rayner, Geoffrey, Chamberlain, Richard and Stapleton, Annamarie. *Artists' Textiles, 1940–1976*. Woodbridge, Suffolk: Antique Collectors Club, 2012.

Success is a Job in New York: The Early Art and Business of Andy Warhol. Edited by Donna De Salvo et al. Exhibition catalogue. Grey Art Gallery and Study Center, New York University, New York; Carnegie Museum of Art, Pittsburgh, Pennsylvania, 1989.

Wrbican, Matt. *A is for Archive: Warhol's World from A to Z*. Edited by Abigail Franzen-Sheehan, with contributions from Blake Gopnik and Neil Printz. New Haven and London: Yale University Press in association with The Andy Warhol Museum, Pittsburgh, 2019.

ACKNOWLEDGEMENTS

Simon Andrews
Stephen Bruce and Serendipity 3, New York
Trevor and Elaine Chamberlain
Maëlle Christien and David Tanguy at Praline
Mark Eastment
Michael Eftihiou
The staff of the Fashion and Textile Museum, London
Melissa French
Hilary Hammond
Michael Dayton Hermann
Julie Hrischeva
Rachel Hughes
Gyr King
Rosie Luck
Paul Maréchal
Metropolitan Museum of Art, New York
David Morris
Dennis Nothdruft
Bethan Ojari
Amy Paladino
Zandra Rhodes
Jonathan Richards
Kelly Robinson
John Rombola
Peter Salmon and Upstage Theatrical Dry Cleaners
Gladys Schondorf
Marta Soriano
Pete Woronkowicz
Matt Wrbican and The Andy Warhol Museum, Pittsburgh

PICTURE CREDITS

All Andy Warhol Artwork © 2023 The Andy Warhol Foundation for the Visual Arts, Inc. / Licensed by DACS London.

Additional copyright and photo credits are listed below.

Photograph by John Ardoin. Courtesy of Stephen Bruce: 30a
Courtesy of Stephen Bruce: 31a, 32a
Esquire: 14a
Glamour: 15a, 29a
Harper's Bazaar: pp. 18 and 19, 17a, 18h, 18j, 23a, 24a
Honolulu Advertiser: 2a
McCall's: 12a
Image copyright The Metropolitan Museum of Art / Art Resource Scala, Florence: 32b
Photograph by Duane Michals. © Duane Michals: p. 23
New York Times: 9b, 28a, 28h
Courtesy of Amy Paladino: 18a
Courtesy of Zandra Rhodes. Photograph by Joan Agajanian Quinn: p. 9
Photography by Jonathan Richards. © Target Gallery: p. 14, 2c–2e, 3a–3d, 4b, 4c, 5b, 5c, 6c, 6d, 7d–7f, 8b, 9c, 10c, 11b, 12b, 13c, 14c, 15b, 16c, 17b, 17c, 18k, 19b, 19c, 20c, 21b, 22a, 22b, 23c, 24c, 25b, 25c, 26b, 27b, 28c–28g, 28i, 29c, 29d, 30d, 31c–31g, 32c, 32d, 33a–33e
Sony-BMG Entertainment: 6a, 25a
Vanity Fair: 4a, 5a
Vogue: 14b
© 2023 The Andy Warhol Foundation for the Visual Arts, Inc. / Licensed by DACS London/Artimage London: 30c, 31b
The Andy Warhol Museum, Pittsburgh: 18b–18f

Every effort has been made to obtain copyright clearances and permissions. Any queries or corrections should be addressed to the authors.

First published by Yale University Press 2023
302 Temple Street, P. O. Box 209040,
New Haven CT 06520-9040
47 Bedford Square, London WC1B 3DP
yalebooks.com | yalebooks.co.uk

Published to accompany the exhibition
Andy Warhol: The Textiles
at the Fashion and Textile Museum, London
31 March 2023 – 10 September 2023

Library of Congress Control Number: 2022946629
ISBN 978-0-300-27051-8
A catalogue record for this book is available from
the British Library

10 9 8 7 6 5 4 3 2 1
2027 2026 2025 2024 2023

Designed by Praline (David Tanguy, Maëlle Christien)

Printed in Italy by Printer Trento

Front cover: Andy Warhol, 'Ice Cream Cones', purple and green colourway. Detail of silk dress by Castelli. Manufacturer: Stehli Silks Corporation, Inc.

Back cover: Andy Warhol and Stephen Bruce at Serendipity 3, 1961. Photographer: John Ardoin. Courtesy of Stephen Bruce.

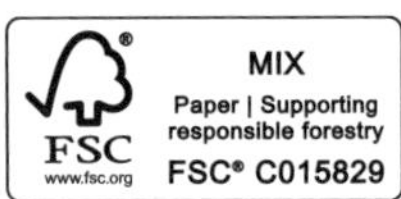